Private Wealth Tactics

Private Wealth Tactics

Legal tools like trusts, offshore accounts, and quiet banking

Matthias Lorenz

Mindful Pages

Published in 2025

ISBN: 9789371343763 (PB)
ISBN: 9789371345910 (eBook)

Published by

Mindful Pages
Imprint of Alpha Editions LLC
312 W. 2nd St #1834
Casper, WY 82601, USA

This book was developed using advanced writing tools to support the drafting and ideation process. All content has been thoughtfully curated, refined, and reviewed to ensure quality and relevance.

Content

Introduction Power in the Shadows ix

Chapter 1 The Myth of Visibility – Why Privacy is the New Wealth 1

Chapter 2 Control Without Ownership – The New Rules of Power 23

Chapter 3 Trusts – Structures of Intent and Protection................. 44

Chapter 4 Offshore Accounts – Jurisdiction as a Strategy 65

Chapter 5 Quiet Banking – Silent Leverage in a Loud World....... 86

Chapter 6 The Invisible Paper Trail – Structuring for Strategic Obscurity. 107

Chapter 7 From Reactive to Proactive – Designing Your Asset Shield.. 131

Chapter 8 Wealth and Identity – Who Are You Without Your Assets? 158

Chapter 9 Global Arbitrage – Playing the Game Without Being Played... 185

Chapter 10 Legal Doesn't Mean Obvious – The Art of Subtle Compliance 204

Chapter 11 In Case of Emergency – Resilience Tactics for Wealth Survival 225

Chapter 12 The Quiet Billionaire Mindset – Principles for the Next Era 246

Conclusion Legacy Without Spotlight 270

About the Author 278

Introduction
Power in the Shadows

Wealth, in its most visible form, has always carried a performative edge. Tailored suits, carefully managed portfolios, luxury cars, exclusive addresses—all serve as modern-day insignia of success. We're conditioned, almost reflexively, to equate prosperity with public display. A net worth isn't just a figure—it morphs into a marker of significance, a badge of influence, a searchable footprint in the theatre of status. But beyond this elaborate performance lies a quieter, far more enduring kind of capital. It doesn't clamor for attention. It governs, silently and effectively. This book sets out to defend that understated power.

Private Wealth Tactics opens with a deliberately contrarian premise: the most durable wealth is not ostentatiously possessed, but discreetly orchestrated. It asks us to look beyond applause, beyond prestige, beyond the lure of visibility. The foundation of such wealth is not merely fiscal—it is architectural. It is constructed from legal frameworks, psychological acuity, and geopolitical awareness. And what sets it apart is not how much, but how well it can withstand.

The pages that follow do not concern themselves with how to amass, parade, or publicise wealth. Instead, they probe how to safeguard it—how to shield it from shifting tides and, just as crucially, how to position it wisely in an era that increasingly penalises discretion. To engage in this sort of positioning, one must cultivate a distinctly different literacy—one that straddles the realms of global law, behavioural insight, and strategic adaptability in a fractured world.

We find ourselves in an age where the very notion of privacy is under siege. Financial discretion is routinely miscast as guilt. Transparency is demanded—ostensibly for the sake of security—but seldom is any distinction drawn between illicit secrecy and principled confidentiality. Under such pressures, especially among those new to affluence, the default response is exposure. Assets are held in one's own name, capital remains parked in home jurisdictions, and clarity is mistaken for protection. It's a comforting illusion. But it's still an illusion.

This book makes the case that true wealth—the kind that outlives regimes, that weathers downturns, that insulates rather than exposes—requires a different philosophy. Not secrecy for secrecy's sake, but deliberate opacity. Not loopholes, but lawful frameworks. Not fear, but prudence. The strategies examined herein are not about hiding. They are about structuring—intelligently, lawfully, in full view, yet out of reach. Visibility should never be mistaken for invulnerability.

This is not, lest there be any confusion, a technical handbook in disguise. It is a philosophical treatise on a different way of being in relation to wealth. The tools—trusts, offshore structures, banking layers—are available to many who can afford them. But the clarity of mind required to wield them with ethical purpose is another matter. Most are never taught to separate validation from control, or visibility from value. They conflate being seen with being secure. That, in today's climate, is not just shortsighted—it's perilous.

Pause for a moment on this paradox: we live in a time of pervasive surveillance, yet most private wealth remains exposed to the point of fragility. Governments, banks, insurers, litigators—even one's own kin—can, with sufficient motive, chart your financial architecture in unnerving detail. If it can be found, it can be frozen, seized, taxed, weaponised. The old assumption that to own something is to be safe in it belongs to a world that no longer exists. Today, ownership can be a vulnerability dressed as dominance.

So what, then, is the alternative?

It begins with a subtle, but vital distinction—control versus ownership. Ownership is declarative, fixed, visible. Control, by contrast, can be discreet, flexible, concealed. Through mechanisms like discretionary trusts, nominees, layered corporate structures, and jurisdictional diversification, one can orchestrate a financial life that maintains strategic distance—distance from threats, from litigation, from noise. When built within the bounds of the law and guided by ethical clarity, this isn't a loophole—it is stewardship in a complex world.

This book assumes you are not interested in deceit or exploitation. Rather, you seek to build—deliberately, with foresight, and in a manner that grants you sovereignty. The aim is to create a structure resilient enough to shield you from political turbulence, litigious opportunism, and the digital glare of a hyper-connected world.

Each chapter unfolds a distinct pillar of this strategy. We begin by examining the modern myths that bind legitimacy to visibility, drawing on history and psychology. Power, throughout the ages, has always understood how to retreat from sight. Dynasties, clerical empires, secretive states—these entities mastered structural invisibility not as subterfuge, but as a guarantor of survival. The Vatican, the Rothschilds—these were not accidents of inheritance, but deliberate architectural feats. And you needn't be born into a lineage to grasp the logic. These are not arcane secrets. They are tools—available, learnable, deployable.

The book then moves into terrain some would call technical—structures, entities, jurisdictions. But the lens remains human. Each mechanism is introduced not as a plug-and-play device, but as a response to specific personal aims. You won't just learn *how* a trust works, but *why* one type might better suit a particular temperament or risk profile. We will explore why a corporation isn't just about tax, but about containment, buffer, and narrative separation. You'll come to see that multi-jurisdictional planning is not about adventure—it's about insulation.

And then, we go deeper. Most treatments of wealth strategy ignore what lies beneath the mechanics: the emotional substrate. But here, we confront it directly. What compels someone to overshare? To title assets in their own name? To crave the digital applause of disclosure? These behaviours, though common, are rooted in misaligned emotional frameworks. They feel like control. They are, in fact, surrender.

Chapter 1
The Myth of Visibility – Why Privacy is the New Wealth

To speak of wealth today is, almost reflexively, to speak of its visibility. Financial capital and social capital have become so entwined that the distinction is no longer clear—and increasingly, affluence is measured not by what one quietly controls, but by what one boldly displays. The high-net-worth individual, once enveloped in institutional discretion, now finds themselves algorithmically mapped, indexed, nudged—if not shoved—into the light. Lifestyle media, regulatory imperatives, and peer culture dressed up as "professional openness" all contribute to the same pressure: Be seen. This chapter poses an unsettling question—when, exactly, did exposure become a proxy for legitimacy? And more importantly, what have we lost in the exchange?

The global financial system, while geographically expansive, is psychologically narrow. It rewards those who present neatly: with clear titles, orderly declarations, and traceable metrics. Yet this obsession with clarity is a historical anomaly. For the greater part of civilisation's arc, enduring wealth—the kind that spans generations, that withstands upheaval—has operated in deliberate opacity. The merchant dynasties of Venice, the estate-holding gentry of Georgian England, the Rothschilds' transnational banking matrix, the layered corporate empires of Asia's dynastic families—all understood one essential principle: to last, one must be architected, not advertised. In their world, visibility wasn't leverage. It was a liability.

To assume that wealth must be visible in order to be real is not just naïve—it betrays a startling ignorance of history. Exposure, after all, serves the observer far more than the subject. It benefits the tax authority, the adversary, the opportunist. And in today's increasingly centralised, digitised, and politically volatile landscape, visibility is not merely inconvenient—it is dangerous. Still, the myth persists: that if your assets are visible, they are safe. If disclosed, they are shielded. If transparent, you are beyond suspicion. This is not strategy. It's a sedative.

What's needed to untangle this confusion isn't just financial acumen—it's a reintroduction to historical and psychological context. Think of the Medici—whose real power wasn't displayed in florid excess, but encoded into a banking infrastructure aligned with both church and state. Consider the Ottoman vakif—a charitable trust structure that deftly preserved family assets across generations while evading state appropriation. Or look to the merchant families of Africa and South Asia, who understood that genuine wealth wasn't tallied in ledgers, but diffused through kinship networks and social obligation. In all these cases, discretion wasn't a luxury—it was a core design principle.

And yet here we are, in a time of unprecedented structural capability—offshore foundations, nominee layers, jurisdictional arbitrage—and the average affluent professional remains curiously exposed. Not by force, but by habit. We've been trained—conditioned, really—to disclose. To present. To narrate. Success is no longer something to be experienced quietly; it must be demonstrated. Even in private wealth circles, clients are urged to create legacy brochures, host family office summits, craft carefully packaged philanthropic narratives. As if the wealth itself required an Instagram account to be taken seriously.

Legal frameworks have followed this cultural drift. KYC, FATCA, CRS—necessary, in some respects, but often blind to nuance. They don't distinguish between transparency for accountability and transparency as vulnerability. As a result, privacy has ceased to be a neutral stance. It's become suspect. This is the cost of conflating privacy with secrecy, and secrecy with guilt. In reality, privacy—done well—is not evasive. It's intentional. It's protective. It's wise.

This is not an argument against compliance. It is an argument against conflation—the kind that mistakes noise for legitimacy, or exposure for virtue. The modern cult of visibility flatters the ego, even as it hollows out the balance sheet. The litigator doesn't care about your narrative of purpose. They care about what you own and where it is. The political regime doesn't care for your Instagram philanthropy. They care about jurisdiction. Visibility is seductive because it appeals to our instincts. But instincts, unchecked, have a poor track record when it comes to preserving capital.

The psychological undercurrent is, of course, even more difficult to confront. Financial fragility is often born not of bad planning, but of emotional hunger. The need to be seen. To rank. To dazzle. To be the article in the glossy magazine. And we live in a culture that confuses quiet strength with weakness. Modesty is mistranslated as mediocrity. Silence, as fear. The impulse to signal success—to broadcast it—is rarely rational. It's a defence mechanism. One that works well—until it doesn't. Until the yacht is seized. The account frozen. The asset contested. These aren't failures of wealth. They are failures of exposure.

And this is not a problem confined to the ultra-rich. It reaches entrepreneurs, upwardly mobile professionals, even digital nomads with modest portfolios. They assume legality equals safety. They believe that because their holdings are earned and taxed, they are protected. But legality and structure are not synonyms. Nor are ownership and control. Protection, crucially, is not the same as performance. These distinctions matter—urgently so.

To think of privacy as strength requires a shift in narrative—personal, not just political. It is not about evading the world. It is about crafting your interface with it. Strategic discretion is not a retreat. It is a form of authorship. It allows you to decide—deliberately, precisely—which parts of your life intersect with which systems, under what terms. This is not theoretical. It is practical. Whether it's via private trusts, layered ownership, or cross-border vehicles, privacy can be woven into the very spine of your financial structure.

But—and here lies the catch—structure without philosophy is a castle built on sand. Without a clear inner compass, even the most elegant setup becomes susceptible to poor decisions, compromised judgment, and ethical drift. That is why this chapter pushes beyond tactics into terrain more difficult to navigate: motive, belief, assumption. What compels you to share? What prevents you from withholding? Why does silence feel subversive? These aren't idle musings. They're prompts for responsibility—not just over your financial architecture, but over the identity that shapes it.

In the pages ahead, we will delve into the history of hidden power—not to romanticise secrecy, but to extract intelligence. We'll examine the visibility epidemic—not as a cultural annoyance, but as a structural liability. We'll trace the unspoken logic that turns exposure into exploitation. And we'll begin to sketch an alternative: privacy not as retreat, but as resistance; not as absence, but as design.

If any of this feels extreme, it is only because the modern narrative has veered so far in the opposite direction. But that narrative is not immutable. Tides turn. And as we edge further into a future defined by regulatory expansion, algorithmic oversight, and widening economic divides, those who know how to operate with intentional opacity will not merely endure. They will retain sovereignty.

This chapter, then, is your first aperture into that mindset—not of evasion, but of elevation. Not of hiding, but of designing with discernment. It challenges the deeply embedded assumption that what is unseen must be unreal. As we will see, reality is not bestowed by spotlight. It is revealed, in its truest form, when the lights go out—and what remains still stands.

Wealth and the Illusion of Exposure

Modern finance, for all its sophistication and abstraction, remains oddly theatrical. The perception of wealth—how it is signalled, narrated, and broadcast—often carries more cultural weight than the underlying reality of ownership or control. To be *seen* as wealthy is frequently mistaken for *being* wealthy. This confusion, while seemingly superficial, has deep consequences for how individuals build, protect, and ultimately lose their assets. Visibility has become a modern fetish, one that mistakes exposure for legitimacy, publicity for prudence, and status for security. But as we'll examine, this equation is not only flawed—it is dangerous.

The rise of exposure as a proxy for success is not accidental. It is the product of intertwined forces: cultural, regulatory, psychological, and technological. What was once a private matter—one's net worth, holdings, or financial intent—has, over time, become a curated persona. Social media accelerated this shift, but it did not create it. Long before Instagram portfolios and crypto influencers, financial visibility had already begun to supplant substance in both public and professional consciousness. The result is a generation of asset-holders—some genuinely affluent, others aspirational—who mistake performance for protection.

Yet history tells a different story. In the most enduring financial dynasties, discretion was never an afterthought—it was the architecture. The Rothschilds, whose wealth and influence shaped European banking for over two centuries, understood the value of silence better than most. Their empire was built on private channels of communication, decentralised family branches, and layered ownership structures that were deliberately hard to map. Similarly, family offices in Switzerland, Singapore, and Luxembourg have long prized strategic opacity—not to deceive, but to defend. These structures were not expressions of fear; they were expressions of control.

Contrast that with the contemporary obsession with exposure: public shareholding announcements, venture capital brag sheets, high-profile real estate acquisitions, and Forbes lists that function less as journalism and more as scoreboard. The implicit message: if it isn't visible, it doesn't count. This is the financial equivalent of shouting into a crowded room in hopes that validation will equate to safety. But exposure is not security. It is vulnerability, repackaged.

There is a persistent myth in Western finance that disclosure equals integrity. That the more one reveals—whether in public filings, digital footprints, or curated lifestyle— the more trustworthy one becomes. In reality, this is a confusion of categories. Legal compliance is necessary. Public display is not. The conflation of the two has created a cultural environment in which privacy is mistaken for guilt, and visibility is presumed to be moral. But the truth is more nuanced: *what is visible is often manipulated, and what is private is often deliberate.*

The danger in this myth lies not only in social perception, but in structural misunderstanding. To be visible in today's financial system is to be traceable, taxable, and—at times—targetable. Your name on a property deed, your personal signature on a corporate document, your passport linked to an account in a politically unstable jurisdiction—each of these increases your exposure without necessarily increasing your power. You may *own* more, but you *control* less. And when scrutiny arises—whether from litigators, hostile family members, creditors, or regulators—visibility is the first breach point.

This does not imply that wealth must be hidden, nor that transparency is inherently flawed. It does mean, however, that *intelligent discretion* is more important now than ever before. And that requires a paradigm shift: from reactive exposure to proactive structure.

Psychologically, this shift is difficult. The ego craves confirmation, especially in societies where wealth is intertwined with identity. We are conditioned from a young age to associate financial success with recognition. Academic achievement is measured in grades, career progression in titles, and wealth in visible consumption. Even the language betrays this mindset—*he's worth a billion*, *she made the list*, *they're high net-worth.* These are not statements of liquidity or structure; they are statements of perceived significance. In such an environment, choosing privacy feels like stepping off the stage. But sovereignty begins the moment applause no longer defines your direction.

This psychological vulnerability is compounded by social platforms, which have turned visibility into a default condition. Financial disclosures are no longer confined to regulators—they are posted, liked, and shared. A successful exit from a start-up, a luxury home purchase, a round of fundraising—these moments are no longer private milestones; they are content. But what happens when visibility becomes habitual, even addictive? What happens when the digital persona becomes inseparable from your financial posture?

You expose yourself to entities you do not control. Governments, hackers, journalists, litigators—each can leverage public information in ways you cannot reverse. This is not speculation. Numerous cases now exist where social media posts have been used in court to assess asset ownership, where offshore accounts were identified not by forensic audit, but by online breadcrumbs. The cost of exposure is rarely immediate—but it is cumulative.

Let us consider an increasingly common case: the high-net-worth individual who builds first-generation wealth through entrepreneurship. Eager to prove legitimacy, they keep their name attached to every entity, sign every deal personally, and showcase every success online. Initially, this generates respect. But over time, visibility turns toxic. They are sued by a former business partner. A journalist investigates their cross-border holdings. A government agency flags inconsistencies in their filings. None of this would have happened had their structures been built around *control*, not *ownership*. They confused being seen with being safe.

Contrast that with a well-structured private family office in Liechtenstein or the Cayman Islands. The beneficial owners may control hundreds of millions in assets. But their names are not publicly tied to those assets. Their operational footprint is quiet. Their reporting is compliant, but minimal. Their exposure to reputational risk is drastically reduced—not because they are hiding, but because they have architected *distance.* Not distance from the law, but distance from volatility.

This concept of *distance* is central. A well-structured wealth plan inserts distance between the individual and their assets—through trusts, corporate vehicles, nominee agreements, and geographic diversification. These tools are not exotic. They are legal, well-documented, and widely available. What is lacking is not access—it is education. Most financial advisors are not trained to think in terms of exposure. They focus on growth, yield, and tax. Few ask: *Who can see you? Who can touch you? Who can challenge your claims in court or public opinion?* But these are the questions that determine whether wealth becomes a burden or a fortress.

There is also an ethical dimension here, often ignored in mainstream discourse. Critics argue that private structures breed inequality or hide wrongdoing. That is true *when used maliciously.* But to equate privacy with misconduct is to ignore both intent and legality. A family shielding assets from geopolitical instability in Venezuela is not morally equivalent to a corporation laundering funds. The tools may overlap; the ethics do not. The question is not whether privacy is suspicious, but *how it is used, and why.*

Indeed, in an age where surveillance capitalism and regulatory overreach co-exist uncomfortably, privacy can be a moral stance. It is a way of asserting boundaries—not from society, but from systems that mistake disclosure for virtue. To be private is not to be opaque. It is to be *selectively transparent*—visible where required, silent where permitted, and structured in ways that reflect both legal prudence and personal philosophy.

Ultimately, the illusion of exposure persists because it flatters. It tells you that your presence in the headlines equals protection. That your name on the asset is proof of control. That your digital persona is your reputation. But these are superficial truths, designed for consumption, not continuity.

Real wealth does not need to shout. It does not need to appear in league tables or interviews or curated bios. Real wealth is designed to endure scrutiny without collapsing, to pass through crises without seizure, and to operate quietly while the noisy world distracts itself with rankings and performance metrics.

To reject the illusion of exposure is not to retreat—it is to lead with structure. To understand that ownership is not the point; *positioning* is. And that in the decades to come, when the divide between the visible and the sovereign becomes starker, those who chose discretion over display will not just survive—they will shape the future.

A History of Hidden Power

Power, when it wishes to endure, tends not to shout. It structures. It distances. It conceals in plain sight. Contrary to the modern tendency to conflate influence with attention, history is littered with examples that point in the opposite direction—where the most consequential individuals and institutions have shaped events, controlled capital, and secured dynastic legacies precisely because they mastered the art of discretion. Visibility was rarely a strategic advantage. It was a liability to be minimised, an exposure to be engineered out of the equation. If you want to understand wealth that lasts—not simply accumulates, but survives—then you must study not only how it was built, but how it was *hidden*.

The idea that visibility is a modern affliction is only partly true. Even in antiquity, the exercise of power often relied on obscurity. The Roman elite, for instance, understood the use of proxies, patronage networks, and layered property holdings to insulate themselves from public scrutiny. While emperors were omnipresent in civic iconography, the senatorial class—the real locus of generational wealth—operated through familial alliances and silent partnerships. Roman landowners would frequently register properties under the names of freedmen or distant relatives to avoid excessive taxation or political targeting. The appearance of modesty concealed extensive control.

This foundational insight—that ownership can be separated from control—is not a modern innovation. It is ancient practice, continually reinvented. The medieval Catholic Church offers a particularly sophisticated case study. It amassed staggering land holdings across Europe, not by openly claiming territory, but through trusts—proto-legal vehicles like the *mortmain*, which allowed land to be held "in the dead hand" of the Church, immune to seizure or inheritance disputes. By legally owning nothing in a personal sense, Church authorities controlled vast resources without exposing individual clerics or papal representatives to legal risk. It was institutional invisibility designed for permanence.

Move forward a few centuries, and you find the Venetians—one of the most commercially successful societies in pre-modern Europe—developing early forms of financial opacity. The wealth of Venice did not lie solely in trade; it lay in how that trade was structured. Venetian patricians often financed expeditions indirectly, using "commenda" contracts that blurred the lines between investor and operator. These agreements allowed for limited liability, risk dispersion, and—crucially—private capital flows that were hard to trace. The city's fortunes were not declared on ledgers open to scrutiny but embedded in agreements, networks, and family trusts.

Perhaps no family in modern financial history has mastered the concealment of power as elegantly as the Rothschilds. By the mid-19th century, they controlled one of the most influential banking networks in Europe. But unlike their industrial contemporaries, the Rothschilds did not seek public adoration. They cultivated a deliberate invisibility. Their holdings were fragmented across sibling-run banks in different countries, linked by confidential correspondence and informal partnership agreements rather than formal consolidation. Their fortune was protected not just by wealth but by *opacity*. While other magnates courted monarchs with titles and displayed their influence through estates and patronage, the Rothschilds wrote in code, diversified across borders, and minimised personal exposure. It wasn't humility. It was strategic foresight.

This ethos of concealed control extended beyond Europe. In the Indian subcontinent, centuries of political volatility bred a similar instinct. Merchant families—such as the Marwaris or Chettiars—built informal banking systems (*hundi*) and intra-family lending networks that functioned as shadow economies. These systems operated in trust, rather than law, and enabled financial continuity through multiple invasions, colonial transitions, and currency collapses. Their power was built on what *wasn't* visible in the colonial books. While foreign companies built factories, these families built networks—less vulnerable, less fixed, and therefore more resilient.

It is tempting to dismiss these cases as the product of bygone conditions. But the principles they embody—*distance, decentralisation, discretion*—remain just as relevant in today's hyper-regulated financial landscape. The difference is that modern systems are more invasive and standardised. Technology has accelerated asset discovery. Compliance protocols increasingly require disclosure of beneficial ownership, real-time reporting, and cross-border transparency. But even within this framework, power continues to favour those who understand that visibility can still be managed—legally, ethically, and architecturally.

Consider the post-World War II emergence of the family office as a vehicle for discrete wealth preservation. The truly powerful did not put their assets in personal accounts or in their own names. They put them into holding companies owned by trusts, overseen by professional managers, domiciled in favourable jurisdictions. While the legal apparatus may have evolved, the logic remains ancient: preserve power by distancing the individual from the asset. If you are named directly, you can be targeted directly. If you control indirectly, through structure, you are resilient.

More recently, sovereign wealth funds and large philanthropic foundations have carried forward this legacy of strategic obscurity. These entities often operate behind front-facing missions—stewarding public good, funding research, supporting infrastructure. But behind their stated purpose is a sophisticated machinery of asset control, tax efficiency, and political insulation. The Gates Foundation, the Qatar Investment Authority, the Vatican Bank—each navigates intense public scrutiny while maintaining considerable operational opacity. This is not evasion; it is institutional design.

Yet modern culture pulls in the opposite direction. In an age of media saturation, where value is often tethered to attention, discretion is mistaken for absence. The noise of celebrity wealth—the Tesla stock surges, the crypto billionaires, the high-profile acquisitions—distorts our understanding of how lasting power is structured. True influence, especially financial influence, does not crave audience. It craves continuity. And continuity is only possible when risk is dispersed, ownership is engineered at a distance, and the operator does not need to perform visibility for validation.

This misalignment between cultural expectation and strategic necessity creates a problem for the contemporary wealth builder. If you are accumulating assets in today's environment, you are not just playing a financial game—you are operating inside a narrative that expects you to narrate yourself. You are expected to signal progress, to account publicly for your holdings, to broadcast success. But these signals—however good for brand or ego—rarely protect you. And when the environment turns hostile, it is often the most visible who fall first.

To understand this more clearly, consider the selective enforcement of laws and sanctions. In high-stakes environments—whether it's geopolitical unrest, financial crashes, or legal retaliation—those who are visible are disproportionately targeted. Sanctions on Russian oligarchs following the invasion of Ukraine were not simply a matter of legality. They were a matter of *visibility*. Assets that were easily found—superyachts, London properties, bank accounts tied directly to names—were seized. Meanwhile, wealth held in trusts, layered through entities, or distributed across jurisdictions often remained intact. This is not moral justification; it is empirical observation. Those who understand exposure as a variable, rather than a necessity, tend to survive better.

This brings us to a core philosophical distinction: *is power the capacity to display, or the capacity to endure?* In almost every serious historical case, the answer is the latter. Families, empires, and institutions that survived regime changes, economic implosions, or cultural revolutions did so not because they were seen, but because they were structured. Their wealth did not rely on spectacle, but on insulation.

This is not a romantic appeal to secrecy, nor a cynical exaltation of the elite. It is a sober look at how power is actually preserved across time. Discretion is not weakness. It is design. Opacity is not dishonesty. It is discipline. And hiddenness is not the opposite of legitimacy—it is often its precondition.

The modern investor, entrepreneur, or professional would do well to study these examples not as curiosities, but as models. Not everything from the past can be recreated. But the principles—build quietly, decentralise control, avoid naming yourself unnecessarily—are enduring. The tools may be different now: offshore entities instead of land grants, trusts instead of ecclesiastical law, encryption instead of handwritten code. But the strategic imperative remains the same.

If you want your wealth to perform, make it visible. If you want it to *last*, structure it so that you can *disappear*. That is not cowardice—it is calculus. The loudest fortunes are rarely the most secure. And history, when read with clarity, confirms this again and again.

The Psychology of Financial Vulnerability

We rarely speak honestly about the emotional roots of financial fragility. Technical explanations—lack of diversification, tax inefficiencies, poor risk management—are comfortable, because they are external and quantifiable. But beneath these surface-level issues lies a more complex reality: many people become financially exposed not because they lack information or tools, but because their decisions are driven by unresolved psychological dynamics. *Fear, ego, and societal conditioning* are not minor footnotes in the story of wealth; they are often the invisible authors of its undoing.

This subchapter takes a deeper cut than most books on asset protection or personal finance are willing to take. It argues that the way we disclose, declare, and structure our wealth is rarely neutral. Instead, these choices are shaped by subtle pressures: the need to be seen, the fear of being irrelevant, the internalised belief that success must be visible to be validated. These forces do not just skew our decisions—they quietly erode resilience, leaving otherwise intelligent individuals structurally vulnerable.

Let us begin with ego—not as a caricature of narcissism, but as a deeper mechanism of identity. For many, money is not merely a tool or resource. It becomes an extension of the self. The portfolio becomes a biography; the net worth becomes a scoreboard; the investments, an encoded value system. This personal identification with capital is culturally reinforced from every direction.

Advertisements suggest that your purchases reflect your personality. Business school rankings conflate personal worth with financial achievement. And on social media, success is quantified in likes and impressions as much as returns or revenue. *To possess wealth silently in this environment is to resist the psychological current of an entire culture.*

The result is a compulsion to *over-disclose*—not for legal or strategic reasons, but for affirmation. Professionals publish earnings milestones on LinkedIn. Entrepreneurs narrate their exit valuations to near-strangers. Even those working in ostensibly private sectors often find ways to signal affluence—through lifestyle markers, digital presence, or network positioning. None of this feels excessive in the moment. But collectively, it produces a portfolio of exposure that is unnecessary, unprotected, and often irreversible.

This is not theoretical. Legal case files are filled with examples of financial disclosures—public or semi-public—that have been weaponised in litigation, divorce, or political retaliation. What you say casually today may become admissible evidence tomorrow. A seemingly innocuous business biography that details your holdings, a media profile that connects your name to a trust or entity, a real estate purchase registered in your personal name—these can all become breach points in scenarios of stress or scrutiny. *The line between affirmation and ammunition is dangerously thin.*

Fear operates along a different axis but often leads to the same outcome. Insecurity—particularly among first-generation wealth builders—can drive people to disclose prematurely. There is a desire to establish credibility, to prove that the wealth is "legitimate" or "earned." This can manifest as over-cooperation with financial institutions, over-reporting in family or professional contexts, or structuring assets in ways that are too direct—registering them in one's own name, combining business and personal holdings, or foregoing protective legal vehicles for the sake of perceived simplicity.

Fear also influences how people interpret regulations. Many confuse transparency with vulnerability, believing that the only way to be compliant is to be *fully visible.* But the law does not require self-sabotage. It requires accuracy, not nakedness. Strategic privacy—when designed legally and intentionally—is not evasion. It is good governance. And yet fear, particularly fear of being "found out" or "audited," causes many to default to maximal disclosure. This is not virtue. It is miseducation.

Societal conditioning is the most subtle of all forces. It shapes not just what we do with wealth, but what we believe is *appropriate* to do. In much of the Anglo-American world, the cultural script is clear: wealth should be displayed, taxed, and occasionally confessed. Anything else appears unpatriotic, suspicious, or worse—elitist. This conditioning is internalised even by those who intellectually understand the value of discretion. The result is a conflict: between what is legal and what is culturally rewarded, between what is strategic and what is socially acceptable.

This tension becomes especially acute when navigating cross-cultural wealth. An individual raised in a Western democratic context may feel morally conflicted using structures that are common and entirely legal in Swiss, Singaporean, or Middle Eastern financial circles. The discomfort doesn't come from illegality—it comes from stepping outside a narrative of virtue-through-visibility. But wealth structuring is not about optics. It is about *risk-adjusted autonomy.* And that often requires unlearning the social scripts that have shaped our beliefs about money.

Psychology also influences how individuals respond to perceived threats. People who have not examined their emotional relationship to money often react to stress by *tightening their grip*—consolidating control, naming themselves directly on accounts, dissolving trusts they feel distant from. These reactions are almost always counterproductive. True protection comes from *distributed control, legal insulation*, and *jurisdictional diversification*. But these strategies require emotional detachment—the ability to see wealth as a system, not a personal trophy cabinet.

This is why financial privacy is not just a legal or strategic stance. It is a psychological threshold. It requires the individual to step outside of ego and into structure. To move from *performance* to *positioning*. To accept that the safest wealth is not the most visible, but the most intelligently obscured.

Therapists and financial advisors rarely sit at the same table, but perhaps they should. Unexamined beliefs about money—learned in childhood, shaped by trauma, or distorted by cultural messaging—manifest not just in spending habits but in structuring decisions. A client who grew up in scarcity may over-consolidate out of fear. Another who feels unworthy of success may reject complex structures as "too much." A third may anchor their identity in performance, choosing branding over buffering, aesthetics over architecture.

To build resilient wealth, then, one must first build emotional fluency. This does not mean turning financial planning into therapy. It means recognising that *structural clarity without psychological clarity is fragile*. No amount of offshore layering or tax optimisation will protect someone who cannot emotionally tolerate distance, privacy, or delayed validation.

So what does psychological sovereignty look like in practice? It begins with a disciplined refusal to conflate exposure with legitimacy. It accepts that disclosure should be a *choice*, not a compulsion. It favours structures that align with long-term control, not short-term affirmation. And it remains humble in the face of uncertainty—understanding that the goal is not to signal wealth, but to protect the freedom it provides.

Ultimately, the greatest vulnerability in finance is not volatility, litigation, or taxation. It is *unexamined identity*. When wealth becomes a mirror for the ego, it becomes brittle. When it becomes an extension of fear, it becomes overexposed. When it becomes a performance, it becomes predictable—and therefore easy to attack.

By understanding the psychology of financial vulnerability, we gain more than insight. We gain leverage. Leverage to design better. To disclose wisely. To operate with strength, not noise. And to live not in the shadow of our assets, but with the full clarity of having built something that does not need to be seen in order to endure.

Privacy as a Philosophical Stance

To treat privacy merely as a tactical measure is to miss its deeper significance. Privacy is not simply a method of risk mitigation, nor is it an evasion mechanism reserved for the paranoid or the powerful. When understood clearly, financial privacy becomes something far more substantial: *a declaration of personal sovereignty*. In a world increasingly structured around visibility, compliance, and interconnected surveillance, the deliberate act of preserving one's financial privacy is not retreat—it is resistance. It is a statement that autonomy has value, and that value is worth protecting with intentional architecture.

Let's begin with the prevailing misconception. Privacy is often framed as absence: absence of disclosure, absence of participation, absence of transparency. But that is a shallow definition. Properly framed, *privacy is not about withholding—it's about boundary-setting*. It is not a negation of social or economic responsibility, but a form of self-determination. It defines where your obligation to disclose ends and where your legitimate right to operate quietly begins.

To understand why this matters, one must first recognise the broader cultural forces that have normalised exposure. We live in a society where visibility has become moralised. The more we share, the more authentic we are presumed to be. The more public our choices, the more legitimate they appear. Tech platforms reward this with engagement metrics. Governments increasingly legislate it through financial disclosure laws. Social expectations reinforce it by treating discretion as something suspect. *In this environment, to assert financial privacy is to step outside the moral default—and that act carries philosophical weight.*

Privacy, in its truest form, is not just about secrecy. It is about authorship. It allows individuals to choose the narrative by which they are known—or not known at all. This idea has philosophical roots that go beyond finance. In political theory, John Stuart Mill argued that liberty is grounded in the capacity of the individual to decide the contours of their life without unnecessary interference. Financial privacy is an extension of that principle. It is the freedom to define the contours of your economic life, without having to perform it for public, corporate, or state approval.

This is not a licence for irresponsibility. The law must be respected, and ethical obligations met. But there is a meaningful difference between legal transparency and public exposure. A compliant trust registered in a privacy-respecting jurisdiction does not evade law—it operates within it, intelligently. A corporate structure that masks direct ownership without hiding beneficial control is not deceptive—it is strategic. These are not evasive acts. They are expressions of *jurisdictional and structural choice*, grounded in an understanding that not all stakeholders deserve access to all information.

To see financial privacy in this light is to shift the entire conversation. It is no longer about what one has to hide. It is about what one has the right to *protect.* The rise of surveillance capitalism has collapsed many of our traditional boundaries. Algorithms track spending patterns. Databases triangulate wealth indicators from lifestyle choices. Regulators trade financial data across borders through automatic exchange agreements. In this context, privacy becomes not just a preference but a form of resistance—a way of defending against systemic overreach. *It is not about avoiding visibility entirely; it is about deciding when, where, and to whom you are visible.*

Historical analogues support this interpretation. The Quakers of 18th-century England, despite being deeply engaged in commerce, maintained a strict ethic of financial discretion. Their quiet wealth funded abolitionist campaigns, scientific research, and early social housing—all without public self-congratulation. Their financial privacy was not a shield from scrutiny, but a shield from distraction. They believed that influence should come from design, not display. In more recent times, certain dynastic families in Europe and Asia have cultivated entire legacies without public presence. Their wealth is not less real because it is unbroadcast. If anything, it is more secure—and more sovereign—because it is unperformative.

Contrast this with the prevailing ethic of performance in many contemporary financial cultures. The startup founder who posts quarterly wins on social media. The investor who speaks more about their holdings than they structurally control. The family office that operates as a branding engine rather than a shield. These are not failures of intelligence. They are failures of philosophy. They mistake applause for autonomy.

Privacy, properly understood, is not motivated by fear. It is motivated by clarity. Clarity about who has the right to know, and who does not. Clarity about the risks of exposure, and how they compound. Clarity about the distinction between public virtue and private capacity. This kind of clarity requires discipline—and that discipline is not always easy to cultivate in a world that equates transparency with virtue.

But there is also a deeper moral logic to privacy. It is not simply a right to conceal; it is a responsibility to *structure*. To make deliberate choices about stewardship, succession, liability, and risk. Financial privacy that is built on ad hoc secrecy is brittle. But privacy that is architected—through trusts, multi-layered entities, and cross-jurisdictional systems—is robust. It becomes a framework not for escape, but for continuity.

This distinction is essential. Privacy is not a passive condition. It is an active construction. It must be thought through, maintained, reviewed, and—above all—aligned with one's values. The goal is not opacity for its own sake. It is *selectivity with intention.* Who knows what, and why? What jurisdictions can demand access, and under what rules? What liabilities are you personally exposed to, and which have been legally transferred? These are not administrative questions. They are philosophical ones—because they speak directly to the kind of autonomy you are claiming in your financial life.

Critics will argue that privacy allows for bad behaviour. That it creates asymmetry in power, privilege, and access. And it is true that secrecy has been abused by bad actors. But to conflate *abuse of privacy* with privacy itself is to miss the point entirely. The solution to misuse is not the dismantling of discretion, but the improvement of accountability mechanisms. *You do not make systems stronger by making all actors visible—you make them stronger by ensuring that visibility is earned, not coerced.*

Ultimately, financial privacy as a philosophical stance is an act of adult citizenship. It recognises that freedom is not given. It is designed. It understands that wealth, in the modern context, is not simply a number—it is a structure of power, influence, and responsibility. And it asserts that the *right to discretion* is not morally inferior to the *obligation to disclose*—they are complementary, not oppositional.

This is a difficult balance to strike. But it is a necessary one. Because the opposite of privacy is not openness. It is *exposure.* And exposure, without intention, is neither noble nor safe. It is merely available—for consumption, targeting, or theft.

To claim financial privacy is to claim authorship over your own narrative. It is to understand that wealth is not something to prove, but something to protect. And that in a system designed to extract visibility, the quiet act of structuring your affairs thoughtfully, legally, and privately is not merely a tactic. *It is a declaration of who you are—and who you are not willing to become.*

Chapter 2
Control Without Ownership – The New Rules of Power

Ownership has long been considered the gold standard of economic identity. Deeds, share certificates, property titles—tangible affirmations that something is "yours." From early adulthood, we are trained to equate ownership with control: if your name is on it, you have dominion; if it's registered to you, it answers to you. Yet, behind the polished façade of modern wealth, a different, more intricate story unfolds. Increasingly, true power over capital lies not with those whose names appear on official records, but with those who've learned to operate from the shadows of formality. They hold the reins—quietly, effectively—without ever standing in the spotlight. This chapter unpacks that paradox, and considers what it means for the future of financial sovereignty.

At the core of this quiet evolution is an idea as old as it is contemporary: that ownership and control are not synonyms. This separation is no longer theoretical—it is now a working design principle. Enabled by modern legal infrastructure and a fluid landscape of transnational entities, it allows individuals to structure capital in such a way that influence is retained, even as formal ownership disappears. What emerges is not some legal sleight-of-hand, but a calculated architecture—one that rewrites how wealth is held, shielded, and stewarded.

Consider, for a moment, a simple exercise. Make a list of everything you believe you own. Now make another of all the things you truly control. Where those lists diverge, insight begins. The difference isn't rhetorical—it's practical. In the event of litigation, investigation, or financial disruption, it is the first list that becomes a target. That which you own outright is vulnerable by default. The second list—if properly designed—remains structurally insulated. And yet, the material reality might be identical: you enjoy the use, benefit, and influence. You live in the property, direct the fund, benefit from the return. You're in command—but you don't legally "own" it. That's not avoidance. That's evolution.

This isn't a manifesto for concealment. It's a meditation on where power really resides. For all its symbolic comfort, direct ownership introduces risk. Names on registries become invitations—often unspoken—for scrutiny. They mark you out for attention, and not always the kind you'd choose. Legal databases, journalistic exposés, asset disclosure regimes—once your name is attached, the structure is exposed. In calm times, this might seem a tolerable price. But crises, whether personal or political, rarely announce themselves in advance. And when they do arrive, it's the visible assets that are attacked first. Those who understand this design accordingly: trusts, holding companies, layered entities, nominee frameworks—all deployed not to obscure wealth, but to protect it.

This, then, is the essence of the corporate veil. Entities like LLCs, foundations, and corporations are not simply business mechanisms. They're legal membranes. They relocate liability, fragment control, and dissolve the neat trail that so often leads directly to the individual. But they do more than shield. When properly constructed, they introduce governance mechanisms that improve both resilience and continuity. The power centre shifts—from the person to the structure. And with that shift comes protection from personal downfall. The structure, not the individual, becomes the single point of failure.

Take a typical arrangement: a Cayman exempted company owns a Delaware LLC, which in turn controls an IP asset licensed to a UK-based operating firm. The individual at the centre may have created this network, may even direct it day to day—but their name appears nowhere. Perhaps their family trust holds the shares; perhaps a fiduciary acts under a durable power of attorney. Either way, their exposure is radically reduced. Journalists will find paperwork. Creditors will encounter delay. Adversaries will face complexity. The benefit flows, the asset remains active, but the trail leads nowhere simple. That, precisely, is the point.

Naturally, this raises ethical questions. Where, one might ask, is the boundary between prudent insulation and outright deception? Public discourse tends to collapse the distinction, smearing all asset protection under the same cloud of suspicion. But legal systems themselves recognise the nuance. There is lawful structuring, and there is fraudulent concealment. They are not the same thing. The tools in question—trusts, holding companies, jurisdictional arbitrage—are not illicit in themselves. They are instruments. Their character lies in their use. Intent matters. Disclosure where required matters. Ethics, inconveniently, lives in the grey space between transparency and opacity.

This becomes particularly salient when succession enters the frame. Many assume that passing on wealth means handing over ownership. But direct ownership comes with a price: probate delays, estate tax inefficiencies, the risk of fragmentation. By contrast, wealth held within a well-governed entity can transition seamlessly. Shares transfer according to shareholder agreements. Trustees are appointed in advance. Powers shift on a defined schedule. The individual passes on, but the structure endures. Continuity isn't disrupted. The wealth isn't scattered or contested. It's preserved—architecturally, not sentimentally.

There's also room for nuanced control without micromanagement. A founder might cede formal titles yet retain strategic veto rights. An heir might benefit from a trust without ever directing distributions. Family councils or holding company boards may oversee long-term strategy, balancing governance across branches or generations. These are not hypotheticals. They are real-world practices—standard among families whose wealth has survived political collapse, litigation, or the entropy of poor planning. Control here is not egocentric. It's structural. Embedded. Durable.

That said, transitioning from direct ownership to indirect control can feel uncomfortable, particularly for those new to wealth. It may feel like giving something up. In reality, it's quite the opposite. Holding everything in your name may feel like command, but it centralises risk. A single court order can unravel an entire financial edifice. One publicly recorded asset can become a beacon for opportunists.

Indirect control, on the other hand, disperses liability and builds in distance. It requires foresight, legal design, and a willingness to relinquish the illusion of immediate access. But it offers, in return, resilience.

One of the most common missteps made by newly wealthy individuals is defaulting to personal ownership for the sake of simplicity. A founder exits a venture and deposits the proceeds in a personal brokerage. A family buys homes in their own names. Intellectual property is registered to the individual rather than an entity. These decisions feel transparent, even responsible. But structurally, they are naive. When litigation arrives—or political conditions turn—these assets become low-hanging fruit. Restructuring after the fact is rarely effective. The opportunity to design usually precedes the threat.

There's another dimension too—strategy. In negotiations, being known as the owner of a particular asset can weaken your position. You lose ambiguity. You lose leverage. But when an entity sits between you and the asset—be it a trust, a nominee, or a special purpose vehicle—you regain optionality. The counterparty negotiates with a structure, not a personality. You remain protected. The asset remains valuable. And the deal unfolds on your terms. This isn't avoidance. It's positioning.

Here lies the deeper shift: power has migrated. It no longer resides in possession, but in the design of systems. The most secure individuals are often those who appear, on paper, to own very little. Their names are absent. Their influence is not. Their wealth, meanwhile, flows—calmly, efficiently—through latticed frameworks of control. This inversion of visibility and power remains alien to popular understanding, but is second nature to the truly sophisticated. It is why the world's wealthiest often appear asset-light. Their affluence has not diminished. It has been encased—by choice, by design.

This chapter opens the door to that world. We will walk through the mechanisms—foundations, LLCs, hybrid trusts—and examine how they alter the calculus of risk. We'll look at real case studies—some anonymised, others widely known—to see how elite individuals use indirect control to preserve wealth and autonomy. We'll wrestle with the moral lines, and ask difficult questions: when does structuring become camouflage? When does strategy lapse into subterfuge? And, crucially, how can you audit not just what you hold, but how—and why—you hold it?

This is not about secrecy for its own sake. It is about intelligent, principled positioning. To be visible only when it serves you. To be structured everywhere else. Ownership may impress. But control—silent, embedded, resilient—is what endures. And in an age increasingly defined by its hostility to visibility, the rules of power now belong to those who understand how to vanish from the register, without ever losing command.

The Legal Fiction of Ownership

Ownership, as it is typically understood, is a story we've been taught to believe without ever interrogating its internal contradictions. From an early age, we are told to own our homes, own our ideas, own our success. The very language of self-worth is tied to the act of possession. But in legal and strategic terms, outright ownership is often *not* a position of power—it is a point of exposure. It invites liability, attracts scrutiny, and collapses distance between you and risk. What the law calls "ownership" is, more often than not, a formal placeholder for responsibility, not control. In private wealth strategy, the critical distinction is not what you own—it's what you *control.*

To grasp this, we must start by understanding ownership as a legal fiction—one that serves tax authorities, creditors, and courts more than it protects the individual. When your name appears on a title deed, a shareholder registry, or a public filing, you have not merely acquired an asset. You have assumed legal and reputational responsibility for everything that asset implies. You are now liable for litigation, claims, regulatory demands, and unforeseen contingencies. The asset is not just in your portfolio—it is tied to your name, your passport, your jurisdiction, and often, your physical freedom. This is not sovereignty. It is exposure, formalised.

Consider the concept of *beneficial ownership*, now aggressively tracked under global transparency initiatives such as the OECD's Common Reporting Standard and the FATF's beneficial ownership disclosure regimes. These frameworks operate on the assumption that naming and identifying the real people behind assets is a path to fairness and accountability. But for private individuals, this visibility can become a strategic liability. If your assets are known, they can be contested. If they are registered in your name, they can be seized. If they are owned directly, they can be taxed, divorced, litigated, and politicised. *Outright ownership, far from offering control, often invites its loss.*

This is not a fringe insight. It is well understood at the top of the wealth pyramid. Many of the world's most sophisticated asset holders own remarkably little on paper. Their names are absent from land registries. Their investment portfolios are held through nominee accounts. Their companies are directed by proxies. Their real estate is owned by holding entities, which are in turn held by discretionary trusts. To the casual observer—or even to an auditor without legal cause—they appear modest. But in practice, they exercise full control. They decide who lives in the house, when the shares are sold, how distributions are made. *They control without owning—and are safer for it.*

This distinction has historical roots. Roman law, which still underpins much of modern Western jurisprudence, recognised the concept of *usufruct*—a legal right to use and enjoy the benefits of property without holding title. Feudal systems separated the rights of tenancy from the obligations of lordship. In Islamic jurisprudence, the *waqf* structure allowed property to be held perpetually for charitable or familial purposes, with no individual owner. These legal mechanisms were not designed to obscure ownership—they were designed to *neutralise its burdens.*

In modern financial planning, this principle finds its strongest expression in *trusts* and *corporate entities.* A properly constructed discretionary trust, for instance, removes legal ownership from the settlor. The assets belong to the trust—not the individual. The trustee has fiduciary duty, but the control mechanisms can be carefully drafted to reflect the founder's wishes. This layered design ensures that no single person "owns" the asset in a strict legal sense, even though it continues to serve the economic and strategic interests of those involved.

Similarly, an LLC or foundation can act as a control vehicle, allowing an individual to make decisions over assets without assuming the legal burdens of ownership. A foundation in Liechtenstein or Panama, for example, can be structured with a council that implements the vision of a founder while shielding them from personal liability. These are not shell games. They are *legal reclassifications of power*, designed to separate control from risk.

This becomes particularly important in volatile environments—where courts are politicised, divorce laws are punitive, or regulatory enforcement is arbitrary. Owning a valuable asset in your own name in such jurisdictions is not just inefficient. It can be existentially foolish. When governments collapse, when family disputes escalate, or when courts are captured, *direct ownership becomes the most dangerous position one can hold.*

There are, of course, ethical tensions in this terrain. The line between protection and concealment is thin. A structure designed to preserve family wealth from political instability may look identical to one built to avoid tax or shield criminal proceeds. This is why *intent and legal compliance* must be foundational. Using corporate or trust vehicles to avoid legitimate obligations—such as spousal maintenance, lawful tax dues, or creditor repayment—is not asset protection. It is asset evasion, and courts are increasingly willing to pierce such structures when abuse is evident.

The goal, then, is not to *escape* responsibility. It is to *distribute it wisely.* Control over possession means designing your asset architecture so that no single failure—personal, legal, political, or relational—can collapse the entire system. If your holdings are all in your name, you are the single point of failure. If they are structured through layered control, governed by independent entities, and protected by legal distance, you become *insulated rather than exposed.*

To internalise this concept is to adopt a new philosophy of wealth. It is no longer about accumulation. It is about positioning. Where is the asset held? Who has signing authority? Which jurisdiction governs its legal status? What disclosures are triggered, and to whom? These questions define whether your wealth is protected—or simply parked under your name, waiting to be attacked.

A useful analogy is that of a military command. The general does not fight on the front line. Their power lies in coordination, strategy, and command. They do not personally possess every asset in the field, but they determine how those assets are deployed. That is *functional control without operational exposure.* In wealth structuring, the same logic applies. The effective principal is not the registered owner. They are the orchestrator—the one who designed the system, who defines its movement, but who remains outside the blast radius of litigation or audit.

This framework also forces a reassessment of what "wealth" really means. If we measure wealth by what we own, we are adopting a 19th-century mindset—one in which land deeds and stock certificates defined influence. But if we measure wealth by what we *can control, shape, or preserve*, we arrive at a more relevant and robust definition for the 21st century—one that reflects legal complexity, geopolitical volatility, and the need for strategic ambiguity.

This is not a technicality. It is a shift in worldview. To own is to be known. To control discreetly is to remain agile. And agility—not visibility—is the true currency of modern power.

In the chapters ahead, we will explore the mechanics of how this fiction is constructed: how control clauses in trusts work, how nominee directors are appointed, how corporate layering can reduce risk without undermining legality. But at the centre of it all is this core insight: *ownership is no longer the endpoint of financial success. It is often the beginning of strategic vulnerability.* If you understand this, you begin to structure not to possess, but to protect. Not to signal, but to steward. And not to anchor wealth in your name, but to anchor it in design.

The Corporate Cloak

A legal entity is not merely a business tool. It is a boundary—a deliberate separation between person and asset, control and liability, identity and function. When used with clarity and intent, entities such as limited liability companies (LLCs), foundations, and corporations offer more than just operational convenience. They create *legal membranes* that redefine ownership, obscure exposure, and enable control without possession. This capacity to cloak—strategically, lawfully, and intelligently—is foundational to modern wealth preservation.

To the untrained eye, a company is a vehicle for commercial activity. In legal terms, however, it is a person: a distinct juridical entity, capable of owning property, entering contracts, suing and being sued. This distinction is not academic. It is structural. When an asset—be it real estate, intellectual property, equity, or a luxury asset—is held in the name of a company rather than an individual, the legal relationship to that asset changes. The individual no longer *owns* the asset. The company does. The individual may still control it, benefit from it, or even manage its use—but from the perspective of courts, creditors, and registries, they are no longer synonymous with it. *This is not concealment. It is reclassification.*

This reclassification matters profoundly. It transforms risk. Suppose a litigation claim is brought against you personally. If your key assets are held in your own name, they are exposed. If, instead, your shares in operating businesses are held by an offshore holding company, and your properties by special purpose vehicles (SPVs), you have functionally isolated the threat. The claimant may succeed in court but find the spoils protected by corporate shells with no direct link to your name or personal liability. You haven't hidden the asset—you've distanced it.

This legal distancing is the essence of the corporate cloak. The LLC, one of the most widely used structures in wealth strategy, illustrates this elegantly. It combines pass-through taxation with limited liability and operational simplicity. But its deeper utility lies in flexibility: ownership can be held through nominees; management rights can be assigned separately from ownership; and jurisdictional selection can tailor visibility to the needs of privacy or compliance. An LLC registered in Wyoming or Nevis may offer member anonymity, while a counterpart in the UK or Singapore offers credibility and regulatory reputation. In both cases, the core value is the *buffer* it creates between the individual and the asset.

Foundations operate on a slightly different philosophical basis. Unlike corporations, which are owned by shareholders, a private foundation typically has *no owner.* It exists as a self-standing entity governed by a charter and overseen by a council or board. This distinction creates powerful legal distance. A Liechtenstein or Panama foundation, properly drafted, can act as the central node of a family's wealth architecture—holding companies, properties, and intellectual assets—while legally insulating the founder from direct ownership. Even the founder's influence can be layered: they may retain rights to appoint or remove council members, issue letters of wishes, or control key decisions through reserved powers, but they remain technically outside the ownership chain.

This creates a paradox that many struggle to understand: *you can design a structure in which you hold no official title, yet control outcomes entirely*. The courts, regulators, or adversaries see a network of companies and entities. You see a system you authored—one that continues to serve your family, business, or legacy, without tying your name to any particular asset.

This approach is not reserved for the ultra-wealthy. Middle-market entrepreneurs, investors, and globally mobile professionals increasingly use the corporate cloak to achieve the same ends. A British expat in Dubai may use a BVI holding company to manage international rental income. An e-commerce business owner may isolate brands in separate LLCs to limit cross-liability. A family concerned about political instability in their home country may consolidate their estate into a Dutch foundation for governance continuity. In each case, the individual has moved from *ownership to architecture*. And with that shift comes strategic leverage.

Of course, leverage without clarity breeds danger. The misuse of entities—whether for evasion, obfuscation, or fraud—has rightly drawn regulatory scrutiny. Shell companies have been linked to tax abuses, money laundering, and capital flight. But to conflate abuse with use is a category error. *The structure is neutral. The intent is what matters*. A hammer can build a house or break a window. Similarly, an LLC can enable multi-generational asset protection—or it can conceal illicit flows. Legal frameworks across jurisdictions increasingly reflect this distinction, introducing transparency registers, substance requirements, and mandatory disclosures for beneficial owners. Responsible structuring must account for this—compliance is not optional, and ignorance is not a defence.

Yet even within compliant frameworks, the corporate cloak remains essential. It is the difference between being personally accountable for every commercial risk—and being shielded. Between being an individual on a registry—and being a decision-maker behind a governance firewall. Between losing assets in a single litigation—and preserving them through layered holding chains.

Ethically, this demands a specific mindset: *stewardship over entitlement.* You are not building structures to hide from responsibility. You are building them to *assign responsibility rationally*, to ensure continuity, and to separate the personal from the operational. This requires psychological discipline. Many founders are uncomfortable giving up legal title. They want to "own" their company in name, hold the real estate themselves, or sign as director on every deal. But control without insulation is not strength—it is fragility disguised as ownership. The corporate cloak invites us to redefine what it means to lead: not through proximity, but through design.

Consider also the psychological effect of detachment. When assets are held in your own name, every event—market dip, property issue, business lawsuit—feels personal. When those assets are held through structured layers, you can engage more strategically. Decision-making becomes less reactive. Governance becomes more intentional. You shift from *operator* to *architect.*

From a legacy perspective, the benefits are even clearer. Assets held in personal name require wills, probate, and exposure to estate taxes. Entities, by contrast, are durable. A family trust can hold a foundation, which owns various companies, each with succession protocols embedded. Control passes not through inheritance, but through structure. The family's economic engine persists, regardless of personal transitions.

But none of this works if the design is sloppy, superficial, or self-deceiving. Entities must have real substance—bank accounts, books, directors, contracts. Founders must relinquish enough legal control to avoid recharacterisation by courts. Nominee arrangements must be documented, ethical, and legally defensible. In short, *the corporate cloak must be tailored—not mass-produced.* And it must be integrated with a broader philosophy of wealth: clarity, continuity, and lawful discretion.

To operate effectively in today's world, you cannot afford to think in binaries—visible vs hidden, owner vs non-owner, legal vs illegal. You must think in layers. In shields. In designed opacity that enhances stability. The corporate cloak offers this. It is not an artefact of offshore opportunism. It is a strategic necessity in an environment where visibility is vulnerability.

In the chapters ahead, we will examine how these entities interface with trusts, banking jurisdictions, and privacy laws. But for now, let this be the foundation: *You are not building structures to hide assets. You are building boundaries to preserve freedom.* The company is not a mask. It is a membrane. And learning how to wear the corporate cloak well may be the most durable financial skill of the 21st century.

Shadow vs Substance: What You *Actually* Own

Walk into a room of affluent individuals and ask what they own. Most will respond with a familiar list: a portfolio of equities, several properties, shares in a business, perhaps a trust or two, and some digital assets for good measure. The inventory is offered with confidence, even pride—each item representing perceived security, power, and independence. But dig deeper, and another picture often emerges: many of these assets are registered in jurisdictions the owner doesn't understand, tied up in vehicles they don't control, or exposed in ways they never intended. The distinction between *what you think you own* and *what you actually control* is not trivial. It is, in fact, foundational.

This subchapter challenges the reader to conduct a forensic audit—not of what sits on paper, but of the *structural truth* behind their financial architecture. It asks a deceptively simple question: if tomorrow morning you were sued, politically targeted, or unable to access your accounts, which of your assets would remain secure, functional, and legally within your influence? The answer, for most, is far less reassuring than their balance sheet suggests. *Wealth without control is not wealth. It is exposure.*

To understand the difference between shadow and substance, we must first reframe what it means to "own" something. Ownership, in common usage, implies exclusivity: that you have full rights to use, sell, transfer, or leverage an asset. But legally and strategically, ownership is often a proxy for liability. The real question is not *do you own it?* but *can you control it without being directly exposed to its risks?* That distinction is what separates resilient wealth from fragile capital.

Take real estate. Owning property in your personal name feels straightforward. It is legible to banks, understandable to courts, and psychologically satisfying. But it also places you in the direct line of attack. A lawsuit, tax dispute, or regulatory event can lead to a charging order, asset freeze, or public exposure. Now compare that to a scenario in which the same property is held by a trust, which in turn is owned by a holding company, with a nominee director and registered in a jurisdiction that doesn't publicise ownership data. The asset is functionally the same—you still enjoy it, rent it out, or sell it—but your personal liability has been rerouted. The ownership is a shadow. The control, however, is substantive—and durable.

This structure is not theoretical. It is how many of the world's wealthiest families preserve their financial ecosystems. The public might believe a billionaire owns several homes. In reality, the person may own nothing directly. Their role is managerial, directional, perhaps even consultative—but not registered. Their control is real.

Their liability is not. *They understand that visible ownership attracts attention; functional control preserves autonomy.*

Yet many high-income earners and first-generation wealth builders conflate visibility with legitimacy. They want to "own" their success, to demonstrate it, to anchor it in names and deeds. This impulse is understandable. It is also risky. The moment your name is tied to an asset, that asset becomes a conduit to you. That's not an abstraction. In asset tracing, lawyers and forensic accountants do not just follow the money—they follow the *names*. If your signature appears on the articles of incorporation, if you're the beneficial owner on a bank record, if your identity is tied to a land title, then you're a legally actionable endpoint. *Substance follows exposure.*

There is, however, another danger—one that occurs at the opposite extreme. In an attempt to obscure ownership, some individuals over-engineer structures they do not fully understand. They delegate too much. They sign away too many rights. They engage advisors who serve compliance checklists, not long-term stewardship. As a result, they end up not with shadow ownership—but with *no ownership at all.* They've built a fortress with no master key. This often becomes apparent only when the founder dies, a beneficiary makes a claim, or a financial institution interprets the structure differently than expected. Complexity without comprehension is not strategy. It is abdication. *If you cannot answer who controls your wealth in a crisis, then you don't.*

This is where inventory becomes essential. Not an inventory of assets, but of *control pathways*. For each significant holding, ask:
– Who holds legal title?
– Who can transfer, liquidate, or encumber the asset?
– Which jurisdiction governs the entity or vehicle involved?
– What level of personal liability attaches to the asset?
– What would happen to the asset if you were incapacitated, exiled, or audited?

These questions cut through narrative. They expose how much of your wealth is structurally yours—and how much merely appears to be.

Real control is not reactive. It is architected. A Singapore-based family office may sit atop a web of global assets, but if all investment decisions are routed through a Cayman master fund, and all beneficial rights flow through a Jersey trust, then control rests in the documents—not in the founders. This is by design. It allows for adaptability, risk dispersion, and operational silence. The founder can shape, influence, and even enjoy the wealth—but without appearing as its owner. *They have replaced ownership with authorship.*

This is not merely a legal exercise. It is philosophical. What does it mean to "have" something, if you cannot protect it, reassign it, or access it under pressure? Conversely, what does it mean to not "own" something, but to guide its every movement? These are not rhetorical questions. They force us to reconsider whether our wealth strategies are designed for visibility—or viability.

Ethical reflection is also crucial. Structures that distance ownership can be used responsibly or irresponsibly. To shelter assets from legitimate creditors, divorce obligations, or tax authorities in bad faith is not sophisticated. It is reckless—and increasingly penetrable by courts. The principle at stake is not concealment, but *containment.* You are not avoiding the law. You are designing within it, to minimise unnecessary exposure and maximise long-term resilience. That is not deception. It is discretion.

Shadow ownership becomes problematic only when it lacks transparency to the right audiences—your advisors, your heirs, your fiduciaries. A well-structured estate plan, for example, may legally deny any single party full ownership, but it should ensure that the intended beneficiaries receive benefit, and that trustees or directors understand their roles. The illusion that "no one owns anything" should be a legal truth, not a practical chaos. *Opacity without clarity creates the illusion of control—but not its substance.*

A meaningful exercise for any serious asset holder is to periodically collapse their own illusion. Remove the titles, the valuations, the vanity metrics. Ask: what do I *actually* control? What can I still command if I'm not in the room? If my name is removed from the equation, what still works? The answers to these questions will reveal not just your assets—but your exposures, your dependencies, and your blind spots.

This is what differentiates temporary wealth from enduring capital. Wealth measured in titles and declarations is always vulnerable to litigation, politics, or personal error. Wealth embedded in structure, supported by legal clarity, and divorced from personal identity is far harder to disrupt. It does not live in the ego. It lives in the blueprint.

As you move through the more technical sections of this book—trusts, corporate layering, offshore jurisdiction selection—this distinction between shadow and substance will become increasingly vital. Strategy is not about owning more. It is about *controlling wisely, exposing selectively, and building systems that outlive your presence.*

Because ultimately, the question is not what your net worth says. It is: what survives when your name no longer does? That is the difference between paper wealth and true power.

Ethics of Invisible Control

The power to act without being seen is seductive. In wealth structuring, it can be immensely protective—allowing individuals to direct assets, influence decisions, and enjoy economic benefit without personal exposure. But there is a fine line between *invisible control* and *deceptive concealment.* Understanding where that line lies is not only a legal and strategic imperative; it is an ethical one. The legitimacy of privacy structures—trusts, foundations, layered corporations—hinges not only on compliance with statutes, but on clarity of intent. The most robust asset protection plan is worthless if it cannot withstand ethical scrutiny, especially when tested under legal or moral pressure.

The purpose of invisible control is not to vanish from responsibility but to *separate ownership from liability*. It is about *designing distance*, not denying existence. This distinction matters. It is the difference between someone who builds structures to mitigate unjust exposure, and someone who builds structures to avoid just obligations. Both may use similar tools. The divergence lies in their intent and how those tools are implemented.

This tension is not hypothetical. It arises frequently in courts around the world. When judges pierce corporate veils or disregard trusts, they do not do so because the structures themselves are illegal. They do so because *the purpose behind the structure was deemed abusive or dishonest.* In other words, the legal tool was ethically misapplied. And courts—contrary to popular belief—are increasingly willing to consider *substance over form* when examining wealth protections.

Consider the landmark case *Prest v Petrodel Resources Ltd* (UK Supreme Court, 2013), which revolved around a divorcing husband's attempt to shield assets using companies he nominally did not own. The court ruled that although the husband was not the legal owner of several properties held by companies, the corporate form had been used to frustrate legitimate claims. The companies were treated as his proxies. Not because they were inherently flawed, but because they were used in bad faith. *It was not the invisibility that failed. It was the motive behind it.*

This forces a critical question: when does legitimate privacy become illegitimate evasion? The answer lies not in public opinion or political narratives, but in principles of fairness, proportionality, and responsibility.

A person shielding their family estate from unjust political seizure—say, in a collapsing or corrupt jurisdiction—acts to preserve their autonomy and generational continuity. Their use of offshore trusts, nominee structures, and layered control is a rational defence against chaos. By contrast, an individual who places assets in foreign structures to avoid alimony payments, settle tax fraud, or hide funds from bankruptcy proceedings is not engaging in strategic discretion. They are abusing legal distance to escape personal accountability. *Ethical wealth structuring does not protect the individual from their responsibilities—it protects them from disproportionate or illegitimate risk.*

Navigating this distinction demands intellectual honesty. It is easy to rationalise any defensive measure under the guise of privacy or security. But effective architects of invisible control ask harder questions: What am I protecting, and from whom? Are my structures designed to honour legal obligations—or to elude them? Would this arrangement stand up to adversarial scrutiny—not only legally, but morally?

These are not abstract dilemmas. In fact, ethical structuring is more resilient in practice. Structures built with sound intent are easier to defend under audit, litigation, or political inquiry. A well-documented trust with independent governance and transparent tax reporting will outlast a hastily formed offshore shell company registered to an unmonitored nominee. *The ethical foundations of your structure are the true test of its durability.*

We should also acknowledge that the public discourse around invisible control is distorted. Media and political rhetoric often conflate all financial discretion with malfeasance. In this worldview, any attempt to separate oneself from one's assets is assumed to be suspicious. This conflation is intellectually lazy. Privacy is not inherently unethical. Just as individuals have a right to physical security, they have a right to financial security. The fact that a few abuse discretion does not invalidate the many who use it wisely.

Nevertheless, public perception matters. A family office that structures assets to avoid unnecessary visibility may be acting legally and ethically—but if its intent appears opaque, it risks reputational damage. This is where transparency *by choice* becomes a strategic advantage. The ability to disclose *when necessary*—to regulators, legal counsel, or beneficiaries—reinforces the integrity of the structure. The smartest architects of invisible control build systems that can flex under scrutiny without collapsing. Their privacy is not absolute; it is *selective, purposeful, and defensible.*

A principled approach to invisible control also requires internal governance. Structures must not only be legally compliant; they must be operationally coherent. If a foundation is created to support philanthropic objectives, it should have records, minutes, and a governing board. If a trust is discretionary, its trustees should act with independence, document their reasoning, and maintain oversight. Empty vehicles are indefensible. Substance—not merely form—makes discretion ethical.

This brings us to a core tenet: *invisible control must be auditable by design, not just in theory.* If your entire structure collapses the moment someone asks a hard question, you haven't built discretion—you've built deception. And no amount of legal architecture can salvage a structure that rests on unethical foundations.

It's also important to reflect on how this impacts successors. Invisible control may work in your lifetime because you understand the architecture and maintain the relationships. But what happens after you? If heirs inherit assets they don't legally own, or can't locate, or can't explain, then you have not passed on a legacy—you have passed on confusion. A principled approach involves succession mapping: clarity about roles, responsibilities, and timelines for when visibility should be increased. *Privacy without continuity is an incomplete strategy.*

For professional advisors, this ethical responsibility is especially acute. Lawyers, trustees, and fiduciaries must resist client pressures to "hide" rather than "structure." They must educate clients on the difference between protection and avoidance, and build systems that can hold up under pressure—not just legally, but morally. That is not idealism. It is sustainability.

Ultimately, the ethics of invisible control are not a side conversation. They are the backbone of every choice in this field. Invisible control is a powerful capability—but only if wielded with proportion, discipline, and clarity of purpose. It enables sovereignty, not secrecy. Stewardship, not concealment.

So as you assess your own architecture, or advise others on theirs, ask not just: *Is this legal?* Ask: *Is this fair? Is this coherent? Could this stand up to honest scrutiny, if needed?* The answers to these questions will not only shape the strength of your structure—they will define its legitimacy.

Invisible control is not about absence. It is about *intelligent distance.* And when that distance is built on principled intent, it becomes the most powerful—and defensible—form of protection available.

Chapter 3
Trusts – Structures of Intent and Protection

At first glance, the trust can seem like an antique—an artefact of old-world estate planning, wrapped in arcane legal formality and wielded by landed families to safeguard their fortunes from the reach of time. Yet that image, persistent though it is, barely scratches the surface. Far from being a fossil of aristocratic excess, the trust is arguably one of the most versatile instruments in modern finance. Not because it hides things—though it can—but because it gives form to intent. A well-conceived trust is more than a vault. It is a vessel of purpose. It lets you transmit not just assets, but values—offering precision that a will, deed, or even the most sophisticated corporate structure simply cannot replicate.

This chapter does not concern itself with the usual checklist of trust options. It is not another primer on basic estate planning. Rather, it offers a deeper exploration—one that treats the trust as a strategic and philosophical artefact. When properly architected, a trust becomes a living, breathing system: adaptive, durable, and deeply expressive of the founder's intent. It is, in short, a form of governance—subtle, structured, and built to outlast its originator.

What's often missed in popular and even professional discussions is this: a trust is not defined by the things it holds. It is defined by the purposes it's built to serve. This makes it astonishingly adaptable. It can preserve a family's cohesion—or its distance. It can ward off creditors, withstand political instability, or preserve wealth from regimes that provoke deep distrust. It can, in essence, serve as a bulwark—not merely of money, but of meaning. A sovereign tool for a sovereign life.

To see the trust clearly, we need to break free from the binary lenses through which it's so often viewed. Revocable versus irrevocable, onshore versus offshore, simple versus complex—these are the taxonomist's tools, not the strategist's. Useful, perhaps, for orientation. But the more important question is not which label fits. It's what the trust is *for.* What function is it meant to perform? And under what pressures must it hold?

This chapter begins at that precise juncture—with a concept we might call functional intent. We'll move through contrasting case studies that reveal how particular trust configurations answer to particular strategic demands. Consider the humble living trust: efficient, lightweight, ideal for bypassing probate and smoothing intergenerational handover. It's not a fortress; it's a filing cabinet—tidy, convenient, unobtrusive. Now contrast that with an "asset armour" trust: irrevocable, discretionary, strategically opaque, often spread across multiple jurisdictions. This isn't about ease. It's about insulation—against lawsuits, surveillance, state encroachment. One is built for flow, the other for friction. Neither is universally better. Each is only as good as its alignment with its environment.

The real danger—and it's far from rare—is misalignment. Time and again, professionals reach for templates. They apply boilerplate structures without ever probing the underlying motivations. The result is depressingly predictable: trusts that are technically valid, but practically inert. They're too inflexible to evolve, too imprecise to protect, or too broad to enforce. Worse still are those designed with one function in mind—family harmony, say—but then conscripted into roles they were never meant to play, like shielding assets during a divorce or withstanding a tax authority's inquiry. A trust cannot become what it was not designed to be. Purpose cannot be retrofitted.

Which is why, before structure, there must be story. And not merely a list of beneficiaries, but a map—an intentional beneficiary map, to be precise. This is not a bureaucratic form. It's a conceptual tool. It asks: who are you protecting, and from what? Are they aligned or at odds? Do they require access, or should they be buffered from temptation and responsibility? Are you encouraging growth, or enforcing boundaries? These are not legal queries. They are matters of design, psychology, and foresight. And they are essential.

A common failure in trust creation is the absence of narrative scaffolding. Deeds are signed. Trustees are appointed. Funds are transferred. But the founder leaves behind no moral compass—no letter of wishes, no philosophical preamble, no human explanation for what the structure is meant to uphold. So when friction arises—and it always does—fiduciaries are left groping through cold legal text instead of being guided by warm intention. This is not simply unfortunate. It is structurally dangerous. A trust without a story is a mechanism without meaning. It may function, but it cannot lead.

Let's make this real. Picture an artist—someone whose life's work is their intellectual property. They want to ensure their royalties are stewarded wisely and channelled into cultural initiatives, long after their death. Or think of a globally mobile entrepreneur—tax-resident nowhere in particular, exposed to a patchwork of legal jurisdictions. Their assets, split across continents, must be both compliant and protected. Then there is the activist—operating under regimes where dissent is penalised. Their priority is to protect their family's safety and wealth from political reprisal, without slipping outside the boundaries of the law. These aren't edge cases. They're the future. And in each instance, the trust must be crafted not just legally, but philosophically and emotionally.

Because—let's not pretend otherwise—trusts carry fingerprints. The choices embedded in their design speak volumes. The jurisdiction selected reveals views on risk and regulation. The identity and independence of trustees speaks to confidence—or lack thereof. Reserved powers signal attachment. Abdicated ones suggest trust. A settlor who clings tightly to every detail hasn't built a trust at all. They've constructed a ticking liability. One who delegates everything without clarity has instead engineered a governance vacuum. Real control lies not in either extreme, but in the architecture that balances discretion with direction.

To navigate this well, one must approach trust planning not as a compliance chore, but as a form of strategic authorship. Jurisdictions vary not only in tax implications, but in how they handle privacy, settlor influence, and conflict resolution. Tools such as protector roles, letters of wishes, and decanting powers can transform a static trust into a dynamic one—capable of evolving in response to circumstance while remaining true to its founding spirit. But these tools require care. And clarity.

This chapter will guide you through all that—jurisdictional subtleties, mechanisms of internal governance, adaptive strategies for trust evolution. But beyond the technical, it also invites you to consider the trust as a human construct. A trust, ultimately, is not a box for money. It's a vehicle for meaning. It transmits more than wealth. It reflects a worldview. And so, it demands something that lawyers and advisors too often sidestep: a confrontation with values. Yours.

Because when done properly, a trust isn't merely established. It is tended. Stewarded. Revisited. The documents may be static, but the circumstances they govern are anything but. Families evolve. Politics shifts. The markets, as ever, tremble. A robust trust must flex without fracturing. And that only happens when structure and philosophy are in constant, if quiet, conversation.

So if you're willing to think past ownership… past tax codes and formality… to let legacy speak in a deeper register—then the trust becomes something altogether different. Not a hedge. Not a loophole. A legacy, codified. A statement of intent that carries not just authority, but soul. Not because you wish to escape scrutiny, but because you've chosen to build something that reflects more than your wealth. It reflects your will.

Anatomy of a Trust: Beyond Definitions

Ask most professionals—lawyers, bankers, even financial planners—to define a trust, and you will likely hear the same formulaic response: *"a fiduciary arrangement in which a trustee holds legal title to property for the benefit of a beneficiary."* Technically correct. Functionally useless. This skeletal description captures the legal fiction but omits the structural intelligence. It says nothing of *why* trusts exist, *how* they are constructed to fulfil diverse strategic purposes, or *what* makes a trust truly resilient in the face of legal challenge, political instability, or interpersonal breakdown. To understand trusts as living architecture—not just legal abstractions—requires going well beyond definitions. It requires looking at their anatomy: not just who does what, but how power, intent, and protection are engineered into the structure itself.

At its core, a trust is a separation mechanism. It breaks the conventional fusion of ownership and control, creating a layered relationship between legal title, beneficial interest, and decision-making authority. This separation allows assets to be insulated from direct claims by creditors, courts, governments, or even family members, depending on how the trust is designed. But this insulation is not automatic. Nor is it absolute. The effectiveness of any trust lies in its *functional anatomy*—the way its components are constructed, interrelated, and governed over time.

To grasp this, consider the essential components. A trust requires at minimum: a settlor (the person creating the trust), a trustee (the legal owner of the assets), a beneficiary or class of beneficiaries (those who benefit economically), and a trust deed or instrument (which dictates the terms of engagement). Yet even these elements are not as simple as they appear.

Take the settlor. Their influence does not end upon signing the deed. In many trust designs, particularly in asset-protection or discretionary trusts, the settlor retains indirect influence through roles such as *protector*, *investment advisor*, or *letter of wishes author*. While not always legally binding, these soft powers—when strategically documented—can shape trustee conduct without violating the principles of separation. This is not manipulation; it is architectural foresight.

The trustee, often presented as a passive administrator, is in fact the structural linchpin. Their legal ownership is not symbolic—it carries fiduciary liability, discretion, and operational responsibility. A poorly chosen trustee—whether inexperienced, conflicted, or inadequately regulated—can unravel the entire trust. Conversely, a professional trustee with independence, track record, and proper governance controls becomes a strategic asset. The distinction between *individual trustees*, *corporate trustees*, and *licensed fiduciary firms* is not merely cosmetic. It has implications for everything from legal continuity to jurisdictional exposure.

Beneficiaries, too, require nuance. A trust is not merely about passing assets down a lineage. It is about *controlling the nature and timing of access*. Beneficiaries may be fixed (with defined entitlements) or discretionary (with interests that depend on trustee judgement). This flexibility is often what gives a trust its power to adapt to changing circumstances—divorce, litigation, economic downturns, or shifts in family dynamics. But with flexibility comes risk. The more discretion granted, the more potential for dispute. Discretionary trusts must therefore be paired with strong interpretive guidance—letters of wishes, review mechanisms, and, ideally, a trust protector to mediate conflicts or replace unfit trustees.

The trust instrument itself—the legal document setting out the terms—should be viewed as a form of constitutional architecture. It defines not just asset distribution, but governance protocols, amendment procedures, dispute resolution frameworks, and succession planning. In high-functioning trusts, the deed does not merely replicate statutory defaults. It pre-empts challenges. It anticipates failure points. It adapts traditional trust law to modern complexity.

Mainstream books tend to stop here. But the real sophistication begins when trusts are built with *purpose-built frameworks*—models that go beyond inheritance planning and enter domains like litigation defence, cross-border asset holding, philanthropic strategy, or political exile preparation.

Consider, for instance, the *dynastic trust.* This is not simply a multi-generational asset container. When constructed thoughtfully, it serves as a perpetual governance engine—funding education, entrepreneurship, or charitable giving across generations, while maintaining oversight through evolving trustee boards and value-aligned provisions. Alternatively, take the *privacy-focused discretionary trust,* used in high-risk environments where the settlor wishes to obscure beneficial ownership from public registries, political authorities, or even familial rivals. Such a trust may involve jurisdictional layering, non-aligned trustees, and strict anti-disclosure clauses to enforce opacity within the bounds of the law.

Then there are *asset segregation trusts*, created to ringfence specific classes of assets—intellectual property, real estate, or minority business interests—from wider estate exposure. These are commonly used by creators, inventors, or founders who wish to distinguish control from revenue participation. In each case, the trust is not just a tool. It is a *design language*—tailored, conscious, and strategic.

It is also a language of *jurisdiction.* A trust formed in Guernsey behaves differently from one formed in New Zealand, Singapore, or South Dakota. Some jurisdictions favour settlor control. Others prioritise asset protection. Some require public registration. Others do not. These variations are not trivial. They define the legal durability of your structure under external challenge. A trust is only as strong as the jurisdiction that governs it—and that jurisdiction must align not only with current strategy, but with *future legal and geopolitical volatility.*

No less critical is the trust's *lifecycle planning.* Trusts are not static. They encounter friction: tax law changes, beneficiary disputes, trustee retirement, political pressure. High-functioning trusts are designed for *evolution.* They include provisions for decanting (transferring assets to a new trust), replacement of trustees or protectors, amendment of clauses under defined circumstances, and the creation of successor vehicles. Trusts that lack these evolutionary valves become brittle. They may protect assets, but at the cost of utility.

This brings us to a final but essential point: a trust is only as effective as the *thinking that precedes it.* No document, however carefully drafted, can substitute for strategic clarity. Before creating a trust, the founder must think like an architect. What is the function? What are the risks? What values are being preserved? Who will implement the vision, and what incentives or protections will guide them? What exit routes exist if the structure ceases to serve its purpose? These are not legal questions. They are structural, ethical, and philosophical.

When this level of reflection is absent, the trust becomes an empty husk. It may exist legally, but it will lack coherence, resilience, and continuity. But when this reflection is present—when form follows purpose—then the trust transcends its conventional role. It becomes a living institution: flexible, adaptive, enforceable, and above all, *intentional.*

This is what is rarely taught. Not just how trusts work, but how they can be built to work *well.* This chapter is a corrective to that omission. Here, we will examine not only technical configurations but strategic frameworks. You will learn how to read a trust as a map of power relationships—not simply a legal tool. And you will come to appreciate that the true anatomy of a trust lies not in its paperwork, but in its *architecture of intent.* That architecture, when designed with clarity and purpose, becomes one of the most powerful expressions of private sovereignty in the modern world.

Living Trusts vs. Asset Armours

In the world of wealth structuring, the word *trust* often suggests something universally beneficial, stable, and protective. But this blanket characterisation is misleading. Not all trusts serve the same function, and not all are designed with the same intent. Much like architecture, form follows function—and without a precise understanding of purpose, even the most elegantly drafted trust instrument can fail its creator. This subchapter examines two fundamentally different strategic orientations of trusts: the *living trust*, often used as an estate management and succession vehicle, and the *asset armour*, a more defensive construct focused on shielding wealth from litigation, creditors, or political volatility. The difference is not semantic. It is structural, philosophical, and operational.

Let us begin with the living trust—a form widely used in common law jurisdictions such as the United States and increasingly popular elsewhere for its simplicity and adaptability. At its core, a living trust (also known as a revocable trust) is designed to facilitate the management and distribution of an individual's assets during their lifetime and after death, *without triggering probate.* Unlike a will, which becomes operational only upon death and passes through public court proceedings, a living trust is a private, ongoing legal relationship. It allows the settlor—who is often also the initial trustee and beneficiary—to manage their estate while alive and stipulate detailed instructions for how those assets should be handled if they become incapacitated or pass away.

The living trust is prized for its practicality. It reduces court involvement, avoids delay, and preserves privacy during transitional periods. In families with significant assets, blended relationships, or special-needs dependents, it offers an elegant solution for orderly succession. It is also amendable; the settlor retains control and can alter beneficiaries or trustees as circumstances evolve. But herein lies both its appeal and its vulnerability. *Because the settlor retains control, the trust is considered transparent for legal and tax purposes.* That means its protective power is minimal. In litigation, divorce proceedings, or insolvency, a revocable trust can be pierced, disregarded, or collapsed—precisely because it is seen as an extension of the settlor, not a separate legal person.

Contrast this with the asset armour trust—a phrase not typically found in legal textbooks, but increasingly relevant in strategic wealth circles. An asset armour is a class of irrevocable, often discretionary trust, established not for administrative convenience, but for *liability insulation.* Its structure is intentionally built to distance the settlor from the assets—legally, operationally, and even philosophically. Once the trust is created and the assets are transferred, the settlor relinquishes legal ownership and control. The trustee becomes the true legal custodian, and beneficiaries may have only contingent or discretionary interests. This loss of control is not a design flaw. It is the very essence of protection.

The effectiveness of such structures lies in the clarity of separation. If litigants or state actors cannot show that the settlor still controls the trust—through explicit powers or covert influence—they cannot claim that the trust assets are part of the settlor's estate. This makes the asset armour a preferred tool for entrepreneurs, professionals in high-litigation fields, politically exposed persons (PEPs), and individuals operating in fragile jurisdictions. But the price of this protection is permanence. Unlike a living trust, an irrevocable protective trust cannot easily be amended. *It demands clarity of intent at inception.* There are no do-overs.

Purpose alignment, then, is the critical axis. Many individuals wrongly attempt to use a living trust as if it were an asset shield—believing that because their name is off the deed, they are insulated. This is a common and costly misconception. If a court finds that the settlor retains control, enjoys benefits, or uses the trust to circumvent obligations, the veil will be pierced. Similarly, some founders establish protective trusts but fail to structure their affairs coherently—continuing to use trust-owned assets as if they were personal property, or issuing informal directions to trustees. This behaviour undermines the credibility of the structure, legally and ethically.

It's also worth noting the jurisdictional dimension. In some jurisdictions, revocable living trusts enjoy no recognition or are treated identically to personal ownership. In others, such as certain U.S. states, they are deeply embedded in estate law. By contrast, asset protection trusts are typically domiciled in asset-protection-friendly jurisdictions—think Nevis, the Cook Islands, or Jersey—where firewall legislation and strong trustee independence are built into the legal code. These jurisdictions actively resist foreign court judgments that attempt to reach into trusts governed by their laws. But selecting a favourable jurisdiction is not enough. Courts examine *substance over form*. If the trust was created in anticipation of a legal challenge, without genuine relinquishment of control, it may be ruled a fraudulent conveyance.

This introduces an ethical dimension often overlooked in discussions of trust structuring. Protection is legitimate. Deception is not. A well-structured asset armour trust is not a loophole to hide from rightful creditors; it is a tool to manage risk responsibly, provided the settlor acts in good faith, complies with the law, and observes the limits of their post-transfer influence. Likewise, a living trust is not a camouflage for secreted assets; it is a governance tool for families who value efficiency and discretion in generational transition.

The stakes here are not theoretical. Consider a real-world scenario: a successful business owner in a high-risk profession—medicine, for example—accumulates wealth over two decades and places her assets into a revocable living trust. She is both trustee and beneficiary. When a malpractice suit arises, her trust assets are claimed in the litigation. She argues that they are protected under the trust, but the court rules otherwise: she retains control, she enjoys all the benefits, and the trust was revocable. The trust offers no protection. If instead, she had established an offshore discretionary trust with a neutral professional trustee, independent governance protocols, and a cooling-off period before litigation arose, the assets might have been ringfenced from the beginning.

This is not an isolated example. The modern landscape of trust litigation is filled with cases where form was present but substance was lacking. Advisors created beautiful legal documents. But the settlors failed to adjust their behaviour, or chose the wrong structure for the job. As a result, assets were exposed—not because trusts don't work, but because *they were used without strategic clarity.*

To navigate this landscape effectively, readers must resist one-size-fits-all thinking. Trusts are not interchangeable. A living trust is a planning tool. An asset armour is a defence mechanism. Each has its place, but only when aligned with purpose. When selecting between them, ask: Am I trying to *manage* wealth or *protect* it? Do I need *control*, or do I need *distance*? Is the priority *family governance*, or *legal insulation*?

These are not legal questions. They are strategic, emotional, and philosophical. They touch on risk appetite, legacy values, and the settlor's willingness to cede power in exchange for permanence. In this sense, the right trust is not the one that offers the most flexibility or the highest yield. It is the one that *honestly reflects the priorities of its creator*, and stands resilient in the face of real-world scrutiny.

The pages ahead will explore specific configurations, variations, and cautionary examples. But the foundational distinction should now be clear. Living trusts and asset armours are not rivals. They are different instruments in a well-constructed privacy and protection strategy. To mistake one for the other is to misunderstand the architecture of modern wealth. And in that misunderstanding, exposure often hides.

The Intentional Beneficiary Map

Too often, the design of a trust is reduced to a checklist: settlor, trustee, beneficiaries, assets, governing law. Legal form is ticked off, boxes are filled, documents are signed—and yet what should be a vessel for vision, continuity, and protection becomes little more than a legal storage unit. The problem is not the trust structure itself. The problem is that it was constructed without *intentionality*. Specifically, without a deep alignment between the settlor's emotional values and the allocation of benefits. A trust is not only about ownership, tax strategy, or asset shielding. At its best, it is a moral and philosophical instrument—an intergenerational architecture of meaning. The Intentional Beneficiary Map is the framework that ensures a trust reflects not only technical correctness but *purposeful human design*.

The starting point is to acknowledge what most estate planners avoid: *beneficiaries are not interchangeable*. They differ not only in age and legal category but in psychological maturity, financial literacy, relationship to the settlor, and potential risk to the trust itself. A trust that treats all beneficiaries equally in form may produce wildly unequal outcomes in effect. This is not an argument for favouritism. It is a call for *nuance*. Equality and fairness are not always the same thing, especially when viewed through the lens of generational responsibility. A wealthy parent may have three children—one an entrepreneur, one struggling with addiction, and one with a developmental disability. Should these three be treated identically on paper? Legally, perhaps. Intellectually, never.

Traditional trust templates often default to either equal shares or discretionary distributions. While both have their uses, they frequently fail to account for the deeper emotional and strategic context in which trusts operate. Equal distribution assumes parity in capacity, character, and need. Discretionary distribution assumes the trustee knows the settlor's heart and priorities without being told. Neither approach adequately resolves the core challenge: how do you balance legal clarity with emotional fidelity?

This is where the Intentional Beneficiary Map becomes indispensable. It is not a legal document, but a planning methodology. Its purpose is to force a higher-order reflection before ink meets paper. Who, precisely, are the individuals or entities being included in this trust—and *why*? What are their personal circumstances, risks, dependencies, and trajectories? How might their inclusion in the trust serve or destabilise them? And what is the settlor actually trying to accomplish—security, opportunity, stewardship, or simply legacy transmission?

Consider a practical example: a trust established by a politically exposed person (PEP) in a fragile jurisdiction. They have three heirs: a son studying abroad, a daughter working in domestic civil society, and a nephew being groomed to take over the family business. A cookie-cutter trust might list them all as equal discretionary beneficiaries. But the Intentional Beneficiary Map would provoke deeper reflection. The daughter's visibility in a sensitive sector may expose her to scrutiny. The son's foreign residency may trigger tax or reporting complications. The nephew's managerial responsibilities suggest he may require different access mechanisms—perhaps through a purpose-built subtrust or a commercial holdco vehicle within the trust. Without this mapping exercise, the trust may not only fail to meet its goals; it may actively increase exposure for its beneficiaries.

The process of mapping begins with segmentation. Each potential beneficiary must be understood through four primary lenses: *relational, behavioural, situational,* and *strategic.* Relational considerations include the emotional bond with the settlor—how much trust, influence, or history exists. Behavioural refers to the individual's psychological profile: do they handle money wisely? Are they prone to conflict, dependency, or legal entanglements? Situational factors include geographic location, citizenship, creditor risk, and professional liabilities. Strategic refers to their potential role in the broader structure—are they simply recipients, or are they actors in the long-term governance of the trust's assets?

Once these dimensions are clearly articulated, the settlor can make far more precise decisions about allocation. A discretionary trust may still be appropriate—but with tailored distribution triggers, protective clauses, and role-based benefits. A child in recovery from addiction might be a contingent beneficiary whose access is mediated by a care plan. A financially capable spouse might be appointed as a co-trustee. A philanthropic heir might be named as director of a charitable sub-fund. None of this detail is captured in standard boilerplate drafting, yet it makes the difference between a trust that merely stores capital and one that stewards it.

Critically, the mapping exercise also surfaces hidden contradictions. Many settlors unconsciously import emotional baggage into their trust decisions—rewarding loyalty, punishing dissent, or clinging to outdated family hierarchies. The act of mapping forces these assumptions into the open. Why, for instance, is one child given access to business assets while another is limited to income support? Is this truly based on aptitude, or on unexamined bias? By subjecting these decisions to honest scrutiny, the Intentional Beneficiary Map does not remove subjectivity—but it insists that subjectivity be intentional, rather than reflexive.

From a legal drafting standpoint, the insights from the mapping process can be integrated into several mechanisms: *letters of wishes*, *distribution matrices*, *conditional clauses*, and *custom governance protocols*. These instruments do not replace the core legal deed but operate alongside it as interpretive guides. While not always legally binding, they are frequently decisive in court disputes or trustee discretion debates. More importantly, they provide trustees with *context*. A trustee granted broad powers is far more likely to act wisely and faithfully if they understand not just the what, but the why.

It is also worth noting that the beneficiary map is not static. Lives change. Relationships evolve. New risks emerge. That is why the map should be treated as a *living document*, reviewed periodically—

especially in dynamic family systems or high-risk jurisdictions. This allows the trust structure to retain its integrity without becoming rigid. It also reinforces a culture of stewardship, rather than entitlement. Beneficiaries aware that their role in the trust is defined not merely by birthright but by purpose are more likely to approach their inheritance as a responsibility, not a windfall.

There is, finally, an ethical dimension to this methodology. In a world where wealth is often decontextualised—reduced to digits, structures, and flows—the Intentional Beneficiary Map reintroduces humanity into financial architecture. It asks the settlor to do more than hide assets or reduce tax. It asks them to *design outcomes.* To anticipate how the distribution of capital will shape behaviour, character, and relationships. This is not sentimentalism. It is strategic realism. A poorly designed trust can destabilise a family faster than public exposure ever could.

What, then, is the ultimate purpose of a trust? It is not merely protection. It is continuity—of values, intentions, and vision. The Intentional Beneficiary Map ensures that continuity is not left to chance or generic drafting. It transforms trust design from a legal transaction into a strategic act of leadership. For the thoughtful reader, it offers a tool not just to allocate capital, but to *sculpt its impact.*

In the chapters that follow, we will examine specific drafting strategies, structural alternatives, and narrative case studies—including how artists, expats, and activists have used tailored beneficiary mapping to secure privacy, purpose, and legacy. But before diving into those technicalities, one truth must be internalised: *you do not merely create a trust—you create a worldview.* And the shape of that world begins with whom you empower inside it.

Real-Life Scenarios: The Artist, The Expat, The Activist

Trusts are often misunderstood as instruments of the ultra-wealthy, tied solely to tax avoidance or dynastic wealth. This perception, while partially grounded in history, is increasingly outdated. Today, trusts are more versatile than ever—capable of accommodating not only traditional wealth preservation but also highly individualised aims: intellectual property protection, jurisdictional agility, activist security, or even personal anonymity. To grasp the full strategic power of trusts, one must look beyond the theoretical and into the applied. The following three cases—the artist, the expat, and the activist—demonstrate how trusts serve vastly different functions depending on personal context, political environment, and psychological intent. Together, they reveal one simple truth: *a trust is only as powerful as its alignment with purpose.*

Consider the case of Nadia, a British multimedia artist whose global acclaim came with a rising tide of legal risk. Her work—politically subversive and emotionally raw—challenged authoritarian regimes, sparked protests, and attracted both awards and litigation. While critics dissected her work, Nadia quietly retained full commercial rights. This brought money, yes—but also exposure. Licensing deals across Europe, Asia, and North America complicated her tax position. More dangerously, one of her works was banned in a major jurisdiction, and local officials moved to freeze royalties on the grounds of "national interest." Nadia's personal name was on every contract, making her financially and legally vulnerable.

The solution was neither relocation nor withdrawal. It was structural realignment. Working with an experienced fiduciary team, she transferred her intellectual property into a bespoke purpose trust, domiciled in a jurisdiction with strong IP protection laws and a political neutrality clause in its trust framework. The trust appointed a professional trustee to manage rights and licensing, while Nadia retained advisory input via a letter of wishes. Importantly, she no longer owned the rights herself—*the trust did.* This separation provided both legal insulation and jurisdictional detachment. Royalty income flowed through the trust and was redistributed to Nadia under clearly defined conditions, allowing her to maintain artistic freedom without tying her personal reputation to asset visibility. Her case illustrates how an artist—whose primary assets are intangible—can use a trust not to transfer wealth, but to *liberate creation from ownership.*

Now shift to Karim, a Lebanese software entrepreneur turned expatriate. After relocating to Portugal under the D7 visa programme, he found himself grappling with cross-border reporting obligations, dual tax treaties, and the looming spectre of political instability in his country of origin. His primary concern wasn't tax—it was *continuity.* If Lebanon's political situation collapsed further, how could he ensure that his assets, businesses, and dependants would be protected—regardless of local law or inheritance complications?

Karim's case required a trust not as a vault, but as a *bridge.* He established a multi-jurisdictional trust designed to hold shares in his offshore company, which itself operated his SaaS platforms globally. The trust was governed by the laws of New Zealand—chosen for its robust settlor protections and transparency with international tax compliance frameworks. Beneficiaries included not only Karim's children, but also a contingency allocation for his parents in Beirut, should he become unable to send direct support. What made this structure distinctive wasn't complexity but *clarity.* Each beneficiary's rights were mapped according to both proximity and risk exposure. Karim also included a flexible protector clause, allowing him to replace trustees if their fiduciary posture ever conflicted with the family's needs.

His case underscores a fundamental truth for modern expatriates: residency may shift, passports may multiply, but financial integrity requires a *structural home*. In a world of volatile geopolitics, a well-drafted trust is less about shielding and more about *anchoring*. Karim's assets are no longer tethered to any one country's collapse—or whims.

Finally, consider Lina, a human rights lawyer and dissident from Hong Kong. Facing increasing state surveillance, she fled to Canada, but her digital footprint and financial ties remained exposed. Prior to emigration, she'd sold a memoir manuscript for a substantial advance. Her concern was how to use this income—not just to protect herself, but to support the causes she believed in—without endangering recipients or violating foreign donation laws.

In consultation with a privacy-focused legal team, Lina created a charitable trust with dual-purpose design: first, to provide personal subsistence; second, to fund specific advocacy efforts through vetted third parties. The trust was housed in a jurisdiction with favourable donor anonymity protections, and she deliberately renounced any discretionary control. Instead, a governance board with rotating members—drawn from aligned non-profit circles—was empowered to direct distributions. Lina's role was simply that of named grantor with a moral vision. Her trust became not only a firewall against political reprisal but a living expression of *mission continuity*. Even if she disappeared from public life, the trust could outlast her, funding the very causes she once championed on the front lines.

Lina's case raises deeper ethical considerations. Can one structure a trust to serve both personal needs and collective goals without slipping into self-dealing or opacity? Yes—but only with rigorous design and principled oversight. Her experience illustrates that trusts are not inherently selfish tools; under the right framework, they become instruments of *distributed agency*—protecting both identity and impact.

What binds these three stories together is not wealth level, career path, or nationality. It is *intentional design.* Each trust was shaped to solve a specific problem: exposure to authoritarian interference, interjurisdictional instability, or purpose-based risk. Each settlor began not with a product or template, but with a question: *What must be preserved? What must be distanced? And what must endure, even in my absence?*

This raises an important point: trusts are neither inherently secretive nor noble. They are morally neutral tools, made ethical or unethical by the motivations of their creators and the transparency of their use. There is no virtue in complexity for its own sake. A convoluted trust structure that obfuscates illegal income or hides assets from rightful claims may be legal, but it is not principled. Conversely, a well-drafted, openly declared trust that protects vulnerable beneficiaries or supports public goods may operate discreetly—but it is morally defensible and strategically sound.

For readers navigating the decision to form a trust—whether to protect intellectual property, ensure cross-border continuity, or insulate mission-driven capital—the key takeaway from these scenarios is not to mimic, but to *diagnose.* The trust you build should reflect *your unique context, risks, and values.* Borrowing structures without adapting them to your reality is the fastest path to strategic failure. The artist, the expat, and the activist did not use trusts to escape scrutiny. They used them to *reshape exposure on their own terms.*

As this chapter continues into technical design, the reader should carry forward one simple insight: there is no such thing as a one-size-fits-all trust. Just as no two lives are identical, no two structures should be. The most effective trusts do not merely protect assets. They *protect agency.* And agency, in a surveillance-driven, geopolitically fragile, and reputationally volatile world, may well be the most valuable asset of all.

Chapter 4
Offshore Accounts – Jurisdiction as a Strategy

Few financial instruments are as shrouded in misunderstanding—and, let's be honest, as stained by suspicion—as the offshore account. Say the words aloud and chances are the mind goes straight to images of hidden vaults in Geneva, hastily incorporated companies in the British Virgin Islands, or sun-soaked beaches concealing illicit wire transfers and evasive billionaires. It's a narrative that plays well in headlines and courtroom dramas, but it tells only part of the truth—and a skewed part at that. The popular perception is, in many ways, a fiction: entertaining, politically useful, and intellectually shallow.

What's often ignored—or wilfully overlooked—is that offshore finance is not a shadowy corner of the financial world. It is very much at its centre. Used not just by oligarchs or arms dealers, but by entrepreneurs, philanthropists, multinationals, and yes, ordinary professionals whose lives and assets no longer align neatly with a single flag or tax code. The key to understanding this space lies not in scandal or secrecy, but in governance. Jurisdiction, after all, isn't just a spot on the map—it's a legal and political framework. And where your money lives, in a very real sense, determines how free you are to access, control, and defend it.

Let's be clear from the outset: this chapter is not a how-to guide for evasion. It won't offer tricks, nor trade in ambiguity. What it does do is invite you to engage with a deeper line of questioning. Not just "Where is your bank account?" but "Who has legal claim over your assets?" "Whose laws will govern your capital in crisis?" And perhaps most telling of all: "Is your current financial setup the result of strategic thinking—or simply the default handed to you at birth?"

To properly understand offshore finance, one must grasp the notion of jurisdictional arbitrage. That is, the deliberate choice to have one's wealth governed under a legal regime that best serves their interests. It's not dissimilar to the choices made by corporations every day—Delaware for incorporation, Luxembourg for funds, Singapore for data hosting. Individuals, too, have the right to choose. And many do—particularly those whose earnings, investments, or identities transcend national boundaries. The modern world offers few illusions of permanence. Savvy actors know this, and act accordingly.

This doesn't mean offshore is universally appropriate. It isn't. Nor is it simple. The legal, ethical, and compliance dimensions are complex and evolving. But for those willing to learn the contours, offshore structuring offers real, lawful advantages. We're not talking about secrecy in the cloak-and-dagger sense. We're talking about optionality. Privacy. Durability. The ability to maintain access to one's assets across political changes, reputational storms, or regulatory shifts. Offshore, when done well, is not a loophole—it's a form of resilience.

Before anything else, we must debunk the most persistent myth: that offshore is inherently illicit. The reality, stubborn though it may be, is that there's absolutely nothing illegal about holding a foreign bank account. No more than there is about owning a flat in another country or carrying dual citizenship. What matters—what always matters—is transparency. Is the account disclosed? Are the funds lawful? Has the jurisdiction been selected to enhance protection, not to dodge obligations? The problem isn't "offshore". The problem is opacity. And it's that distinction—between structure and subterfuge—that frames everything that follows.

Now consider what we call The Firewall Effect. It's a simple idea, but profound in consequence. Most people labour under the illusion that their domestic banking system will protect them—that because their account is with a reputable local institution, regulated by a familiar government, it's inherently secure. But ask yourself this: are financial threats really about finances? Rarely. The true risks come from law, politics, reputation—from lawsuits, sudden regulatory shifts, asset freezes, currency devaluations. When all your wealth is held under a single jurisdiction, you are exposed to the full force of that jurisdiction's volatility. That's the danger. Offshore accounts, particularly when combined with holding structures or international trusts, don't eliminate risk—but they help distribute it. They create distance. They preserve access. They give you time to respond.

Of course, not all jurisdictions are created equal. The amateur offshore enthusiast looks only at tax rates. But a wise planner looks further—at judicial independence, creditor rights, political neutrality, regulatory competence. Does the court system actually function? Will the regulator act with integrity? Is the banking environment hostile to foreigners or structured for inclusivity? These aren't theoretical questions. They are, in fact, moral ones. Because at the core of your banking relationship lies trust. And if you wouldn't entrust your health or your children to a certain government, why would you entrust your capital?

The chapter that follows will not only examine the mechanics of offshore structuring, but the ethics. We'll look at case studies drawn from across the spectrum: the startup founder in a fragile state, who safeguards their cash reserves abroad to keep payroll going during upheaval. The human rights lawyer under surveillance, who shifts assets offshore to protect their family, not to obscure their mission. The retiree whose pension and property lie scattered across borders, seeking both efficiency and peace of mind. Offshore, in these examples, is not a shadow—it's a safety net.

And yes, we'll confront the thornier questions too. When does protection become evasion? How do you balance compliance with confidentiality? What duties accompany cross-border wealth management? Offshore doesn't exempt you from these responsibilities—it intensifies them. Sovereignty without integrity is just another disguise for fragility.

In the end, the decision to bank offshore is not about escaping notice. It is about reclaiming autonomy. The world is not getting simpler. Legal systems are converging even as political systems diverge. Wealth is more exposed than ever—not because it is larger, but because it is visible. Against this backdrop, offshore accounts, when executed lawfully and with intent, offer something rare: space. Not to disappear, but to decide. Not to escape, but to endure.

Let me say it plainly: this is not a manual for sidestepping laws. It's a framework for navigating them wisely. Offshore structures are not moral actors. They are neutral tools. Their meaning—like their consequences—depends on how you use them. Used well, they are instruments of strategy. Of prudence. Of independence.

By the end of this chapter, you will have a more refined grasp of what offshore really is—and what it isn't. You'll understand the principles that underpin it, the decisions that drive it, and the pitfalls that threaten to undermine it. More importantly, you'll learn how to approach it not as a gimmick, but as a form of design.

Because, in the final analysis, offshore is not a destination. It is a decision. And the first decision, always, is jurisdiction. Let's begin there.

Why Geography is Political

It is tempting to believe that money is neutral—that once earned, it exists in an abstracted, placeless realm of balance sheets, spreadsheets, and digits. But this belief is not only false; it is dangerously naïve. Where your money resides is not a logistical footnote—it is a political decision with legal, strategic, and existential consequences. Geography, in the context of wealth, is not a backdrop. It is a force multiplier, a risk variable, and a declaration of allegiance. Jurisdiction is power, and the selection of that jurisdiction is one of the most consequential forms of sovereignty a private individual can still exercise.

Jurisdictional arbitrage, a term often heard in tax optimisation circles, is far more than a clever accounting manoeuvre. It is the deliberate leveraging of legal, regulatory, and geopolitical differences across nations to enhance security, reduce vulnerability, and regain control. It means recognising that laws do not operate in a vacuum—they are created, enforced, and interpreted through the lens of national interest, historical legacy, and institutional temperament. And when your assets are subject to a particular jurisdiction, they are not governed solely by abstract statutes, but by the political, economic, and ideological climate of that territory.

Consider the case of Cyprus in 2013. The island, long regarded as a stable offshore banking haven for both Europeans and Russians, became a cautionary tale overnight when the government—under pressure from international lenders—announced an unprecedented bank deposit levy. Private accounts were frozen. Assets were expropriated. Depositors, many of whom had no involvement in Cypriot domestic affairs, suddenly found themselves paying for a national crisis. This was not a failure of banking. It was a failure of geography. Their money was parked in a jurisdiction that lacked the political will, or perhaps the independence, to protect foreign capital when internal pressures mounted.

This is the core argument of jurisdictional arbitrage: *what protects your assets is not the idea of law, but the nature of the state enforcing it.* The strength and predictability of a jurisdiction is not measured merely by its legislation, but by how that legislation is applied when tested by crisis, populism, or external influence. Laws can be reinterpreted. Regulations can be weaponised. Treaties can be suspended. Courts can be packed. And if your wealth lives in the wrong place, it can become collateral damage in a battle you never chose to fight.

To illustrate the point more broadly, consider three types of jurisdictional risk: legal, reputational, and systemic.

Legal risk arises when the underlying framework of asset protection is unstable or politically vulnerable. Countries undergoing legal reform, or those with weak separation of powers, expose asset holders to unpredictable judicial reversals or retroactive legislation.

In such systems, trusts can be unwound, contracts annulled, and ownership redefined with the stroke of a judge's pen.

Reputational risk stems from the association of your wealth with politically exposed or ideologically hostile environments. For example, a U.S. citizen holding assets in a sanctioned country may not be violating any laws directly, but the mere existence of that link can trigger a cascade of compliance headaches, account closures, and public scrutiny. The same applies inversely: a high-profile philanthropist domiciling their charitable trust in a blacklisted tax haven may undermine their credibility, regardless of the legality.

Systemic risk, meanwhile, involves the fragility of a nation's financial and governance infrastructure. Banking in a country with high debt-to-GDP ratios, political instability, or capital controls exposes you to risks that may have little to do with your personal financial behaviour. You are essentially making a bet—not just on the rule of law, but on the sustainability of the entire system in which your money is nested.

In contrast, savvy wealth holders diversify not only across asset classes, but across legal systems. A diversified portfolio that spans multiple jurisdictions acts as a firewall—insulating wealth from localised shocks, legal seizures, or regulatory overreach. The idea is not to evade regulation, but to *distribute exposure* intelligently. One jurisdiction may offer robust asset protection laws. Another may provide banking secrecy. A third may ensure strong property rights or creditor protections. Layering these advantages across sovereign boundaries creates a structural resilience that no single domicile can replicate.

But this strategy requires more than tactical planning—it demands a philosophical shift. Jurisdictional choice is not just about tax minimisation or avoiding regulation; it is about aligning your financial presence with political values, cultural stability, and institutional trustworthiness. It is, in essence, a form of ethical arbitrage.

Some jurisdictions understand this well. Singapore, for instance, has positioned itself not merely as a tax-efficient environment, but as a jurisdiction of strategic discretion. It offers rule-of-law certainty, low corruption, and an institutional culture of reliability. Switzerland, despite its gradual concessions to global transparency efforts, still retains the core principles of private banking confidentiality and legal maturity. Liechtenstein, often overlooked, combines deep trust law traditions with geopolitical neutrality. These jurisdictions signal not just fiscal advantages, but a political philosophy of stewardship and restraint—qualities that appeal to those seeking not just protection, but principled guardianship.

Contrast this with jurisdictions where the state views private capital as a temporary privilege, revocable when politically expedient. In such countries, sudden wealth taxes, retroactive penalties, or forced disclosures are not anomalies—they are instruments of fiscal opportunism, dressed in the language of justice or necessity. In these places, the legal system may still function, but it functions with a subtext: *your rights are subordinate to the regime's priorities*. For those with significant wealth, betting their future on such foundations is not just risky—it is reckless.

It is also worth noting that jurisdictional arbitrage is not solely the domain of the ultra-wealthy. Increasingly, professionals, entrepreneurs, and digital nomads are engaging in what might be termed *sovereignty shopping*—seeking out residencies, citizenships, and financial homes that reflect their desire for autonomy and resilience. The rise of second passports, global incorporation strategies, and remote-friendly banks is not a fringe phenomenon. It is a response to the growing volatility of national governance and the erosion of trust in monolithic systems.

Yet this movement is often misunderstood. Critics argue that jurisdictional arbitrage undermines national tax bases or facilitates illicit activity. But this criticism, while not entirely without merit, often overlooks a deeper point: most wealth holders engaged in strategic jurisdictional planning are not running from obligation—they are seeking refuge from arbitrary power. The right to protect one's assets from unjust expropriation, political persecution, or legal unpredictability is not a loophole. It is a foundational principle of liberty.

In this light, the geography of money becomes an expression of values. Where your wealth lives is, at some level, a reflection of what you believe about law, power, and human dignity. Do you trust your home country to respect your rights under pressure? Does its legal system function independently? Is its political leadership beholden to the rule of law or to the imperatives of populist cycles? These are not theoretical questions. They are due diligence.

To summarise without concluding: jurisdiction is never neutral. It is not simply where your bank is located, but the ecosystem in which your financial future is adjudicated. To leave your wealth entirely under the custody of one nation is to accept a single point of failure. To diversify across jurisdictions is not only prudent—it is, in an increasingly volatile world, an act of informed defiance. Wealth, when paired with wisdom, does not merely chase returns. It builds frameworks of protection that transcend borders, ideologies, and administrations. And that begins by asking the most overlooked but most essential question in finance: *where* does your money sleep at night, and who holds the keys to its dreams?

The Myth of Illegality

Few subjects in the financial world are as misunderstood—or as deliberately misrepresented—as offshore banking. The very term "offshore" evokes a cinematic imagery of hidden vaults, encrypted accounts, and anonymous transactions occurring beneath palm trees, far from the reach of regulators or tax authorities. To the public imagination, offshore often equates to illicit. This perception is not only inaccurate; it is intellectually lazy and legally misleading. The truth is more complex and, importantly, more empowering for those willing to navigate it with clarity and principle.

The association between offshore banking and criminality is the product of a potent cultural cocktail: media sensationalism, political scapegoating, and bureaucratic oversimplification. Headlines about shell companies in Panama, Swiss banking secrecy, or Caribbean tax havens are rarely accompanied by nuanced explanations of legal distinctions, treaty frameworks, or legitimate asset protection practices. As a result, a toolset designed for strategic financial positioning has been painted with the broad brush of scandal. This distortion serves powerful interests, but it disempowers thoughtful individuals seeking lawful, ethical, and intelligent control over their wealth.

Let us begin by establishing a foundational point: *offshore banking is not illegal.* In nearly every developed country—including the United States, United Kingdom, Canada, and across the European Union—citizens are permitted, even encouraged in some cases, to hold bank accounts and assets in foreign jurisdictions. The key legal requirement is transparency—reporting those holdings through proper disclosure mechanisms such as the Foreign Account Tax Compliance Act (FATCA), Common Reporting Standard (CRS), or local equivalents. Provided these disclosures are made, the act of banking abroad is entirely lawful.

What, then, drives the myth of illegality? The answer lies in conflation. Offshore structures have historically been used—by a minority—for unlawful purposes such as tax evasion, money laundering, and the concealment of illicit funds. But this is a misuse of a neutral infrastructure, not a reflection of its essence. To conflate a tool with its abuse is a logical fallacy akin to banning kitchen knives because some are used in crimes. The real question is not *where* the account exists, but *how* it is used and *whether* its existence is lawfully reported.

More crucially, this conflation has become a political strategy. In the wake of financial crises, inequality debates, or budget shortfalls, governments often look for symbols that galvanise public sentiment. The figure of the "shadowy offshore billionaire" fits this need perfectly. It externalises blame, simplifies complex systems, and shifts attention away from domestic policy failures. Offshore becomes not a strategy, but a scapegoat.

This political opportunism has consequences. It deters legitimate actors—professionals, entrepreneurs, and families—from exploring global financial options that are entirely above board, simply because the optics are risky. It also results in poorly drafted policies that penalise transparency and erode financial innovation. The tragedy here is that offshore banking, when properly structured and ethically executed, is not about secrecy. It is about *jurisdictional optionality*.

To understand this distinction, we must decouple offshore from opacity. In the post-2010 world, offshore accounts are far from hidden. Most reputable jurisdictions now participate in automatic exchange of information agreements. Banks in Singapore, Switzerland, the Cayman Islands, and other prominent offshore centres are deeply compliant with international reporting standards. Indeed, the regulatory burden for opening and maintaining an offshore account is, in many cases, *more stringent* than that of a domestic account. Banks require certified source-of-funds documentation, enhanced due diligence for politically exposed persons (PEPs), and often enforce minimum balances that filter out casual or opportunistic users.

What remains, then, is not secrecy, but *structure*. Offshore accounts, trusts, or companies allow individuals to separate asset control from domestic volatility. They provide buffers against local political risk, judicial overreach, and currency debasement. They enable legacy planning through multi-jurisdictional trusts. They support international business operations with currency flexibility. They also allow for asset protection—not against taxation per se, but against capricious litigation or state confiscation.

Take, for example, the case of an entrepreneur operating in a country with a weak legal system, where business disputes often escalate into politically influenced prosecutions. By holding their key business assets or intellectual property in a foreign jurisdiction—perhaps in a properly disclosed offshore company or holding trust—they reduce their exposure to legal abuse. This is not tax evasion. It is legal self-defence.

Or consider a dual citizen living in a country with capital controls. By banking offshore, they preserve their ability to transact, invest, or relocate without being trapped by sudden restrictions. This is not betrayal of one's homeland. It is prudence born from history. Many nations—from Argentina to Lebanon to Zimbabwe—have shown just how quickly domestic financial environments can shift from liberal to punitive. Offshore infrastructure provides an insurance policy.

This insurance, however, comes with ethical responsibilities. Offshore structures should not be used to obscure wrongdoing, deny just obligations, or undermine public interest. They must be *transparent to the relevant parties*—primarily the tax and regulatory authorities of one's home jurisdiction. The challenge is to strike the right balance between privacy and accountability. This is where *legal positioning* becomes an art form.

Legal positioning means aligning one's financial footprint with lawful, strategic intent. It involves selecting jurisdictions not because they are secretive, but because they offer *predictability*, *rule-of-law integrity*, and *asset protection mechanisms* aligned with one's goals. It requires working with skilled professionals to design compliant, purposeful structures—trusts, foundations, holding companies—that serve specific functions: wealth preservation, succession planning, risk mitigation, and cross-border flexibility.

More fundamentally, it involves resisting the binary thinking that dominates mainstream discourse. Offshore is not inherently good or bad. It is a neutral geography in the legal-financial ecosystem—one that becomes powerful when paired with thoughtful intent. The myth of illegality survives because it serves narratives of fear and control. But the reality is that most offshore users are not oligarchs or criminals. They are business owners, retirees, expatriates, artists, and global citizens navigating a complex world with legitimate concerns about sovereignty and security.

It is time we shift the frame. Offshore banking, when understood through the lens of legal positioning, is not a threat to society. It is a defence of individual autonomy. It empowers people to think beyond borders, to diversify risk, and to operate on a more resilient playing field. It reflects a philosophy that values lawful stewardship over passive dependence on any one government or jurisdiction. And in an age of increasing surveillance, inflation, litigation, and financial instability, this philosophy is not fringe. It is *wise.*

Thus, the next time someone raises an eyebrow at the mention of offshore, the more intelligent response is not deflection or apology. It is education. It is explaining that offshore banking, when properly structured and fully disclosed, is no more suspicious than owning foreign real estate, holding a second passport, or investing in international equities. It is an expression of strategic agency—and one of the few tools left that allows individuals to operate at a structural level, rather than merely reacting to policy shifts from above.

Legality is not defined by geography. It is defined by intent, transparency, and compliance. When those elements are present, offshore is not a threat. It is a choice—one that more people should be free to make, without shame or mischaracterisation.

The Firewall Effect: Diversification by Nation

The modern individual, no matter how financially literate, often falls into a dangerous trap: mistaking geographical convenience for structural security. Decades of relative stability in Western economies have lulled many into a false sense of permanence, the assumption that legal rights are immutable, institutions infallible, and currencies inviolable. Yet history—and increasingly, headlines—tell a different story. From capital controls in Argentina to frozen bank accounts in Cyprus, from property expropriations in Zimbabwe to sanctions in Russia, the truth is this: *sovereign risk is not theoretical.* It is geographic, political, and often sudden. That is why multi-jurisdictional banking—commonly caricatured as exotic or evasive—deserves to be understood as what it truly is: a rational hedge. A firewall.

A technological firewall protects digital assets from network intrusion; a jurisdictional firewall protects financial assets from localised institutional failure. The principle is the same: isolate potential threats, limit the blast radius, and ensure continuity of function even under duress. When properly implemented, a multi-jurisdictional banking strategy does not merely diversify currency exposure or optimise tax efficiency. *It safeguards sovereignty at the most fundamental level: control over one's own resources, regardless of one's national backdrop.*

The need for this firewall is not rooted in paranoia. It is rooted in precedent. In 2008, during the global financial crisis, the Icelandic government allowed its major banks to fail, and imposed currency controls that locked citizens into domestic capital. In 2013, Cyprus went further: a state-backed "bail-in" confiscated portions of depositor savings to recapitalise failing banks—legally sanctioned seizure, not theft, under EU emergency powers. In 2016, India demonetised 86% of its cash overnight, ostensibly to combat corruption, disrupting lives and businesses without recourse. These are not fringe nations nor isolated incidents. They are cautionary tales.

The firewall effect functions by de-linking the fate of your assets from the fate of any one jurisdiction. If your home country faces social unrest, your offshore account in a politically neutral state ensures continuity of access. If currency depreciation erodes domestic purchasing power, your diversified holdings in Swiss francs or Singapore dollars retain value. If new regulations retroactively target certain wealth structures—trusts, retirement accounts, even brokerage holdings—your foreign legal entities may lie beyond the immediate reach of domestic authority. This is not evasion. It is architectural resilience.

Critics often argue that such strategies betray civic duty or erode the tax base. But this critique confuses *avoidance* with *evasion*, and assumes that all jurisdictional loyalty must be singular and unconditional. The mature counterpoint is this: individuals are not chattel. They are moral agents entitled to distribute their lives and assets across jurisdictions that align with their values, priorities, and risk appetites. Indeed, as states become more aggressive in their fiscal enforcement and regulatory overreach, the ethical imperative may shift—from passive compliance to active self-determination.

Consider the example of an entrepreneur based in South Africa. With domestic currency volatility, a history of expropriation without compensation, and deteriorating public infrastructure, she opens accounts in Mauritius and Dubai, both of which offer stable financial environments and favourable legal frameworks. Her operations remain lawful, taxes are declared appropriately, and her international structure enables continuity even if local conditions deteriorate. Her firewall is not ideological. It is practical.

Or take a dual national living in the United States. Concerned about increasing regulatory encroachments, politically motivated asset freezes, or social pressures tied to activism, he opts to hold part of his wealth in Liechtenstein via a foundation that provides privacy and long-term legacy planning. The arrangement is disclosed, taxed, and compliant. But it is also a form of positional insurance—protection not from taxes, but from unpredictability.

There is a critical psychological dimension here as well. The firewall effect also neutralises the psychological chokehold of geographic determinism—the unconscious belief that where you were born, educated, or domiciled must forever determine your economic fate. In a hyper-connected world, where capital can move faster than policy can adapt, such determinism is not only outdated. It is dangerous. The modern financial actor must think structurally, not sentimentally.

The selection of jurisdictions matters enormously. Not all "offshore" is equal. Banking in a banana republic with lax oversight may invite more risk, not less. True diversification requires diligence. Is the jurisdiction politically stable? Does it uphold the rule of law? Is its banking system capitalised and secure? Does it participate in treaties that could compromise asset protection in times of stress? Does it recognise and protect non-resident ownership? These are not minor details. They are determinants of whether your firewall will hold when the heat comes.

And heat does come. In times of political crisis, banks often become tools of coercion. Capital controls are enacted not with warning, but by decree. Foreign exchange restrictions render savings illiquid.

Property laws are reinterpreted. Judiciaries, often politicised, are used to punish dissent. In such environments, *compliance does not guarantee protection*. Only diversification can.

Importantly, the firewall effect is not only defensive. It is also a strategic enabler. It allows you to operate from a position of autonomy—able to pursue investment opportunities, lifestyle changes, or geopolitical exits without begging permission. It supports generational planning, global education choices, and location-independent business models. In a sense, the firewall enables a higher order of living—not just wealth preservation, but *wealth agency*.

Critics of this view will claim that it privileges the already affluent. But that critique misses the point. It is precisely those who are *emerging* into wealth—entrepreneurs, digital nomads, independent professionals—who need this knowledge most. Institutional wealth has always diversified geographically. It is the average, aspirationally mobile individual who has been conditioned to think locally. Teaching them to think structurally is not elitist. It is emancipatory.

Ultimately, the firewall effect reveals a larger truth: *money does not exist in a vacuum*. It exists in legal containers, within national frameworks, subject to political will and social mood. Where your money lives is as important as how much you have. A robust financial strategy is not merely about earning, saving, or investing. It is about where your assets can *survive a storm*—and sometimes, where they can stay neutral in a fight that isn't yours.

To build such a structure requires foresight. Not panic. Not cynicism. But clarity. The firewall is not about abandoning your country or evading civic responsibilities. It is about not placing all your trust in one system, however familiar or once-reliable it may seem. It is about building optionality before it is needed, not scrambling for escape when it's too late.

In short, the firewall effect is not a fringe concern of the wealthy or the paranoid. It is a rational, legal, and increasingly necessary strategy for anyone who recognises the geopolitical fragility of the 21st century. It is not about fleeing, but about thinking—thinking across borders, through systems, and beyond complacency.

The prudent do not wait until the building is ablaze to find the exits. They map the firewalls while the lights are still on.

How to Choose a Jurisdiction That Respects You

There is a quiet revolution unfolding in the way wealth holders and global citizens approach the idea of jurisdiction. No longer tethered solely to their country of birth or default tax residency, today's strategically minded individuals are beginning to ask a more profound question: *What does it mean to be in a jurisdiction that respects me—not just my money, but my rights, my autonomy, and my intent?* This question transcends the typical calculus of favourable tax rates or low regulation. It ventures into the realm of values, institutional integrity, and philosophical compatibility.

Jurisdiction, at its core, is not a backdrop. It is a system of contracts, expectations, and enforceable consequences. It is the legal and ethical environment in which your assets exist. And, just like any other environment, it can either support your aims or quietly undermine them. Too often, people select jurisdictions like consumers scanning price tags—choosing the lowest corporate tax rate, or the bank with the highest yield—without scrutinising the underlying culture of enforcement, privacy, or rule of law. Yet tax rates can change overnight. Institutional character, however, reveals a jurisdiction's true long-term posture toward its stakeholders.

Begin by discarding the notion that "offshore" is a synonym for secrecy or exploitation. That association is both outdated and strategically limiting. Jurisdictions should be seen as *partnerships*, not loopholes. You are entering into a relationship with a sovereign state, its banking system, its legal apparatus, and its geopolitical standing. As in any relationship, you must ask: *Do they protect me when I'm vulnerable? Do they honour what they promise? Do they change the rules mid-game? Do they weaponise compliance or treat me as an asset to extract from?*

Consider the spectrum of national temperaments. Singapore is not the same as Belize. Liechtenstein is not the same as Panama. Switzerland's financial privacy is founded on legal neutrality and deeply entrenched banking professionalism. Estonia's digital infrastructure is based on transparency and efficiency, offering e-residency and decentralised governance. Meanwhile, some high-profile "offshore havens"—despite aggressive marketing—are more unstable than their glossy brochures reveal, prone to succumbing to international pressure, or dependent on informal power networks that change with the wind.

One essential framework is to evaluate jurisdictions not just through the lens of *what they offer*, but *how they govern*. Do they demonstrate legal consistency across time and political cycles? Are the courts independent? Is there a real mechanism for contesting abuse? Is due process a function of law, or of wealth and influence? *Rule of law is the single most important, under-appreciated feature of a sustainable jurisdictional strategy.* A 0% corporate tax rate means little if your assets can be frozen arbitrarily or your legal rights evaporate under political pressure.

Also consider the concept of **jurisdictional dignity**—the extent to which a nation treats non-resident investors and entities as partners rather than problems. Some countries encourage foreign incorporation and capital inflow but make it needlessly difficult for outsiders to open bank accounts, resolve disputes, or even understand local regulations. Others design legal systems from the outset with international stakeholders in mind. The distinction is critical. Choose jurisdictions that invite alignment, not constant defensive posture.

Another litmus test is *transparency versus opacity*. Ironically, the most resilient jurisdictions are often not those that promise secrecy, but those that operate with *predictable discretion*. They do not market themselves as tax shelters; they are not reliant on attracting shady actors. Instead, they have earned reputations for high-integrity structuring options—respected courts, modern regulatory regimes, and a track record of non-intervention. These are jurisdictions that won't collapse your asset plan because of some sensationalist newspaper headline or foreign diplomatic pressure.

Practical due diligence should then extend to how a jurisdiction handles conflict. When cross-border disputes arise—between beneficiaries, corporations, tax authorities, or even state actors—does the country resolve them according to principle, or expediency? Does it have treaties that protect your structure or compromise it? Is it part of information-sharing networks like the Common Reporting Standard (CRS), and if so, how is data handled and secured? These questions are not peripheral. They are *foundational*.

It is also important to distinguish between *banking jurisdictions* and *structuring jurisdictions*. These are not always the same. For example, while Switzerland may offer excellent private banking services, a trust structured in the Cayman Islands or Singapore might provide greater flexibility depending on your goals. The most robust strategies do not rely on a single country, but a matrix of complementary jurisdictions—each selected for a specific functional role: asset protection, tax efficiency, privacy, succession planning, or capital deployment.

However, the most neglected factor in jurisdictional selection is philosophical fit. Do you align with the culture of the nation you're anchoring your financial sovereignty to? Are its values consistent with your long-term worldview? If you value privacy, does the jurisdiction protect it or commoditise it? If you value autonomy, does it have a history of coercive legislation? If you want to support institutions that respect human rights, does the country uphold or abuse them? These questions are not abstract—they inform whether your structure will be enduring or exposed the moment norms shift.

Too often, jurisdiction is reduced to a spreadsheet exercise: columns of rates, treaties, and compliance checkboxes. But jurisdiction is also *narrative.* Where your money lives tells a story about what you prioritise. It reflects your tolerance for risk, your attitude toward authority, and your forecast of what the future might demand. The post-national financial citizen is not fleeing accountability. They are *choosing alignment.* They are designing for resilience in a volatile world—legally, ethically, and intelligently.

Let us consider a few contrasting examples. An investor from Argentina, concerned about fiscal instability and capital controls, chooses Uruguay as a secondary base—not because it's secretive, but because its judiciary is independent, its legal system is transparent, and its political class respects contract law. A German entrepreneur, wary of EU surveillance regimes, structures part of her holdings through a Liechtenstein foundation—not as a dodge, but as a way to ensure succession rights are preserved with discretion and control. A Canadian tech founder, living between Lisbon and Dubai, holds banking relationships across Luxembourg and Singapore, not because he distrusts Canada, but because *he trusts diversity* more than singularity.

These are not acts of rebellion. They are acts of foresight. The world is changing quickly. Laws change faster than habits. The jurisdictions that respect you today may not do so tomorrow. Conversely, countries that were once dismissed as obscure may become tomorrow's anchors of financial security. Your responsibility is not to predict the future, but to architect optionality.

Ultimately, a jurisdiction that respects you is one that honours the intent behind your structure. It does not seek to unravel your privacy, or trap your capital, or reinterpret your contracts at will. It supports autonomy, does not presume guilt, and enables lawful complexity without suspicion. It sees you not as a risk to be managed, but as a sovereign actor to be engaged with professionalism.

This chapter is not an argument for any one country. It is an invitation to reframe how you think about financial geography. The ideal jurisdiction is not simply where your money is safe. It is where your intent is protected. Where your complexity is understood. Where your risk is honoured with structure—not punished with suspicion. And most importantly, where your presence—however digital or remote—is treated not with bureaucratic disdain, but *institutional respect.*

Chapter 5
Quiet Banking – Silent Leverage in a Loud World

The present-day financial arena hums—no, roars—with ceaseless distraction. Meme-driven stock frenzies, lightning-fast algorithmic trades, IPOs dressed up for the masses, and a tide of sentiment swayed by little more than viral outrage or celebrity endorsement. Amid all this noise, something quieter persists—less visible, but no less powerful. A different kind of financial practice, refined and composed, continues behind closed doors, absent from the theatre of the markets. This is the domain of quiet banking. It does not shout. It does not advertise. But it shapes legacies in ways no flash trade ever could.

Let's be clear from the outset: quiet banking is not merely a matter of secrecy. It's not about secrecy at all, really—not in the sense often imagined. It's about discretion as strategy, silence as architecture. In a culture obsessed with performance and visibility, it may sound quaint—old-fashioned, even. But for those who understand the mechanics of capital preservation, strategic liquidity, and multigenerational control, this mode of finance offers something the noisy markets never can: continuity with intention.

What underpins this approach is a foundational belief—almost countercultural now—that strength doesn't require spectacle. That real financial power leaves no trace in the headlines. Quiet banking operates through relationships, not transactions; through memory, not churn. The institutions involved know their clients. They don't need to see a spreadsheet to recall the complexities of a family office or the subtleties of a trust deed signed fifteen years prior. Their business is continuity, not conquest.

This is not the stuff of fintech slogans or mobile apps that gamify investment. It is rooted in a subtler calculus, where the client seeks not returns alone, but refuge. Refuge from scrutiny, volatility, overreach. And yes, refuge from the increasingly performative nature of modern wealth. Quiet banking is built for those who prefer resilience to applause.

Crucially, it rests on the principle of architectural leverage—an elegant kind, often misunderstood. Not the leveraged bets of hedge funds or debt-laden plays for control, but the silent, structurally embedded forms of liquidity. Consider, for instance, the distinction between selling shares to raise capital (visible, taxable, potentially destabilising) versus drawing from a credit facility quietly secured against those same shares. The latter doesn't set off alarms. It doesn't reduce ownership. It doesn't invite questions. But it grants access—on terms chosen in advance. This is fluency, not avoidance.

We'll examine, too, how these systems are built. A bespoke lending arrangement backed by cross-border holdings isn't something you request via app. It is negotiated—deliberately, often slowly—with counterparties who understand not just balance sheets, but legacies. Quiet banking isn't fast. It's deep. And what it may lack in novelty, it more than makes up for in clarity of purpose.

The notion of opacity will, inevitably, raise eyebrows. But let's draw a line—sharply—between concealment and discretion. One implies wrongdoing. The other implies design. Quiet banking does not aim to hide assets; it aims to shield them—legally, ethically, and with sophistication. In a world increasingly governed by surveillance—of data, of reputation, of capital—there is a genuine need to retain control over how, when, and to whom visibility is granted.

This is why need-to-know structures matter. Why trustee communication occurs within privileged frameworks. Why even within a family, access can and often should be asymmetric. To those raised on the notion that transparency equals virtue, this may seem uncomfortable. But the more pressing question is: transparency to whom? And at what cost?

To engage in quiet banking also requires a psychological shift. Many are conditioned to think that what can be shown, proved, or displayed is what holds value. Yet, in this paradigm, the inverse is often true. The less visible your structures, the more secure they become. Not because they are secret, but because they are insulated from reaction, judgement, and opportunism. Quiet banking rests on the proposition that control—quiet, calm, calculated control—is the ultimate expression of financial sovereignty.

And the question of risk? It is approached very differently here. Where retail finance sees risk in terms of volatility curves and market exposure, quiet banking looks at institutional integrity, jurisdictional friction, and the long-term enforceability of rights. A few basis points' difference in yield means little if the underlying legal environment is compromised. Quiet banking doesn't chase returns. It secures ground.

Do not mistake this for nostalgia. This is not some wistful yearning for mahogany desks and cryptic ledgers. Quiet banking has evolved—digitally, legally, structurally. It uses encrypted records, multi-layered governance, real-time regulatory compliance. But its principles endure: loyalty over volume, discretion over theatre, stewardship over sales.

Through case studies, this chapter will bring those principles to life. You'll see how a European family office uses cross-collateralised facilities to quietly release capital without tripping tax wires. How a tech founder banks in Switzerland not for secrecy, but to preserve trustee independence across layered trusts. How a politically exposed client maintains liquidity during a reputational storm without triggering asset freezes or legal entanglements.

Each scenario points to the same lesson: this is not about disappearing—it's about designing. It's about safeguarding decision-making capacity when the world becomes hostile to wealth, complexity, or ambiguity. Quiet banking builds systems that absorb tension. It turns financial planning into a form of soft power.

If you're looking for product comparisons or quick wins, this chapter may frustrate you. But if you're willing to look past the noise—to view banking not just as an interface but as an edifice—then the concepts here will offer something more enduring. A framework. A discipline. A philosophy.

Quiet banking, when rightly understood, is neither a loophole nor a luxury. It is an art of structuring: patient, principled, and profoundly relevant in an era where visibility can be weaponised. If you understand that silence is not weakness but intent—then what follows may serve as your blueprint.

Banking Without Noise: The Architecture of Privacy in Modern Finance

There is a profound difference between secrecy and discretion. Secrecy implies evasion; discretion implies intent. And nowhere is this distinction more crucial than in the domain of private banking—a financial architecture designed not to hide criminality, but to *preserve sovereignty*. In a culture obsessed with visibility, noise, and narrative, *banking without noise* has become one of the most underappreciated disciplines in the pursuit of sustainable, strategic power.

The modern client of private banking is not necessarily a billionaire, a tycoon, or a royalty. Increasingly, they are entrepreneurs, professionals, and families who understand that wealth, once accumulated, becomes *a vector of vulnerability*. Visibility invites friction—legal, reputational, even existential. For these clients, the goal is not to escape oversight, but to *control the terms of exposure*. Noise is liability; silence, an asset class of its own.

At the core of quiet banking lies a suite of structures and protocols that form the bedrock of discretion. Chief among these are *nominee accounts*—a practice as misunderstood as it is effective. In a nominee arrangement, assets are held in the name of an appointed party, but for the *benefit* of the true owner. The legal and administrative identity is decoupled from the economic interest. Critics often conflate this with obfuscation, but this misunderstanding arises from an inability—or refusal—to distinguish *ownership from control.* A nominee structure, when ethically designed and legally compliant, is not concealment; it is protection. *It shifts the conversation from visibility to governance.*

Consider a scenario in which a politically exposed person (PEP) receives sudden global attention. A traditionally structured bank account—tied directly to the PEP's name—becomes immediately vulnerable to overreach, whether from regulators, litigators, or even hackers. By contrast, assets held via a nominee account or within a trust structure managed by professionals in a stable jurisdiction remain insulated, because the economic control is *functionally separated* from the surface-level identity. This isn't merely good strategy; it's essential structural hygiene in a world that penalises prominence.

It's important to recognise that *banking without noise* is not about vanishing—it's about *de-risking visibility.* The goal is not invisibility for its own sake, but *functional unremarkability.* A well-designed nominee structure doesn't trigger alarms. It doesn't invite scrutiny. It doesn't broadcast wealth through conspicuous channels. It blends, by design, into the operating framework of legitimate financial architecture. And when combined with well-considered legal entities—such as private interest foundations, offshore corporations, or discretionary trusts—it creates a *matrix of insulation*, not evasion.

Private banks that serve this clientele do not advertise in the usual way. They do not upsell flashy dashboards, AI-enhanced interfaces, or lifestyle perks. Their value proposition is far more elemental: *to be invisible when it matters most.* These institutions excel not because of technological theatrics, but because of legacy, legal clarity, and discretion protocols embedded deep into their organisational culture. They remember who their clients are—even when no one else is supposed to know.

It is within these quiet corridors that some of the most powerful financial instruments are made available—not through retail channels, but through *relational credibility*. Wealth-backed credit lines that never touch the open markets. Foreign currency reserves diversified across jurisdictions to mitigate systemic exposure. Custodial arrangements that enable asset transfers with no public registry events. *The magic lies in what isn't broadcast.* And that restraint, ironically, is what builds long-term financial resilience.

The psychology behind noise-averse banking is equally instructive. Most individuals, upon reaching a certain threshold of wealth, instinctively seek confirmation—through acquisition, exhibition, or narrative. But the most disciplined clients invert this reflex. They begin to view public attention not as validation, but as *operational drag.* They begin asking different questions: *Who needs to know? What do I need to reveal to achieve my objective? How can I structure this to reduce future friction?* The answers to these questions lead directly to unobtrusive banking.

Critically, we must resist the false dichotomy that silence equals impropriety. The truth is far more nuanced. Discretion in banking allows for *family continuity planning without coercion*, *entrepreneurial risk-taking without reputational volatility*, and *jurisdictional manoeuvrability without perpetual exposure.* In short, it restores *strategic agency* to individuals operating in increasingly surveilled environments.

Take, for instance, the common practice of multi-jurisdictional holding structures. A family business in Singapore may be ultimately held by a private foundation domiciled in Liechtenstein, with banking in Luxembourg and asset custodianship in Zurich. On the surface, this seems unnecessarily complex. But each layer exists for a reason: asset protection, succession control, legal neutrality, and banking discretion. Importantly, such a structure does *not* require criminal intent to justify its existence. It simply reflects a mature understanding that *the geopolitical map is also a financial one*—and that decentralising exposure is often a precondition for protecting legacy.

The regulatory environment has, understandably, moved toward increased transparency. Initiatives such as the Common Reporting Standard (CRS) and FATCA have redefined the global rules of financial disclosure. Yet, even within this regime, it remains entirely legal—and strategically essential—to structure one's financial affairs in a manner that *minimises unnecessary noise.* Full compliance does not require maximal exposure. What it demands is intentional architecture—*an intelligent selection of jurisdictions, entities, and custodians that work together to protect identity while fulfilling disclosure obligations in a controlled, lawful manner.*

A critical tool in this effort is the use of *segregated client accounts* and *multi-signatory mandates.* These arrangements create operational buffers within the banking system. They ensure that transactions occur only within tightly authorised frameworks, while simultaneously preventing over-concentration of authority in a single name. Once again, this isn't about paranoia. It's about *designing a system where errors, overreach, or breaches are statistically and structurally minimised.*

Equally important is the cultural component. Banking without noise requires that both client and institution share a commitment to *intentional silence.* This includes avoiding ostentatious patterns of spending, minimising unnecessary movement of large sums, and communicating through privileged channels with legal oversight. True discretion is not just legal—it is behavioural. And it is sustained not through tactics, but through *philosophy.*

In the final analysis, the art of banking without noise is not a trick or a workaround. It is the reassertion of a principle: that *financial autonomy is inseparable from the ability to remain unexposed unless exposure serves a strategic function.* The world rewards volume and visibility, but history favours those who understood when to speak softly—and how to structure power in silence.

This is not a niche concern for the ultra-wealthy. In a world where visibility increasingly equates to vulnerability, quiet banking offers a universally relevant lesson: *what matters most is not what you own, but how, where, and under what name it is held.* The answer to those questions may very well determine whether wealth becomes a burden—or remains a foundation.

The Power of Underwriting Silence: How Discreet Banking Builds Structural Integrity

Part 1

In a world that amplifies noise and rewards performance theatre, *silence remains one of the most underutilised tools of financial intelligence.* Within elite banking circles, underwriting silence is not about avoiding scrutiny; it's about *reconfiguring exposure.* The institutions that understand this do not sell privacy—they operate from it. And the clients who prioritise discretion aren't hiding—they're *governing.* Quiet capital doesn't simply move differently; it is *treated differently.*

At the core of underwriting silence lies a principle both timeless and radically underexplored: *the less noise your capital makes, the more optionality it retains.* This is not a speculative opinion. It is an operational axiom among sovereign wealth desks, elite family offices, and strategically positioned high-net-worth individuals (HNWIs). The value of money is not merely in its quantity, but in its *survivability under stress, scrutiny, and shifting jurisdictions.* That survivability begins with choosing the right custodians—and cultivating relationships that prize confidentiality not as branding, but as *infrastructure.*

True discretion in banking is never accidental. It is *underwritten*—by internal policy, by jurisdictional design, and by cultural norm. It begins with understanding that not all banks are built alike, even if they operate under superficially similar regulatory umbrellas. A Tier 1 international bank with flashy digital interfaces may be excellent for day-to-day liquidity, but utterly inappropriate for legacy capital or sensitive holdings. Conversely, a well-capitalised boutique institution in Liechtenstein or Monaco—while less accessible to the average retail client—may offer *quiet compartments of service*, shielded by jurisdictional neutrality and informed by generations of fiduciary expertise.

This is not about finding a bank that *offers* privacy. It's about engaging with a bank that *enforces* privacy as a foundational precondition of its existence. These institutions embed discretion into everything: from how client data is segmented and stored, to how relationship managers are trained not just to serve, but to *shield*. Clients who benefit most from this ecosystem are those who understand that private banking is *not* about luxury perks or airport lounges—it's about *discreet leverage, embedded legal insulation, and long-horizon trust architecture.*

Consider the power of a banking relationship that never requires you to explain your public exposure, that never markets your portfolio internally, and that never leaks your transaction profile to third-party product teams. This is not a utopian ideal. It exists—but only for those who have built enough relational equity, legal clarity, and jurisdictional thoughtfulness to *qualify for quiet.* Silence, in this context, is not the absence of signal; it is *precision in transmission.*

One of the most telling indicators of a bank's discretionary competence is its *onboarding ritual.* Superficially, all banks perform KYC and AML procedures. But within high-integrity private institutions, onboarding is less about data extraction and more about *risk calibration.* They are not merely verifying your identity—they are assessing *how to protect you.* What sort of exposure profile do you carry? What jurisdictions are relevant to your asset structures? What cross-border disclosures are you legally obligated to manage? Quiet banks take these factors seriously not to reject clients, but to design *predictably silent frameworks for capital custody.*

The nuance extends deeper. Private banks that master underwriting silence do not simply shield names on accounts; they design ecosystems of discretionary operation. This includes:

– *Nominee directors* and *third-party signatories* where lawful and appropriate
– Jurisdictional diversification of entity formation (e.g., a Panamanian foundation holding a Luxembourg account)
– Preference for manual authorisation flows over automated trigger-based alerts
– Relationship officers who do not operate on commission, reducing internal incentives to "upsell" visibility-based services
– Strategic use of custodial layering to keep asset classes segmented across banking silos

These strategies are not merely legal. They are philosophical. They reflect a deep institutional understanding that *exposure is cumulative and often irreversible.* Once leaked, a client profile cannot be "undeclared." Underwriting silence, then, becomes a method of *preventing future risk by limiting present broadcast.*

Let us not mistake this for secrecy in the criminal sense. All high-quality private banks today operate under strict FATCA, CRS, and local compliance regimes. But within those boundaries lies *a universe of legal discretion.* There is a meaningful difference between *reporting to regulators* and *advertising to the world.* Most reputational risks arise not from tax noncompliance, but from *public profile mismatches.* A politically exposed person who keeps assets in a perfectly legal trust may still suffer from social volatility if the structure is reported in a way that lacks context. A quiet bank avoids this by treating *narrative as risk*.

Critically, building a relationship with a discreet bank does not begin with sending in a wire or filling out an application. It begins with *intentional reputation curation*. Banks that underwrite silence do so because *your profile is coherent, legal, and aligned with their risk horizon*. This requires you to think not just about what you own, but *how your ownership aligns with your declared values, residency structures, and legal entitlements*. In other words, underwriting silence is not a service—it is a *mutual trust calibration*. They vet you as much as you vet them.

More than a financial utility, a discreet bank becomes a *sovereignty partner*. It allows you to manage liquidity, leverage, and asset custody in ways that minimise external interference. For families building intergenerational frameworks, this is invaluable. Silent banks become *strategic buffers*—not just against market volatility, but against narrative volatility. They don't just preserve capital; they preserve *intentional privacy* in an increasingly interpretive world.

Part 2

What often goes unspoken—even among financially sophisticated audiences—is that discretion is not an optional layer applied on top of wealth; *it is often the condition under which that wealth remains intact*. Across geographies where public disclosures, political volatility, or regulatory overreach are common, discretion is not just prudent—it is *existentially necessary*. Consider the business owner in a country with capital controls and unstable property rights. A single press article can trigger investigations, asset freezes, or social unrest. In such contexts, *loud capital is vulnerable capital*. Quiet banking becomes a defensive moat, not a luxury.

This is why jurisdiction and institutional culture matter more than brand recognition. Not all "private banks" are structurally equipped to protect your interests. Many large institutions, despite having a private banking division, are beholden to aggressive internal marketing, AI-based client profiling, and increasingly porous data-sharing practices. The very digital modernity that enables frictionless service also weakens the containment of your financial narrative. In contrast, older, more conservative private banks—often in jurisdictions like Switzerland, Liechtenstein, or select Asian hubs—operate on a model that sees discretion not as a by-product, but as a design imperative.

To engage with these banks is to engage with an alternate rhythm of finance. One that favours long-horizon relationships over high-turnover transactions. One that evaluates character as closely as net worth. One that quietly asks: *Who are you beyond your balance sheet?* The intake meeting is not about pushing products. It's about aligning institutional memory with personal legacy. This subtle difference produces structural clarity that no spreadsheet can capture.

The best private bankers—those worthy of the term—do not speak much. They listen. They ask about *intent*, not just asset allocation. They understand that *the shape of your privacy needs is a reflection of the complexity of your life*. A client going through a geopolitical relocation has different exposure concerns than a third-generation family steward managing foundations across multiple continents. The former may need agility; the latter, stability. A discreet bank translates these nuances into infrastructure: who signs what, who sees what, where it is held, and how it behaves under duress.

One illustrative case is the use of *wealth-backed credit lines*—available only through private banking channels that understand and respect opacity. These facilities do not broadcast themselves. They are often extended on the basis of consolidated balance sheet strength, not public documentation. No public filings, no collateral sales, no media footprints. Just liquidity, precision-engineered around privacy and long-term strategy. Quiet leverage, not noisy liquidity.

Of course, discretion without competence is theatre. A silent bank that cannot execute transactions with accuracy, maintain compliance integrity, or navigate global reporting regimes is simply *a liability in disguise.* True underwriting silence rests not only on discretion, but on *discipline and operational sophistication.* The legal team must understand global tax harmonisation trends. The IT infrastructure must be airtight against cyber intrusion. The internal culture must penalise indiscretion as severely as financial error. In such a culture, silence is not neglect—it is *strategic omission.*

There is also a psychological dimension to be addressed. Clients who seek silent banking are not merely avoiding exposure; they are *asserting authorship* over their financial identity. They want to *curate who knows what, when, and why.* This is a different philosophy from the retail investor who seeks optimisation through apps and public platforms. It is a declaration that *control is more valuable than convenience.* In this light, the relationship with a discreet bank becomes *a co-authored architecture of financial identity.* Done well, it is a long-form collaboration in which trust is not marketed, but earned through time, accuracy, and honour.

It is important to stress that not everyone qualifies for this tier of engagement. Discretionary banking requires a level of clarity about one's own position that few have cultivated. It demands *a sober awareness of jurisdictional implications, disclosure obligations, reputational dynamics, and legal structuring.* It is the final form of wealth maturity—not about having more, but about *risking less unnecessarily.* It is about converting vulnerability into strategy, and turning financial noise into strategic signal.

In today's climate of enforced transparency, algorithmic profiling, and weaponised compliance, silence has become a diminishing commodity. But it has not disappeared. It has *consolidated into fewer hands.* To gain access to it is not to disappear—it is to *become unreadable in the ways that matter.* That unreadability, when lawful and intentional, is not deception. It is *integrity preserved through calibration.*

Underwriting silence, then, is not a service you buy. It is *a condition you cultivate through thoughtful alignment of your structures, your disclosures, and your relationships.* And in the world of serious capital, it is perhaps the last remaining form of leverage that cannot be copied, taxed, or stolen. It is *not the absence of sound—but the presence of signal discipline.* It is the bank that knows your name—but never needs to say it aloud.

Banking for the Long Game

Wealth moves differently when the objective is permanence. This truth, often dismissed by fast-money cultures, sits at the heart of private banking philosophy. To the average investor, capital is a tool for chasing returns. To the private client—especially one intent on preserving multigenerational stability—capital is *a foundation for optionality, legacy, and insulation from volatility.* The difference between these two paradigms is not merely quantitative. It is philosophical. It defines how wealth is structured, where it is parked, and how it grows—not loudly, but predictably.

Modern retail investment culture is dominated by narratives of momentum: quarterly earnings, unicorn IPOs, algorithmic trading, and microsecond arbitrage. This environment rewards churn. Brokers are incentivised by volume. Retail investors are hypnotised by dashboards. The financial press perpetually favours "what's moving" over "what's enduring." But *durability is not glamorous.* And yet, it is durability—not performance spikes—that actually defines the wealth of serious families, sovereign funds, and legacy institutions.

Private banking operates under a different gravitational field. Its logic is measured not in months, but in decades—or more accurately, *in generations.* Where traditional investing fixates on extracting value from the market, private banking is concerned with *preserving control within the family*. The aim is not to beat the market quarter over quarter; it is to ensure that one's capital does not become hostage to it. This is a subtle, but profound distinction.

A well-structured private banking strategy is underpinned by a long-horizon framework. It integrates *consolidated reporting, jurisdictional security, intergenerational planning, and credit access* into a coherent architecture. Assets are not scattered across platforms—they are *aggregated under discreet custodianship*. The emphasis is on *resilience*, not adrenaline. The instruments deployed are tailored: bespoke credit lines secured against hard assets, conservative yield instruments with long-term payout schedules, and trustee-managed vehicles designed for tax efficiency and succession clarity.

One of the most misunderstood elements of private banking is its resistance to volatility. The typical private bank client does not seek excitement; they seek *structural asymmetry*—to participate in upside while minimising public downside exposure. For example, rather than liquidating equities to fund a major acquisition, a private banking client might leverage a long-standing relationship to obtain a credit facility against their portfolio—*retaining market exposure while unlocking liquidity*. There is no forced sale, no public transaction, no tax trigger. Only quiet leverage, secured through trust and time.

This capacity for *quiet liquidity* is one of private banking's great unspoken advantages. While public markets are obsessed with accessibility, private capital is obsessed with discretion and precision. When credit is extended through relationship rather than automation, terms are shaped around the person, not just the asset. Covenant light. Collateral flexible. Repayment structured. This flexibility is not available to those who jump banks every few years. It is *earned loyalty reciprocated with institutional latitude*.

Private banking also recognises that *not all risk is financial*. Reputational, political, and relational risks are often more important.

A family patriarch may wish to shield younger generations from visible wealth during their formative years. A business leader in a fragile political climate may need distance between operating income and personal reserves. A philanthropist may wish to fund controversial causes without drawing public scrutiny. These are not investment decisions in the narrow sense. They are *strategic alignments between intent and architecture*. And they require banks that listen closely and speak sparingly.

Where retail investors often fixate on *what* they hold—stocks, funds, property—private clients focus on *how* they hold it: in what entity, under what jurisdiction, through what legal lens, and with what future-proofing mechanisms in place. A diversified ETF portfolio may offer yield, but if held in a personal account subject to domestic regulatory overreach, it is structurally vulnerable. By contrast, the same assets held via a trust administered by a third-party fiduciary in a stable jurisdiction—with private banking custodianship—*transforms the asset from a point of exposure into a node of insulation.*

This is not simply asset management. It is *wealth architecture*. And architecture obeys different laws than trading. The latter seeks returns; the former seeks sovereignty.

Even within this long-game paradigm, private banking is not homogenous. There are varying models across Europe, Asia, and the Americas. Swiss institutions, for example, emphasise continuity and confidentiality. Singaporean banks often combine advanced digital infrastructure with family office services tailored to Asian diaspora families. Liechtenstein blends civil-law heritage with highly specialised fiduciary expertise. Each model reflects local legal tradition, cultural bias, and banking philosophy. But what unites them is a shared ethos: *stability over sensation, longevity over performance chasing.*

It is worth reflecting on how these principles contrast with the increasingly gamified retail environment. Apps deliver dopamine hits. Influencers celebrate daily swings. Financial literacy is reduced to portfolio screenshots and catchphrases. In such a climate, *private banking feels almost monastic.* Its silence is strategic. Its restraint, deliberate.

Yet to dismiss it as outdated is to miss its true power. When a geopolitical crisis erupts, when capital controls are imposed, when tax regimes shift unpredictably—it is the private client with jurisdictional flexibility, durable structures, and patient capital who *sleeps through the storm.* Not because they are smarter, but because they *built differently.* They did not chase the last percentage point—they designed for permanence.

Ultimately, *banking for the long game is a philosophy of control disguised as calm.* It does not advertise itself. It is rarely featured on magazine covers. But it sits at the foundation of quiet empires, family legacies, and sovereign durability. It turns finance from a sprint into a relay—and the baton it passes is not just money, but *clarity, continuity, and choice.*

Those who understand this approach don't ask, "What's the return this quarter?" They ask, *"What will my great-granddaughter inherit—intact, invisible, and unencumbered?"*

That is not speculation. That is design. And it is the beating heart of private banking for those who play not for applause, but for *continuity across time.*

Silent Credit, Quiet Leverage

The wealthiest individuals in the world rarely sell. This is not because they are sentimental about assets or particularly bullish on markets. It is because *liquidity and control are not the same thing as ownership.* For those playing the long game of capital preservation and influence, the goal is not to liquidate, but to *leverage without disturbance*. Credit—when structured with sophistication—is not just a source of liquidity; it becomes a shield, a lever, and a veil. It allows assets to remain intact while generating utility, all without attracting unnecessary attention or triggering regulatory friction. This is the architecture of *silent credit*—a domain of finance where capital moves, but no dust is kicked up.

At the heart of this strategy is an idea that contradicts popular financial advice: *do not sell your best assets to raise cash*. Retail investors are taught to "take profits" when they need liquidity. Private clients are taught to take loans—*secured not against income streams, but against the integrity and stability of their existing wealth*. A blue-chip art collection, a vintage car portfolio, a stake in a privately held firm, or an international real estate holding—any of these can be quietly used as collateral. The public sees permanence. The bank sees a credit line. The result? Capital flexibility without asset visibility.

This style of wealth-backed credit is not new, but it remains misunderstood and under-discussed. That is partly by design. Unlike personal loans or mortgages, these facilities are negotiated quietly, often with terms tailored to the client's entire financial architecture. Interest rates may be nominal. Repayment schedules may be loosely defined. In some instances, the loan is structured as *non-recourse*, allowing the borrower to walk away with no further liability beyond the asset pledged. More importantly, *the transaction never touches the public markets*. There is no sale to be recorded, no gain to be taxed, and often no paper trail beyond the custodian and the lending officer's desk.

To understand why this matters, consider the cascading risks of a visible asset liquidation. Selling triggers tax obligations. It exposes valuation data. It can move markets or alert competitors. In certain jurisdictions, it can flag regulatory authorities or invite scrutiny into other areas of a family's portfolio. *Credit avoids all of that*. Done well, it allows for movement without exposure, liquidity without liquidation. The goal is to keep one's name *out of headlines, out of databases, and out of reach.*

Take, for example, the family office of a third-generation industrial dynasty in Latin America. Their operating company has been cash-rich for decades, but political instability has made direct ownership visibility dangerous. Rather than moving capital between entities, they pledged a slice of equity in a Swiss special-purpose vehicle to secure a credit line from a Liechtenstein-based private bank. The cash—drawn in tranches—was used to acquire foreign property, fund litigation against a hostile partner, and quietly support political advocacy in their home country. The shares never moved. No sale occurred. The family gained capacity without diluting control.

Or consider the example of an ultra-high-net-worth tech founder post-exit. Following a public listing, her wealth was largely illiquid—held in founder's stock with heavy restrictions. Rather than waiting for a lockup to expire and causing a media frenzy with an insider sale, she approached a Luxembourg-based banking consortium. The deal: a revolving loan facility backed by the pledged equity, with flexible drawdown terms, and confidentiality clauses protecting her identity across all banking layers. The public saw a dormant founder. Her legal team saw a war chest.

These are not hypotheticals. They are recurring tactics among those who understand that *access to capital does not require liquidation—only collateral and credibility*. But it's not only the ultra-wealthy who benefit. Discreet leverage structures are increasingly available to the moderately affluent: international entrepreneurs, successful retirees, or dual citizens with diversified holdings. What matters most is not net worth, but *asset character and banking relationships*. A long-standing, conservative investment profile often unlocks better terms than a flashy but volatile one.

The mechanisms for quiet leverage include several instruments, each tailored to client objectives:

– **Lombard Loans**: These are credit facilities backed by liquid securities such as equities, bonds, or mutual funds held with the bank. The advantage lies in speed, discretion, and customisable terms. The risk lies in margin calls during market downturns.

– **Credit Against Private Holdings**: Less liquid, but potentially more powerful, this involves pledging interests in private companies, real estate, or alternative assets. Valuation becomes more complex, but so too does the opportunity for long-term structuring and covenant negotiation.

– **Hybrid Facilities**: A bespoke combination of liquid and illiquid collateral, often tied to broader banking services. These facilities allow for strategic liquidity over years rather than months, often at low interest rates and with minimal visibility.

– **Trust-Integrated Credit**: In certain cases, the credit facility is not extended to the individual, but to a trust or foundation under their control. This adds an additional layer of anonymity and asset protection, with the lender assessing the trustee's authority rather than the grantor's net worth.

Critics often warn that credit introduces fragility. They assume that debt is a liability—something to be minimised or eliminated. In retail finance, this is a fair view. But in private capital, *credit is a tool of engineering*. It allows for timing advantages, tax deferral, estate planning precision, and liquidity without exposure. The liability is calculated, limited, and often counterbalanced by appreciation of the underlying asset. In the most conservative implementations, the borrower could pay off the loan at any time—but chooses not to, *because opportunity cost makes capital deployment more efficient elsewhere.*

The most astute players use this credit not for consumption, but for *strategic reinvestment.* A silent loan backed by one holding funds the acquisition of another—often in a different sector or geography. The original asset remains untouched. The new one is added. Value accrues in both directions. And yet, to the outside observer, nothing appears to have changed. *This is how dynasties are built—not by buying, but by aligning and multiplying through leverage that whispers instead of shouts.*

Silence, in this context, is not a stylistic preference. It is a strategy of resilience. The less movement your financial footprint shows, the fewer entry points it offers to those who would tax, regulate, sue, or politicise it. Quiet credit becomes *a firewall against scrutiny.* And in a world increasingly hungry for transparency, that silence may be the rarest—and most valuable—form of financial power.

To conclude, silent credit and quiet leverage are not the preserve of elites playing esoteric games. They are *disciplines of design*, rooted in principles that anyone with assets, obligations, or aspirations should study: *keep control, build quietly, borrow strategically, and show as little as legally possible.* What builds an empire is rarely visible from the outside. That is not an accident. That is design.

Chapter 6
The Invisible Paper Trail – Structuring for Strategic Obscurity.

At the uppermost tiers of asset protection, the defining factor is no longer the sheer volume of wealth held—it's the degree to which that wealth can be obscured in plain sight. Not by deception, but by design. Not hidden, but distanced. This chapter does not deal in the crude mechanics of tax havens or paper-thin shell companies. Its concern lies deeper, with the sophisticated choreography of legal form and functional power—how those who truly understand the game deploy documents not to mislead, but to shape perception, dictate access, and engineer ambiguity with intent.

To those operating at the surface of the financial world, ownership seems simple: binary, even. You either own something, or you don't. But peel back the layers and this black-and-white premise fades into a spectrum—one scattered with gradations of control, title, influence, and exposure. Somewhere between "mine" and "not mine" lies a complex terrain in which real protection is born. Strategic obscurity lives there. It is not about erasure; it is about reconfiguration. To appear at arm's length while retaining direction is not a trick. It's a technique.

The trouble is, most who attempt such structuring do so with a false sense of comfort. A trust is established, a nominee named, a company incorporated. The box is ticked. But often the paperwork says one thing while the behaviour says another—and that, more than any regulatory change or legal reform, is what introduces danger. It's not bad faith that causes these structures to unravel. It's misplaced faith in form over function.

Here's the uncomfortable truth: complexity does not guarantee safety, and simplicity does not guarantee transparency. One trust, thoughtfully crafted, may offer more insulation than a multi-tiered, offshore tangle. Conversely, a brilliantly drafted corporate structure may collapse in court the moment behavioural patterns suggest the founder still calls the shots. In this chapter, we'll explore that tension—the quiet conflict between appearance and influence, between what's on the record and what's behind the curtain.

This is not an abstract concern. It's the fault line between effective shielding and full-blown legal exposure. Imagine a founder who places shares into a trust, appoints an independent trustee, and pats themselves on the back, believing they've put the asset beyond reach. But in practice, they continue to give orders, approve decisions, and refer to the company as their own. When scrutiny comes—and it will—it won't be the paperwork that's decisive. It'll be the emails, the meeting notes, the fingerprints on every decision. What was built as a wall of protection becomes, under pressure, a trail of breadcrumbs.

To navigate this terrain, one must understand the mechanics of distance layering—not as mere decoration, but as design with purpose. Nominee directors, third-party custodians, shadow governance—all are tools. But tools only. Their power lies in their alignment with actual conduct. Throughout this chapter, we'll examine three foundational principles that mark the difference between credible protection and elegant failure:

1. **Form Must Mirror Function**: A structure cannot just exist on paper—it must reflect reality. If you are still emotionally, operationally, or financially tethered to the asset, your structure must account for that truth. Pretending otherwise only increases your vulnerability.
2. **Influence Without Footprint**: True protection lies in being able to guide outcomes without being seen to do so. This is where layered directorships, trustee instructions, and disaggregated custodianship become essential—not to obscure illegally, but to operate strategically.
3. **Audit the Narrative**: Think like your adversary. If a hostile party were to read through your emails, minutes, agreements—what story would emerge? Does the narrative reflect the form you've built, or does it betray it? Paper trails aren't merely records; they are scripts in litigation.

This isn't just a matter for tax lawyers and estate planners. Courts, investigators, regulators—and increasingly, journalists—have developed a language for dismantling poorly conceived structures. The doctrines of "beneficial interest," "piercing the corporate veil," and "sham arrangements" aren't fringe tools anymore. They're part of the legal mainstream. The scrutiny has intensified, and so must the sophistication of design.

Take, for instance, the case of a Southeast Asian magnate who tucked his shipping conglomerate into a pristine Cayman trust. The documents were immaculate, the trustee seasoned and professional. But during a high-profile divorce trial, private correspondence emerged showing the settlor routinely giving operational directives—albeit labelled "suggestions." The court saw through the semantic dance. What mattered wasn't the letter of the trust deed, but the lived reality it failed to conceal.

Contrast that with a quieter success story: a Central European financier who foresaw an impending asset freeze amid political unrest. In anticipation, he moved funds across a series of custodial accounts spread over four jurisdictions. None stood out individually; none revealed the full picture. But the whole, taken together, formed a resilient web—one that held firm when the sanctions came. There was no deceit, no illegality. Just foresight, fragmentation, and timing.

These examples are not anomalies; they're instructive. They demonstrate that ownership in the modern era is no longer a matter of possession, but choreography. What appears inert on paper may conceal a live wire of influence. What looks inactive may be calibrated for rapid response. If you want to understand protection today, you must stop asking, "Who owns this?" and start asking, "How does this move? Under whose instruction? With what constraint?"

Philosophically, this chapter asks you to reconsider what it means to hold. Not just to possess—but to direct, to steward, to shelter. Asset protection, at its highest level, is not a vault. It's a performance. And like any good performance, what's visible is only part of the story.

By the time you reach the final page, you'll be equipped not simply with terminology—nominees, fiduciaries, veil-piercing—but with a new lens. You'll know which questions to pose when drafting, which habits to monitor, and which behaviours may one day be read back to you in court. You'll learn how clarity can become a liability, and how discretion, if done right, can be a form of integrity—not just protection.

This isn't about disappearing. It's about appearing—carefully, intentionally, and on your own terms. Some marks are meant to last. Others are better drawn in pencil, with the option to erase when the context changes. Welcome to the architecture of strategic invisibility.

What Shows, What Doesn't: The Discipline of Legal Invisibility

In high-stakes asset protection, visibility is often vulnerability. The wealthiest individuals in the world tend not to ask "How much do I own?" but rather "What does the world believe I own—and what can they prove?" This distinction is not a matter of arrogance or secrecy. It's a calculated response to a legal and economic environment where perception drives action. Creditors don't seize what they can't locate. Litigants don't sue what they can't attach. And governments don't regulate what appears to reside elsewhere. *To survive scrutiny, one must understand what is visible by design, what becomes visible by discovery, and what can remain invisible—lawfully—by structure.*

This is the terrain of asset tracing. Not as an act of concealment, but as a strategic exercise in informational discipline. Asset tracing is the forensic art of following financial footprints—from the tangible (real estate, bank accounts, securities) to the intangible (intellectual property, beneficial control, nominee relationships). Practised by litigation firms, intelligence units, investigative journalists, and state actors, asset tracing exposes what the structure *forgot* to hide. In this context, the issue is not "what's legal." The issue is "what's *legible* to an adversary."

To operate in today's financial landscape without understanding asset visibility is like walking across a minefield with a blindfold: each step risks catastrophic exposure. A name on a registry, a signature on a shareholder resolution, a careless reference in an email—these fragments build a narrative that can collapse years of structural protection. *Your real asset is not the asset itself. It is your relationship to its visibility.*

Let's begin with the basics: what does show?

What Shows—By Default and By Design

1. **Public Registries:** In many jurisdictions, corporate and land ownership is recorded in searchable public databases. Transparency laws, especially in the UK, EU, and parts of the Commonwealth, now require registers of beneficial owners for companies, trusts, and partnerships. While these databases may appear limited, they often reveal more than intended: timelines, nominee patterns, and connections between entities.

2. **Transactional Activity:** Every wire transfer, property purchase, or investment recorded in a financial institution leaves a trail. Institutions subject to Know-Your-Customer (KYC) and Anti-Money Laundering (AML) regimes will flag patterns—even if no laws are broken. The record exists, and under subpoena, it can speak volumes.

3. **Legal Proceedings:** Any asset listed in court documents—wills, divorce disclosures, or creditor lawsuits—enters the public record. This is often how investigators triangulate visibility: they look for assets that are *not* on a balance sheet but are *implied* by income, lifestyle, or behaviour.

4. **Reputational Databases:** Investigative firms maintain grey databases of politically exposed persons (PEPs), high-risk clients, and known associates. These are not criminal records; they

are pattern analyses based on leaked data, press mentions, and offshore leaks like the Panama or Pandora Papers.

The mistake made by many emerging wealth-holders is assuming that what doesn't appear on a balance sheet cannot be discovered. But *what shows is often more behavioural than structural.* That is where most fall.

What Doesn't Show—And Why That Matters

Now, contrast this with what *doesn't* show—when structured properly.

1. **Nominee Shareholding and Directorships:** A nominee, when legally appointed and backed by indemnity agreements, can serve as the public-facing "owner" or director while holding no beneficial interest. So long as instructions are not overtly documented or suggestive of shadow control, the real principal remains insulated.

2. **Discretionary Trusts:** If a trust is truly discretionary, with an independent trustee who has latitude to decide how assets are distributed, the beneficiaries have no fixed right to claim. This means the trust assets are generally not treated as belonging to the beneficiary—even in legal proceedings.

3. **Custodial Ownership:** Securities held through global custodians—especially in jurisdictions with no public beneficial ownership disclosure—can exist in legal limbo. The asset exists. But identifying who *controls* it becomes difficult without cooperation between banks, governments, or intermediaries.

4. **Tiered Holding Structures:** A well-layered holding structure, distributed across multiple jurisdictions, can create what professionals call *jurisdictional fatigue.* This means tracing assets becomes so administratively or politically complicated that it becomes cost-prohibitive for most adversaries to continue.

None of these mechanisms are illegal. But they are rarely well executed. Why? Because the human behaviour beneath the structure betrays it.

Visibility is Often a Matter of Behaviour

A common thread in asset tracing cases is not flawed documentation—but *careless action.* A wealthy individual establishes an offshore trust, appoints a nominee director, and feels protected. But they then use personal email to issue instructions, refer to the trust assets as "mine," or guarantee loans as if they still control the funds. The structure may be legally sound—but the behaviour implies control. And in court, implication can outweigh form.

This is why *visibility is not a legal status—it is a behavioural signal.* To remain structurally invisible, you must align not just your documentation but your actions, communications, and language. Your legal position must be mirrored in your functional distance. Anything less is performance art—and forensic investigators are trained critics.

Case Study: The Disguised Family Office

Consider the case of a Central American tycoon who operated a family office via a Singapore-based foundation. On paper, the foundation held a network of entities across Europe and the Caribbean, all with professional directors. No document tied the principal to the operations. However, in the discovery phase of a lawsuit, an email surfaced from the tycoon to his accountant saying, "Please wire $3M from the Bahamas structure to fund my nephew's project." That single instruction collapsed the structure. The court ruled that he retained "substantive control" and pierced the veil across multiple entities.

This was not a failure of secrecy—it was a failure of *discipline.*

The Ethical Line: Invisibility Without Illegality

The pursuit of structural invisibility must not drift into unlawful concealment. The goal is not to deceive regulators, evade taxes, or obstruct justice. The goal is to *create friction between asset discovery and asset seizure.* In a world where the burden of proof is often reversed—where one must prove innocence rather than be proven guilty—*strategic opacity* becomes a legitimate defensive architecture.

This requires not only legal compliance, but ethical clarity. Ask:

– Am I protecting against illegitimate seizure or avoiding rightful obligation?
– Would I be comfortable if this structure were reviewed by a neutral judge—not one with political motivation or personal vendetta?
– Am I relying on deception, or am I relying on design?

The answers to these questions determine whether invisibility becomes a shield—or a trap.

The Tools of Structured Discretion

While this chapter is not a toolkit, it is worth highlighting the structural mechanisms that professionals use to maintain lawful opacity:

– **Contractual Disassociation:** Private agreements that outline roles, responsibilities, and disengagement between principals and agents.

– **Legal Distance Through Delegation:** True delegation—not symbolic appointment—of trustees, directors, and managers with demonstrable autonomy.

– **Jurisdictional Arbitrage:** Placement of structures in legal systems where asset tracing faces higher thresholds of evidence or lower cooperation across borders.

– **Data Hygiene Protocols:** Enforcing operational rules where no sensitive instructions are sent via traceable mediums (e.g., email, SMS), and no ownership language is used informally.

These are not shortcuts. They are disciplines. And like any discipline, they require understanding, training, and consistency.

The Bottom Line: Asset Tracing Is the New Litigation Weapon

The modern adversary—whether governmental, corporate, or private—is not breaking down doors with armed bailiffs. They are tracing your assets via data brokers, leaks, subpoenas, and forensic accountants. They are constructing narratives from registry entries, transaction patterns, social media posts, and careless correspondence.

And unless you design for *narrative resistance*, not just legal compliance, you are exposed.

What shows is more than what you own—it is what can be proved. What doesn't show is not hidden. It is constructed. Therein lies the difference between evasion and insulation, between recklessness and resilience, between short-term concealment and long-term sovereignty.

Paper Structures vs. Living Realities: The Illusion of Protection in Legal Architecture

In private wealth strategy, nothing is more dangerous than mistaking legal form for functional power. Sophisticated structures—trusts, companies, nominee accounts, layered holdings—are often treated as impermeable shields. They are drafted with Latin phrasing, notarised by specialists, and stored in vaults as if sacred instruments. But a document does not defend itself. A contract does not act. A structure is only as strong as the alignment between its written intention and its operational behaviour. *The map is not the terrain.*

This subchapter confronts one of the most neglected truths in asset protection: *a perfect legal document can offer zero real protection if the facts on the ground tell a different story.* Courts do not adjudicate paperwork in isolation. They examine patterns, timelines, behaviours, control, and intent. And when those elements clash with the paperwork, the veil is lifted.

Wealth holders, attorneys, and advisers alike often overestimate the power of form and underestimate the weight of function. This false sense of security is not theoretical. It has collapsed fortunes, unravelled dynasties, and exposed structures that were technically legal—but practically useless.

Let us examine why.

The Legal Form Is Not the Legal Reality

In fiduciary structuring, "control" is the axis on which legitimacy spins. The question in litigation or tax inquiry is not, *What does the trust deed say?* It is, *Who behaves as if they own or direct the assets?* If you sign the trust deed as settlor and then instruct the trustee as if they are your personal assistant—sending routine emails with orders, approving distributions, vetoing investments—then the reality is clear: *you remain the de facto controller.* In many jurisdictions, this will be grounds for the trust to be declared a sham.

Consider the 2013 case of *Antle v. Canada*, where a trust was deemed invalid because the actions of the parties contradicted the trust's stated independence. The trustee exercised no real discretion. The beneficiary (also the settlor's spouse) had no functional autonomy. The judge stated that the trust "existed only on paper," and the structure was ignored entirely for tax purposes.

The lesson? *Law responds to substance, not signatures.* If your structure says one thing but your behaviour says another, you are exposed.

Corporate Veils Are Thinner Than They Appear

Similarly, in corporate structuring, the illusion of separation between individual and entity is often pierced. Asset holders set up companies in the British Virgin Islands or Nevis, appoint nominee directors, and assume that this alone creates a firewall between personal and corporate assets. But if they then sign contracts as "owner" of the company, fund it from personal accounts, or take unilateral decisions without board meetings, they risk veil piercing.

Courts have repeatedly ruled that where there is commingling of funds, inadequate corporate formalities, or personal misuse of company assets, the corporate veil may be lifted. This is not rare. It is the norm in high-stakes litigation involving offshore structures. *The critical variable is not geography or statute—it is governance and discipline.*

A nominee director who has no record of meetings, no autonomy, and no traceable compensation for independent thought is not a director. They are a liability. A company that files no audited reports, keeps no formal minutes, and serves only as a conduit for personal assets is not a company. It is a red flag.

Power Is Demonstrated, Not Declared

The failure to distinguish between paperwork and practice often stems from a fundamental misunderstanding of what courts and regulators seek: *not the appearance of separation, but the reality of separation.* When a trust or company is scrutinised, investigators ask:

– Who has the ability to access funds?
– Who gives day-to-day instructions?
– Who benefits economically and makes discretionary decisions?
– Are there internal controls, or is the entity effectively a personal proxy?

These questions are not answered by trust deeds, incorporation documents, or notarised letters. They are answered by emails, transaction histories, behavioural patterns, and testimony.

Case Study: The Collapsed Fortress

In a high-profile litigation involving a Russian industrialist, over £100 million in assets were routed through a Guernsey trust. The trust had been drafted by a leading fiduciary firm. It featured discretionary language, multiple protector provisions, and offshore banking. On paper, it was unassailable.

But when the industrialist's divorce proceedings began in London, a different picture emerged. The court found that the settlor regularly contacted the trustee to approve distributions, often dictated investment decisions, and treated the trust account as his own. He even referred to the trust assets as "my money" in text messages. The judge declared that while the structure was "formally offshore," the control was "functionally domestic." The entire trust was treated as a personal asset pool—and included in the divorce settlement.

The problem was not in the drafting. The problem was in the conduct.

Why Simplicity Betrays Sophistication

Modern wealth often operates across borders, currencies, and asset classes. Simplistic structures—like a single offshore company or a one-layer trust—fail not because they are inherently flawed, but because they lack resilience under stress.

A single-layer structure is easy to map. If one nominee cracks, if one jurisdiction complies with a request, the entire apparatus is exposed. Sophisticated wealth requires *operational complexity aligned with real independence*—not just multi-jurisdictional opacity, but behaviour that matches the paper.

It is tempting to think that minimalism equals elegance. But in asset protection, *simplicity often equals fragility*. What appears efficient to a layperson appears suspicious to an investigator. Robust structures must *earn* their legitimacy through consistent separation of roles, real delegation of power, and clear operational protocols.

The Behavioural Audit: A Forgotten Safeguard

Every six months, any serious wealth structure should undergo a behavioural audit. This means evaluating not just the paperwork, but the reality of how decisions are made:

– Who initiates wire transfers?
– Who signs resolutions?
– Who attends meetings?
– What language is used in emails?

If the answers point back to the settlor or beneficial owner—even subtly—then the structure may be legally sound, but practically penetrable.

This is not about hiding. It is about alignment. If a trustee is meant to be independent, they must act independently. If a company is meant to have its own governance, it must observe governance practices. If an entity is meant to be discretionary, no personal entitlement can be implied.

Where Philosophy Meets Protection

This discussion is not merely technical. It is philosophical. At its heart is the question: *What are you trying to protect—and from whom?* If your goal is merely to "own without owning," you will design structures that look impressive but crumble under inquiry. If your goal is resilience—through legal insulation, ethical clarity, and behavioural alignment—then the structure becomes more than a façade. It becomes a fortress.

This requires maturity. Many high-net-worth individuals treat structuring as a game: the right document, the right jurisdiction, the right nominee. But real asset protection is not a game. It is a discipline grounded in *consistency between structure and substance*. It is not about misleading adversaries—it is about leaving them with nothing legitimate to attack.

Final Insight: Protection Lives in Coherence

The mistake most people make is over-investing in paperwork and under-investing in practice. The law doesn't protect the clever. It protects the coherent. A structure that is poorly documented but consistently observed may withstand attack better than a perfectly documented one that is functionally a puppet show.

Paper structures are the skeleton. Living realities are the muscle. Without harmony between the two, your asset protection is not defensive architecture—it is theatre. And in litigation, theatre rarely ends well.

Nominees, Custodians, and Layers of Distance: Engineering Strategic Ambiguity in Ownership

To the casual observer, ownership appears binary. One either possesses something or does not. But in the world of private wealth architecture, ownership is anything but straightforward. It can be direct or indirect, legal or beneficial, transparent or obscured. And for those seeking both lawful protection and discretion, it is rarely absolute. *Control without exposure*—this is the ideal. And legal intermediaries such as nominees and custodians are the instruments through which this ideal becomes operational.

This subchapter explores the often-misunderstood roles of nominees and custodians, and how the strategic layering of ownership, control, and possession can create a protective distance between an individual and their assets—without breaking the law, or the spirit of it. It is not a guide to secrecy for secrecy's sake. It is a blueprint for resilient, compliant structuring where discretion serves as a safeguard, not a shield for misconduct.

The Nominee as a Mirror: Illusion or Instrument?

A nominee, in its most distilled form, is someone who holds legal title to an asset on behalf of someone else—the beneficial owner. This is common in jurisdictions with robust financial privacy laws. In theory, the nominee has no discretion and acts solely under the direction of the beneficial owner. But in practice, the integrity and risk exposure of such arrangements vary enormously depending on how the relationship is managed.

Consider the nominee director of an offshore company. They may appear in official registries as the controlling mind of the entity. But if they act solely on instruction, document nothing, and are easily displaced, they provide no legal insulation in a dispute. The courts may view them as an administrative proxy—irrelevant to the determination of actual control.

Contrast this with a nominee who insists on formal instructions, documents every meeting, charges independent fees, and maintains their own legal counsel. Their role then becomes substantive, not superficial. The nominee relationship functions not as a fig leaf, but as a firewall. It is not the appearance of distance that matters—it is the *functional behaviour* of the intermediaries involved.

Custodians: Holding Without Owning

Where nominees are the face, custodians are the vault. A custodian holds an asset—often securities, physical bullion, or critical documents—on behalf of the owner, without appearing to control it. Custodianship is a neutral role by design, and its value lies in creating *physical separation without surrendering economic benefit.*

This distinction is vital in scenarios where immediate control may become a liability. For instance, in countries with volatile political climates or shifting regulatory frameworks, assets held by a neutral custodian in a stable jurisdiction may be shielded from domestic seizure or coercive taxation. Yet unlike a trust or foundation, custodianship does not transfer ownership. It suspends it—functionally—at a legal distance.

A practical example: An investor with dual citizenship places bearer bonds into the custody of a Swiss vault service under a discretionary storage contract. The bonds remain his. But the government of his country of origin, under investigation for capital flight, cannot seize what he does not possess in-country. *Custodianship becomes the mechanism through which possession is rendered non-local.*

Layering: The Geometry of Deterrence

One intermediary creates distance. Several create *strategic ambiguity*. When structured properly, a multi-layered system—where a nominee holds shares in a company, that company owns assets managed by a custodian, all of which are monitored by a fiduciary trust—produces a geometry too complex for casual scrutiny. Each layer must be legitimate in its own right, but together they form an architecture of deterrence.

Deterrence is not concealment. It is *friction*. The more difficult it is for a third party to trace, claim, or interfere with an asset, the less likely they are to try. This matters not just in litigation, but in reputation risk, business disputes, and even family governance. A sibling who sees a direct inheritance may litigate. One who sees a discretionary trust structure, with assets managed by corporate custodians and governed by layered fiduciaries, may reconsider.

That said, layering must be intentional, not gratuitous. Excess complexity without functional purpose is not protection—it is fragility. Each entity in the chain must serve a legal and operational role. Otherwise, the structure risks collapse under judicial scrutiny or operational stress.

Case Study: The Sovereign Dissident

In 2019, a former diplomat from a Middle Eastern monarchy faced internal investigations for alleged dissidence. Anticipating asset freeze orders, he had—years prior—structured his portfolio through a Liechtenstein foundation with professional directors, which owned a holding company in Luxembourg. The Luxembourg entity, in turn, held a brokerage account in Singapore, with assets custodied through a Swiss private bank.

On paper, none of the assets were in his name. In practice, he retained influence through well-documented powers of recommendation—not instruction. The key? At every level, the intermediaries were real: directors who refused informal requests, custodians who required written compliance, and advisers who acted in accordance with regulated duties.

When the investigation reached full tilt, the domestic government issued orders for asset repatriation. But they had no legal path to the funds. The diplomat was not the shareholder, not the signatory, not the director. The structure had no falsehood—only distance. And distance protected him, not deception.

Ethics of Obscurity: Distinction, Not Evasion

Critics may argue that these tools are designed to hide, to frustrate justice or taxation. But such critiques conflate *obscurity with evasion.* The legality of nominee and custodian structures depends not on their opacity, but on the transparency of intent. If these layers are disclosed in compliance filings, if their roles are demonstrably operational, then the structure is neither illicit nor unethical.

Indeed, obscurity in ownership has legitimate applications: protecting whistleblowers, shielding dissidents, defending intellectual property in hostile markets, or preventing extortion attempts. In high-profile divorces, media attacks, or business partner fallouts, clarity is not always protective. Sometimes *ambiguity is the only shield that works*—so long as it is lawfully built.

Legal Doctrine: Possession Is Not Nine-Tenths

A common myth in asset tracing is that whoever holds the asset must be its owner. Legally, this is inaccurate. Courts increasingly distinguish between *legal title*, *beneficial interest*, and *control.* Possession—especially where intermediaries are involved—is no longer prima facie evidence of ownership.

In fact, recent jurisprudence in both the UK and Singapore has clarified that nominee and custodian arrangements, when properly documented and executed, are to be respected unless there is clear evidence of abuse or fraud. This places a heavy burden of proof on claimants who wish to challenge such setups. What matters is whether the structure reflects a *functional separation of roles*, not just a formal one.

Behavioural Integrity: The Weakest Link Is You

The structure is only as strong as its weakest participant. A nominee who signs off without internal controls, a custodian who acts on verbal requests, or a beneficial owner who refers to "my assets" in emails—all can collapse the architecture. Courts are not impressed by certificates. They are persuaded by behaviour.

Thus, the use of nominees and custodians must be paired with discipline. This includes:

– Written mandates and engagement letters
– Logs of correspondence and minutes of meetings
– Compliance protocols that reflect genuine autonomy
– Regular legal audits to validate separation of duties

Without these, layers of distance are illusion. With them, they are law.

Conclusion Without Saying It

The core lesson of this subchapter is simple: *ownership is a spectrum, not a status.* Nominees, custodians, and layered intermediaries allow wealth to be held—not hidden—in a manner that protects without deceiving. But their effectiveness lies not in the paperwork, but in the practice. Strategic distance is not something one declares; it is something one *demonstrates consistently*—across jurisdictions, through conduct, and under scrutiny.

Used well, these tools do not just provide legal insulation. They grant sovereignty. Not to escape the law, but to live above the noise—with clarity, resilience, and discretion.

When Simplicity Betrays You: The Legal Cost of Under-Structuring

In wealth structuring, simplicity is often marketed as a virtue. Consultants promise "clean" frameworks, "streamlined" ownership, and "minimalist" strategies. These promises appeal to intelligent clients who are busy, risk-averse, and allergic to jargon. But simplicity, when misunderstood or applied without strategic thought, becomes something else entirely: a liability dressed in elegance.

The purpose of this subchapter is not to advocate for complexity for its own sake. Rather, it is to *deconstruct the mythology of simplicity*—to examine the legal and operational blind spots that emerge when structuring decisions are made for aesthetic ease rather than strategic durability. In the high-stakes world of litigation, regulatory investigation, or cross-border enforcement, what was once an "elegant" structure can become dangerously fragile. And by the time that fragility is exposed, the damage is often irreversible.

The False Comfort of the "Clean Line"

The archetype of the simple structure is the individual who owns all assets directly, or through a single-layer holding company with minimal documentation and flat control. On paper, it looks straightforward. There is clarity of ownership, minimal governance cost, and a short chain of command. But simplicity becomes perilous when the underlying purpose of structuring—*asset protection, jurisdictional distancing, fiduciary delegation*—is sacrificed at the altar of visual tidiness.

Consider a UK-based entrepreneur who owns significant real estate through a local company, with shares held in their personal name. It's clean. It's understandable. It also makes them *the direct target of every claimant*, whether from civil litigation, creditor action, or divorce proceedings. In court, simplicity becomes transparency. And transparency becomes vulnerability.

Contrast this with a more resilient alternative: the real estate held by a holding company in a neutral jurisdiction, whose shares are owned by a discretionary trust, advised by an independent protector, and administered through a regulated fiduciary. To the untrained eye, this appears complex. But it is, in fact, *calibrated complexity*—each layer serving a distinct protective function. And when challenged in court, it resists interpretation as a mere extension of the individual's personal estate.

Simplicity Cannot Absorb Shock

Structures, like buildings, must be evaluated not in calm but in crisis. A single-layer entity can function perfectly well during periods of legal peace. But when challenged—by an ex-spouse, tax authority, political regime, or international regulator—it may offer no insulation. Every document, email, and financial statement will be scrutinised for indicators of control. And where there is control without distance, *the court imputes ownership*—no matter what the paperwork claims.

History provides abundant cautionary examples. In the 2014 case *Prest v Petrodel Resources Ltd*, the UK Supreme Court ruled that assets held by a company could be considered part of the owner's estate in divorce proceedings if the company was deemed a façade. The legal doctrine of "piercing the corporate veil" is applied *not on the structure itself*, but on its misuse, undercapitalisation, or lack of independent governance.

What failed in this case was not law—it was *oversimplification*. The companies were wholly owned, minimally documented, and demonstrably controlled by the individual. There were no legitimate commercial purposes, no independent directors, and no operational separation. Simplicity created a direct line from individual to asset—and the court used that line to dismantle the shield.

Risk Concentration in Single Points of Failure

Another hidden hazard of simplicity is the over-concentration of risk. When one entity or one jurisdiction holds everything, you are one regulatory change, one lawsuit, or one banking policy away from catastrophic exposure. In contrast, *modular structures*—where assets are siloed by class, function, or geography—allow for containment of shocks. Simplicity, by definition, cannot provide that.

This is not a theoretical risk. In 2013, Cyprus enacted emergency legislation to seize portions of large bank deposits in response to a national banking crisis. Thousands of clients who held funds in a single Cypriot entity, under a single banking relationship, were wiped out overnight. There were no fallbacks, no secondary custodians, and no structural insulation. Their simplicity made them visible. Their visibility made them vulnerable.

A more advanced framework—holding cash in three separate custodians, using trust-owned investment vehicles with geographic spread—would have taken longer to set up. But it would have survived. *Survivability requires redundancy. Simplicity forbids it.*

Operational Fragility Masquerading as Clarity

There is also an operational dimension to the risk. Simple structures often rely heavily on the personal involvement of the principal. When everything is centralised in one signature, one login, or one trustee, operational control becomes bottlenecked. If that individual becomes incapacitated, indicted, or politically exposed, the system stalls.

Sophisticated frameworks, on the other hand, use delegated authority, pre-approved protocols, and tiered access rights. These systems may appear more complex, but they are *built to function under stress*—whether personal, legal, or geopolitical. Delegation is not dilution of power; it is institutionalisation of continuity.

When Courts Don't Believe You

The irony of a minimalist structure is that its very simplicity can be used *against you.* When a trust appears thin, with no meetings, no trustee independence, and all decisions made unilaterally by the settlor, courts may treat it as a sham. In such cases, *simplicity erodes credibility.*

Judges are not impressed by sleek diagrams. They are persuaded by functional substance. If you are the settlor, protector, and beneficiary of a trust, and you give all instructions by WhatsApp, you should not be surprised when the court treats the trust as your personal piggy bank. A better structure—yes, more complex—would ensure professional trustees, real advisory boards, and a documented separation of powers.

Substance beats simplicity. Every time.

The Psychological Appeal—and Its Cost

Part of the problem lies in human psychology. Simplicity is cognitively appealing. It feels clean, manageable, and safe. Busy professionals dislike ambiguity. They want dashboards, not flowcharts. But wealth structuring is not a productivity tool. It is a shield. And shields must be judged by what they can stop—not by how nice they look.

The temptation to streamline is strong. But one must ask: streamlined for what? For tax filings? For personal understanding? For perceived transparency? If these goals come at the cost of legal protection, discretion, or survivability, they are *false efficiencies*. And in the face of regulatory aggression or litigation, false efficiency becomes very expensive indeed.

The Future Is Structurally Literate

As courts, tax authorities, and investigative journalists become more sophisticated, the old tricks—paper trusts, one-man boards, straw nominees—are being exposed with ease. The next generation of private wealth structuring will demand *functional legitimacy*. This means structures that hold up under forensic examination, not just formal review.

What will that require?

– Independent parties with auditable roles
– Functional purpose behind every layer
– Documentation of decisions, not just deeds
– Jurisdictional diversity tailored to geopolitical risk
– Dynamic governance that evolves with regulation

None of this is "simple." But it is robust. And robustness is what endures.

Final Reflections

The thesis of this subchapter is not that simplicity is inherently flawed—but that *simplification without strategic thought is structurally suicidal.* Private wealth frameworks are not spreadsheets to be optimised. They are legal architectures that must stand under pressure—judicial, regulatory, familial, and geopolitical.

If you are structuring for long-term protection, then complexity, when thoughtful, is not a cost. It is the cost of sovereignty. Simplicity may give you clarity on Day One. But wealth is not judged on Day One. It is judged on the day everything goes wrong. And when that day comes, only one question matters: *Did your structure survive the pressure?*

If it was too simple, it probably won't.

Chapter 7
From Reactive to Proactive – Designing Your Asset Shield

Most people don't give asset protection a second thought—until the moment they must. A lawsuit lands, a tax authority takes sudden interest, a trusted partner defects, or a geopolitical tremor shakes the ground beneath their portfolio. Only then does the search for safeguards begin, often in a panic. By that point, the damage has either been done or the window to act meaningfully has shrunk to the span of a long weekend. The real failing here isn't a lack of financial acumen—it's a failure of strategy. Unstructured wealth is exposed by default. And no amount of eleventh-hour caution can substitute for what should have been architectural foresight.

This chapter invites a shift in mindset. It moves the conversation away from crisis management and toward pre-emptive design. Instead of asking how to respond once the threat has materialised, we ask a more productive question: What would it mean to engineer your financial architecture *before* disruption arrives? How might a private individual—with tangled holdings, unpredictable exposure, and finite attention—trade reactive worry for proactive control? The answer rests on three structural foundations: a layered and intelligent risk map, a codified personal privacy ethic, and an adaptive architecture that evolves in tandem with your life.

The world, after all, is not idle. Legal frameworks shift. Precedents harden into norms. Regulators grow bold. Governments redraw the line between legal and illicit at the stroke of a pen. The asset shield that seemed airtight five years ago might now leak at the seams—not because the structure was faulty, but because the terrain changed beneath it. This is the fundamental insight: asset protection is not a one-time act. It's a living discipline.

The Price of Inaction—Paid Quietly, Often Too Late

Inaction tends not to announce itself. There's no invoice, no immediate blowback. Instead, its cost accumulates offstage—until suddenly, there's a frozen account, a compelled asset disclosure, or an order from a foreign court you never expected to engage with. Among the wealthy, these events rarely arrive with drama. They creep in under the cover of procedural updates, small disputes, or reputational hiccups that spiral.

What's most troubling isn't that such events occur. It's how many affected individuals believed, often with complete sincerity, that they were protected. Why? Because somewhere in a drawer, a trust deed exists. A holding company too. Perhaps even an offshore account. But the architecture has no unifying philosophy—no hierarchy of risk, no policy for recalibration, no guiding framework. In these cases, protection becomes static. It's not a shield. It's paperwork. And paperwork doesn't adapt. It certainly doesn't anticipate.

The Framework: Risk Isn't Monolithic—So Why Are Your Defences?

To construct meaningful protection, you must first abandon the idea that risk is generic. It isn't. A lawsuit from a disgruntled former employee is not the same creature as state surveillance in a shifting political regime. A reputational crisis triggered by a media leak has almost nothing in common with the scrutiny of a multi-jurisdictional tax audit. Each scenario calls for its own structure, its own tactics, its own legal cadence.

This chapter introduces a tiered matrix—an organising tool for thinking about vulnerability. Not as a vague threat, but as a taxonomy. Five domains anchor the matrix: legal, regulatory, reputational, geopolitical, and relational. You'll learn to assess your exposure in each, stress-test existing arrangements, and build responses suited to both asset type and adversarial vector.

Think of it this way: A technology entrepreneur who holds valuable IP is playing an entirely different game than a retired investor with real estate scattered across borders. And yet, in practice, both might employ identical trusts or companies. It's backwards. Some portfolios are overdefended in low-risk zones, and wide open where the risk is actually acute. Correction requires clarity—and clarity begins with audit.

What are the assets? Where do they sit? Who can touch them? What does a worst-case scenario look like in each threat category? Until these questions are answered, no structure—however polished—can claim to be protective. And no lawyer, however skilled, can deliver a universal solution. You must define the threat before you select the tools.

Clarity, then, does not arise from saying to your adviser, "Protect me." It comes from sitting with the uncomfortable but essential question: *What exactly am I afraid of?* Once you can name that fear, you can start to design around it—using layers, jurisdictions, and operational protocols that do more than decorate. They insulate. They endure. And most importantly, they think ahead when you no longer have the luxury of time.

Personal Risk Tolerance: From Emotion to Policy

But asset protection is not merely technical. It is deeply personal. Every structuring decision is a reflection of your *privacy philosophy*. Some individuals are comfortable with partial transparency if it means easier banking. Others want maximum opacity even if it introduces operational friction. Some will tolerate regulatory scrutiny. Others prioritise discretion above all. There is no universal answer—only a coherent strategy aligned to *your values, your anxieties, and your endgame.*

This chapter will challenge you to define your own tolerances: How visible do you want to be? How many intermediaries are you comfortable relying on? What jurisdictions do you trust not only with your money—but with your identity, your legal rights, and your safety?

The most robust structures do not begin with tax optimisation. They begin with *self-knowledge.* The purpose of wealth is not just accumulation. It is sovereignty. And sovereignty requires decisions—often uncomfortable ones—about what trade-offs you are willing to make in the name of protection. Structuring is not just legal. It is psychological.

The Living Document: Why Your Shield Must Evolve

Perhaps the greatest flaw in most asset protection plans is that they are treated as static. Once drafted, the trust deed or holding structure is filed away—unchanged for years. This is an error not of law, but of mindset. *Your wealth changes. Your risks change. Your life changes.* The legal architecture surrounding it must change too.

This chapter advocates for a dynamic approach: treating your asset protection system as a *living document*—reviewed annually, stress-tested against plausible threats, and adapted as your portfolio, geography, or political context shifts.

Consider the rise of digital asset regimes, citizenship-based taxation, or automatic exchange of financial information (CRS/FATCA). A structure built in 2010 may no longer offer the same cover in 2025. The goal is not to constantly rebuild from scratch, but to build *with future revision in mind.* Just as a well-governed company adapts its strategy over time, so too should your personal asset shield.

This requires more than legal support. It requires governance mechanisms: advisory boards, conditional triggers, multi-party consent protocols. Structures must anticipate—not merely react to—life events: divorce, inheritance, regulatory shifts, emigration. A living asset shield doesn't wait for change. It integrates change into its very logic.

Beyond Avoidance: Designing with Purpose

There is an unfortunate assumption that asset protection is about *dodging obligations*. This is a narrow and ethically dubious lens. At its most strategic, structuring is not about avoidance. It is about *designing systems that match your values, protect your dependents, and preserve optionality in an uncertain world.*

You may wish to shield assets from predatory litigation, but still provide transparency to regulators. You may want to build in flexibility for charitable giving, succession planning, or shifting geopolitical allegiances. You may want your structure to preserve anonymity without sacrificing credibility.

None of this can be accomplished with a generic trust or a single offshore vehicle. It demands *design*—with intentionality, technical fluency, and personal conviction. This chapter will walk you through how to combine legal vehicles, philosophical clarity, and structural agility into something that serves you not just legally, but *strategically.*

Why This Chapter Matters Now

We are living in a time where traditional privacy rights are eroding, information-sharing between states is expanding, and wealth itself is becoming a political flashpoint. Courts are growing more aggressive. Regulators are more emboldened. Activist groups increasingly use legal discovery, media exposure, and cross-border alliances to unearth structures once deemed private. In such an environment, the cost of being reactive is rising.

This chapter is not a how-to manual for hiding wealth. It is an invitation to *reclaim agency*—to think clearly, act deliberately, and structure wisely. You will learn how to tier your exposure, translate your values into legal form, and evolve your shield over time. It is about transforming protection from a last-minute scramble into a continuous act of strategic sovereignty.

You cannot predict the next threat. But you can choose whether you'll meet it with fragility—or with a system that was *built to withstand it.*

The Reactive Trap

Most people don't realise they've already lost control until someone else is holding the reins. That moment—whether it comes in the form of a legal summons, a regulatory inquiry, a frozen account, or a leaked document—reveals a stark truth: *protection is not something you can assemble once the threat has materialised.* And yet, that is precisely when most people start looking for it.

Asset protection, in its most potent form, is invisible. It's a pre-emptive architecture built long before the crisis emerges. But in practice, it's often triggered reactively—after a lawsuit is filed, after a marriage deteriorates, after a government introduces new capital controls, or after someone Googles your name and decides you are worth targeting. The timing is not just unfortunate—it is legally, strategically, and structurally *too late.*

This subchapter explores the systemic tendency to delay, the psychological mechanisms behind reactive thinking, and the legal limitations that render last-minute structuring not just ineffective, but often damaging. Most importantly, it makes the case that *proactive asset design is not a luxury for the ultra-wealthy.* It is a necessity for anyone operating in a world where courts can reach across borders, information travels without friction, and wealth itself is becoming a political flashpoint.

Why People Wait: The Myth of Timing

One of the most common rationales for delaying asset protection is the belief that one can always "set it up when needed." This view misunderstands both the legal nature of asset structuring and the scrutiny under which last-minute changes are viewed. Once a legal claim becomes reasonably foreseeable, any restructuring of assets is liable to be interpreted as *fraudulent conveyance*—a transfer intended to frustrate creditors or obstruct justice.

This legal principle is not obscure. It's a staple of litigation strategy. Courts in most jurisdictions have broad authority to *look through* post-threat transfers, freeze assets, unwind trusts, and impose penalties on parties deemed to have acted in bad faith. The mere act of protecting oneself too late can be construed as an admission of liability or deceit.

By the time you feel the threat, it's already too late to move assets invisibly. You've entered the reactive trap.

Psychology of Delay: Why Smart People Still Stall

The delay is not always rooted in ignorance. Many financially sophisticated individuals still fail to take action. Why? There are several converging psychological dynamics:

First is the illusion of invincibility—especially among entrepreneurs, professionals, or new-money wealth builders. They trust their own competence and assume legal threats are manageable events that can be negotiated or settled. Until one day, they aren't.

Second is discomfort with perceived paranoia. To design asset shields in advance feels, to many, like anticipating betrayal, conflict, or collapse. It contradicts the social conditioning of optimism, and appears, at best, as overengineering—or at worst, as evidence of guilt. Few people want to think of themselves as someone who "needs" a trust in Liechtenstein.

Third is inertia. Asset protection requires making decisions that are simultaneously financial, legal, ethical, and psychological. It demands the engagement of multiple professionals—lawyers, tax advisors, fiduciaries—and coordination across jurisdictions. It's much easier to say, "I'll look into this next quarter."

The result is inaction—until a trigger event strips away the option to act strategically.

The Legal Freeze: What Courts Can—and Will—Undo

Most jurisdictions allow courts to reverse transactions that appear designed to frustrate an imminent legal claim. These are known as "clawback" or "voidable" transfers. The window of clawback can range from months to several years, depending on the context and the jurisdiction.

Imagine a business owner sued for breach of contract. If she places her home or investment assets into a trust after receiving a legal notice, the court may void the transfer entirely. If she moves money offshore after an investigation is launched, the same rule applies. Even if the transfer is legally valid, the court may freeze or seize the assets pending litigation. In more aggressive jurisdictions, judges can issue *worldwide freezing orders* that bind third parties, including foreign banks and trustees.

The lesson here is blunt: *Protection delayed is protection denied.* The structure must be in place before it is relevant. Its irrelevance is precisely what makes it unassailable.

Reactive Structuring Often Makes You a Bigger Target

There's a counterintuitive but important point here. When you start protecting assets after a threat arises, you don't just risk ineffectiveness—you may increase scrutiny and suspicion.

Opposing counsel are trained to look for changes in ownership, sudden withdrawals, new trust deeds, and jurisdictional moves. Each of these sends a signal: this person *has something to hide* and *just tried to move it.* That suspicion colours everything—from the aggressiveness of legal strategy to the likelihood of settlement.

In the worst cases, late structuring invites allegations of criminal intent—money laundering, tax evasion, obstruction. Even if unfounded, these claims add pressure and cost. What could have been a strategic shield becomes a legal vulnerability.

Case Study: The Cautionary Tale of Post-Threat Action

Consider the case of a successful tech founder based in California. After a rapid exit, he received notice of a potential class action regarding data privacy issues from his former startup. Within weeks, he transferred $20 million in liquid assets into an offshore trust in the Cook Islands, believing this would place them beyond U.S. court reach.

What he failed to realise was that the timing of his trust creation—*after* notice of legal action—rendered the entire transfer suspect. The plaintiffs filed an emergency motion. The court froze his domestic accounts and placed pressure on foreign institutions. Not only did the trust offer no protection, it actively harmed his case. He was later forced to repatriate funds under threat of contempt.

A trust, had it been set up a year earlier, would have been virtually untouchable.

Proactivity as a Moral and Strategic Posture

Some assume that proactive structuring must reflect guilt or greed. This is a false binary. Protection is not about *hiding*. It's about *organising*—legally, ethically, and strategically—in a world where trust in institutions is declining, legal norms are shifting, and economic systems are growing more adversarial.

There is a dignity in preparation. A parent setting up trusts for their children, a dissident safeguarding assets from authoritarian seizure, a business owner ringfencing operations from personal liabilities—all are acting *before the crisis*, not to evade justice, but to maintain continuity, autonomy, and stewardship.

Proactive structuring is not about escaping law. It is about anticipating change.

The Architect's Advantage

When you act early, you don't just avoid danger. You gain range. You can select better jurisdictions, build more complex ownership chains, create layered governance systems, and implement controls that add legitimacy. You can work with credible institutions that demand time, diligence, and transparency—luxuries unavailable in panic mode.

Most importantly, you can design around *your values.* Want transparency to regulators but not to the public? Want family succession built in but with strict access rules? Want flexibility for relocation or capital flight contingencies? All of this becomes possible with lead time. *The architect has options. The respondent has compromises.*

The Closing Insight

There is no virtue in waiting. Risk doesn't announce itself before it arrives. It builds in the background—quietly, sometimes invisibly—until one day the structures you thought were fine are revealed as paper-thin. Wealth, power, and freedom require *not just defence, but foresight.* And foresight means acting when you least feel the need to.

This chapter is a call to exit the reactive trap. To stop believing that asset protection is something you implement after the emergency. And to begin thinking of it as something you *design precisely when there is no emergency*—so that when one comes, you are already beyond its reach.

The Protection Blueprint

Wealth without structure is not wealth—it's exposure. Ownership in today's global environment comes with visibility, and visibility carries consequence. Courts do not recognise good intentions.

Regulators do not delay enforcement to give you time to reorganise. And adversaries—be they legal, political, or personal—rarely attack when you're prepared. They exploit what you thought you'd handle later.

To navigate this landscape wisely, one must do more than accumulate assets. One must architect protection. And to do that credibly, methodically, and lawfully, you need a framework—not superstition, not myths, and certainly not a patchwork of informal advice from offshore "consultants" with no fiduciary duty to you.

This subchapter outlines *The Protection Blueprint*: a rational model for evaluating your exposure and creating a legal architecture that matches the *real structure* of your life—your income streams, asset classes, jurisdictional presence, personal vulnerabilities, and political context. It doesn't propose a one-size-fits-all solution. Instead, it presents a hierarchy of risk, a vocabulary for describing threat levels, and a series of considerations that align your asset structure with your tolerance for risk, privacy, and control.

A Foundation in Reality: Understanding What Risk Actually Is

Most people talk about risk abstractly. They imagine the "worst-case scenario" as some theoretical event without analysing its probability, jurisdictional reach, or enforceability. But *risk is not fear*. It is the *measurable possibility* that your legal or financial position could be undermined by another party with enough leverage to succeed. This can include:

Civil litigation: contractual disputes, employment lawsuits, defamation claims, shareholder disagreements.

Regulatory interference: tax audits, compliance breaches, politically motivated investigations.

Political turbulence: capital controls, asset freezes, bank nationalisations, expropriation.

Family vulnerability: divorce, inheritance claims, or incapacity challenges.

Data exposure: leaks, breaches, or voluntary disclosures through weak structures or careless intermediaries.

The key is to *map your vulnerabilities against a spectrum of threat actors*—and understand that not all risks are equal in gravity, duration, or remedy.

Tier One: Commonplace Civil Risk (Negligence, Contracts, Divorce)

At this level are the threats that arise from ordinary life and commerce. They include lawsuits from customers, vendors, former employees, business partners, or ex-spouses. These are not theoretical—they are *statistically likely* over a multi-decade professional career or long-term business operation.

For example, a successful surgeon may be sued for malpractice. A property developer may face breach-of-contract claims from contractors. A founder may be accused of breaching fiduciary duty post-acquisition. These risks do not require criminal intent, nor do they stem from unethical behaviour. *They are simply the price of being active in the world.*

The protection strategy at this level should include:

Segregated legal entities for distinct activities

Domestic asset protection trusts (in jurisdictions where these are permitted)

Clear prenups and postnups

Contractual clarity with arbitration clauses

Passive ownership through holding companies or family trusts

At Tier One, protection is primarily about limiting the damage from foreseeable, statistically probable disruptions.

Tier Two: Political and Regulatory Targeting

This level involves *not what you do*, but *who you are* or *where you are.* You may find yourself at odds with a government agency or political faction—not because of a failure in conduct, but because of your profile. This is especially relevant for journalists, political donors, nonconforming business owners, activists, and expatriates.

Regulatory targeting includes selective enforcement, backdated tax interpretations, asset disclosure mandates, and surprise audits. In some jurisdictions, especially those with weak rule of law, this extends to outright asset seizure under vague statutes like "economic sabotage."

At this level, effective protection requires:

Geographic diversification of accounts, trustees, and custodians

Offshore foundations or trusts in neutral jurisdictions with strong fiduciary regimes

Separation of control and ownership

Second residencies or alternative citizenship planning

Relationships with banks that value client discretion and are insulated from political pressure

The goal at Tier Two is to design a structure that cannot be arbitrarily undone by local state action.

Tier Three: Systemic Collapse and Jurisdictional Arbitrage

This tier is often ignored because it feels apocalyptic. But recent history offers plenty of precedent: Cyprus' banking freeze in 2013, Argentina's recurring capital controls, Venezuela's currency collapse,

Russia's flight bans and foreign asset seizures. If your wealth is geographically concentrated in a single country, you are vulnerable to structural collapse—currency debasement, nationalisation, frozen withdrawals, or even reclassification of what counts as "your" asset.

This tier is not about your personal risk. It's about *systemic fragility.*

Protection at this level requires:

Multi-jurisdictional asset placement: not just accounts, but property titles, corporate registries, and insurance vehicles.

Offshore banking in nations with a history of financial neutrality and strong privacy laws.

Holding assets in forms not easily politicised—such as physical bullion held in custody, or globally recognised real estate.

Implementing layers of legal distance between yourself and your assets without violating substance or anti-money laundering rules.

The defining feature of Tier Three is not the scale of risk, but the absolute loss of recourse if risk matures. You don't get to fight in court. The system is the attacker.

The Philosophy of Layered Protection

Rather than chasing the "perfect" structure, strategic asset protection is about designing *layers*—each one addressing a different kind of risk, each one adding friction to intrusion, each one tailored to a specific legal system's blind spots. This is not hiding. It's hardening.

A U.S.-based founder might combine a Wyoming holding company (for internal liabilities), with a Nevis trust (for external shielding), a Liechtenstein foundation (for legacy and reputational anchoring), and private accounts in Singapore (for banking resilience). Each layer is legal. Each layer serves a function. None depends on secrecy—only *positioning.*

Effective protection doesn't make your assets invisible. It makes them inaccessible without due process that rarely succeeds.

Designing Your Own Blueprint: Questions That Matter

No professional can design a credible structure without knowing *you*—your fears, your jurisdictional footprint, your operational exposure. The process begins not with forms or fees, but with questions:

What legal systems do you operate in or under?

Where is your revenue generated, and how mobile is it?

What relationships might deteriorate into litigation?

Are you publicly visible in ways that draw attention or resentment?

How diversified are your custodians—by geography, institution, and asset class?

What jurisdictions could treat your identity, speech, or nationality as a liability?

These are not paranoid questions. They are foundational. Ignoring them is not virtuous. It's negligent.

Avoiding the Illusion of Control

The blueprint also exists to guard against a different enemy: *false security*. Many people believe that having a trust, or a holding company, or a second passport means they are "safe." But a trust without jurisdictional strength is a brochure. A passport without banking privileges is a souvenir. A holding company without proper governance is a liability magnet.

True protection is not paperwork. It is function.

That function is achieved when every piece of your structure has clarity of purpose, tested resilience, and a professional ecosystem that treats your structure not as a gimmick, but as a mandate.

Final Thought: You Must Build Before You're Threatened

The Protection Blueprint works only when it's enacted early—when your profile is still quiet, when your movements are still flexible, and when your decisions cannot be misinterpreted as reactive. You are not building an escape tunnel. You are *designing a fortress.*

And like all good fortresses, its success lies not in how often it is used—but in the fact that when the world grows unstable, *you don't have to move.* You already did.Personal Risk Tolerance as Policy

Wealth, once accumulated, is not merely a matter of numbers—it becomes an expression of philosophy. And that philosophy, if left undefined, defaults to convenience or consensus, not strategy. One of the most overlooked aspects of asset protection is this: *you cannot delegate your tolerance for exposure.* Lawyers may draft structures. Bankers may offer products. Consultants may pitch jurisdictions. But without a conscious framework to express your personal threshold for visibility, scrutiny, and control, you risk constructing a legal edifice that aligns with someone else's assumptions—not your own.

This is the core premise of turning *privacy philosophy into strategic design*: you must begin not with tools, but with truth. What are you actually trying to protect, and from whom? How much interference are you willing to accept? Where is your boundary between transparency and autonomy? And how do those answers evolve across jurisdictions, life stages, and external conditions?

This article argues that personal risk tolerance—typically confined to portfolio theory—must expand to include *institutional, reputational, and sovereign risk.* The purpose is not to encourage paranoia, but to encourage precision. If you cannot articulate your privacy boundaries, you cannot enforce them—because no system can protect what its owner does not value clearly.

The Illusion of Uniform Exposure

Privacy is not binary. It is contextual. Most people assume their exposure is "moderate" without ever defining the parameters. But there is no single exposure profile. An individual's risk landscape is layered across:

Regulatory exposure: How easily can a state actor gain visibility into your holdings, transactions, or business interests?

Litigation exposure: How traceable are you through registries, account records, or known affiliations?

Reputational exposure: Can third parties use public records to craft misleading narratives?

Data exposure: How widely is your personal or financial information replicated in third-party systems?

And most crucially: *how does your level of exposure align with your personality, life goals, and worldview?*

Two individuals with identical wealth may require radically different structures if one is a public figure with geopolitical interests and the other a discreet technologist with a distrust of institutions. Their privacy philosophies should not converge simply because a lawyer handed them the same trust agreement template.

Mapping Privacy Like a Policy Statement

Just as investors write *investment policy statements* to guide decision-making under stress, asset holders must formalise a *privacy policy* for themselves. This is not a legal document. It is a philosophical anchor—a short, structured articulation of how you think about control, visibility, and resilience.

It might include ideas such as:

I am willing to disclose assets when legally required, but not voluntarily.

I prioritise control over appearances. I will tolerate complexity to retain authority.

I prefer to operate in jurisdictions where financial discretion is a cultural norm, not an exception.

I do not wish to rely on secrecy. I wish to rely on legal insulation and jurisdictional distance.

This policy is what keeps your strategy coherent across time. Without it, your privacy decisions will be reactive, often triggered by fear, headlines, or pressure from advisers more focused on compliance than on alignment.

If you don't set your own limits, others will define them for you.

Control, Ownership, and the Architecture of Visibility

Modern asset protection offers a sliding scale between *control* and *opacity*. The key is not choosing one or the other, but understanding what you're trading. For example, if your privacy philosophy values *discretion with real-time access*, you may lean toward nominee structures with robust contractual backup. If you prioritise *total firewalling from litigation*, you may accept reduced operational control in exchange for irrevocable distance.

The danger lies in *contradictory expectations*: wanting complete control and zero attribution. These structures rarely survive audit, litigation, or internal scrutiny. They are brittle, not sophisticated. True structural privacy emerges when you engineer *distance with integrity*—

meaning the structure performs as intended *because it reflects your actual preferences and tolerances*, not because it pretends to be something it isn't.

Case Study: The Tech Founder and the Philanthropist

Consider two hypothetical profiles.

The tech founder has assets across cryptocurrency, intellectual property, and venture equity. He values speed, control, and platform flexibility. He lives under a regime known for capital controls and is wary of government overreach.

The philanthropist is based in a relatively stable jurisdiction but has family ties in countries with volatile political environments. She is legacy-oriented, comfortable with trusteeship, and cares more about protection from future political regimes than from commercial litigation.

Though both are high-net-worth individuals, their privacy philosophies differ markedly. The tech founder may structure around multi-signature wallets, offshore foundations with revocable control, and anonymity-preserving banking. The philanthropist may prefer irrevocable dynastic trusts with tiered beneficiaries, custodian separation, and geographic triangulation to insulate future generations.

One size not only does not fit all—it actively undermines both.

Psychological Risk: The Invisible Variable

Much of wealth structuring fails not because it's technically incorrect, but because it ignores the psychology of the owner. A person who is constantly anxious about whether they "did it right" may be better served by slightly less protective but more understandable structures. Likewise, someone who thrives on autonomy may resent any framework that delegates control—even if it's safer on paper.

That's why privacy philosophy must include *emotional thresholds*. These include:

How much ambiguity can I tolerate?

Do I prefer simplicity I can manage or complexity I can outsource?

Would I rather comply predictably or resist selectively?

Is my anxiety rooted in perception, or in actual risk?

If your structure produces constant second-guessing, it isn't working—regardless of how legally sound it may be.

Jurisdiction as a Reflection of Philosophy

Where you bank, where you register companies, where you hold trusts—these are not just compliance decisions. They are *expressions of belief.* Choosing Singapore over Panama, or Liechtenstein over Delaware, is not only about technical privacy. It's about institutional trust, historical stability, and political neutrality. And if you are unaware of the values embedded in your jurisdictions, you may find that your privacy exists only on paper.

To that end, define what you want in a jurisdiction. Is it discretion? Enforcement neutrality? Rule of law? Banking depth? Cultural respect for wealth? These elements form your operational *value alignment*—and they must match your privacy philosophy if you want a system you can live with over time.

Advisers Are Not Architects of Identity

Professionals can only design structures around the data you give them. If that data lacks philosophical clarity—if it is merely a spreadsheet of holdings and goals—you will receive a structure that may technically "protect" you, but not reflect you. That disconnect becomes obvious under stress, when you're asked to explain the rationale of your decisions to a court, regulator, or family member.

That is why before you solicit trust diagrams, you must define your own comfort with transparency, control, and consequence. Otherwise, you are not buying protection. You are buying decoration.

Revising Your Philosophy Over Time

Privacy is not static. As your life changes—through marriage, children, relocation, or public exposure—your tolerances must evolve. A privacy philosophy written in your 30s may no longer reflect your risks in your 50s. Yet many people treat wealth structures like monuments: permanent, frozen, absolute.

Instead, treat your philosophy like a compass. Review it annually. Test it under hypothetical crises. Ask yourself, "If my name were in the news tomorrow, what would I wish I had changed?" Your structure should not just survive audit. *It should survive hindsight.*

Conclusion Without Saying "Conclusion"

Personal risk tolerance is not just a matter of temperament. It is a critical design input that, if ignored, leads to structural weakness, misalignment, or overexposure. The goal is not paranoia, but intentionality.

A structure that reflects your actual worldview—your real comfort with control, visibility, and decentralisation—will be easier to manage, easier to defend, and far more likely to endure.

Clarity is the highest form of privacy. Begin there.

The Living Document Approach

Every structure—legal, financial, institutional—is at risk of becoming obsolete the moment it is finalised. The paperwork may be flawless, the jurisdictional layers immaculate, the trusts appropriately layered with trustees, protectors, and letters of wishes. Yet even the most artfully engineered structure decays in usefulness if treated as a finished product. Wealth preservation is not about building fortresses. It is about cultivating *ecosystems*—adaptive, self-monitoring, and responsive to change. That is the heart of the *Living Document Approach.*

This subchapter presents a philosophy that resists the illusion of permanence. It insists that no matter how expertly designed, a wealth structure must evolve alongside the personal, legal, geopolitical, and technological realities it is meant to navigate. Not because the law demands it, but because *relevance demands it.* If your structures are not moving, they are dying.

Wealth is a dynamic expression of intention, risk, and power. To treat its architecture as static is to quietly invite vulnerability.

Legacy Planning vs. Structural Stagnation

Most private wealth structures are constructed in phases: legal incorporation, asset injection, trustee appointments, and distribution pathways. This front-loaded design process gives the false impression of completion. Families, founders, and fiduciaries often treat the signed documents like sacred scripture—fixed, untouchable, and permanent unless legally challenged.

But this rigidity is precisely what undermines effectiveness. Structures formed during periods of optimism may not account for economic downturns. Trusts drafted in politically neutral climates may become dangerously exposed under regime shifts. A governance framework that once protected against family disputes may later *cause* them when generational interests diverge.

The Living Document Approach rejects the notion that legacy means immobility. It posits instead that legacy is only as secure as its capacity to adapt.

Designing for Change, Not Perfection

A common failure in asset protection design is the pursuit of a "perfect" plan. Perfection implies finality. It encourages overengineering—multiple jurisdictions, layered entities, rigid clauses—under the assumption that more complexity equals more safety. But in times of crisis, complexity without agility becomes paralysis. The best-designed structure is not the one that tries to account for every hypothetical. *It is the one that allows for controlled evolution as the facts change.*

This is not an abstract principle. It manifests in questions such as:

How easily can we change trustees, protectors, or directors without losing strategic advantage?

Does the structure allow for migration to a safer jurisdiction if geopolitical conditions deteriorate?

Are the beneficiaries' needs and vulnerabilities being reassessed as they age, marry, divorce, or take on new roles?

Can liquidity be rebalanced if a major asset class underperforms for a decade?

The Living Document Approach means designing mechanisms of amendment, not just mechanisms of defence. *It means asking: who gets to rewrite this playbook when the rules change?*

Feedback Loops: Treating Wealth Like a System

Biological systems thrive because they contain *feedback loops*—real-time responses to internal and external stimuli. Most wealth structures, by contrast, are static blueprints: if-then-else diagrams that rely on outdated inputs. A trust deed written twenty years ago may still name a deceased family lawyer as protector. A holding company might still route through a jurisdiction blacklisted by a major trading partner. An investment control agreement may not contemplate cryptocurrency or decentralised assets.

These aren't flaws of intention. They're failures of *iteration.* The Living Document Approach insists that wealth design incorporate regular review cycles, *not just legal compliance audits, but strategic recalibration.* These reviews should involve:

Shifting legal precedents (e.g., increasing pressure on common law trusts to disclose)

Tax treaty reconfigurations (especially under OECD or FATCA frameworks)

Technological disruptions (e.g., tokenisation of assets, smart contract enforceability)

Macro-political movements (e.g., anti-offshore sentiment, asset seizure in unstable states)

This is not maintenance. It is strategic governance.

Case Example: The Family Office that Rewrote Itself

Consider a multi-generational family office based in Switzerland with initial holdings structured in Jersey, the British Virgin Islands, and the United States. The founder's vision had been relatively conservative: protect the core assets, avoid publicity, and manage a tax-neutral inheritance pathway.

Over twenty-five years, the external world transformed. FATCA and CRS rewired reporting obligations. The U.S. began aggressively extraterritorial asset scrutiny. Crypto exposure introduced valuation volatility. A major European bank collapsed, prompting a review of counterparty risk.

Instead of treating the original trust and holding company structures as immutable, the family used these disruptions to *retool rather than react.* They:

Replaced their static letter of wishes with a codified, regularly reviewed family constitution

Introduced conditional migration clauses for trusts and holding companies

Created a "jurisdictional risk index" updated quarterly to assess political drift

Reframed succession triggers to allow dynamic role reassignment based on merit, not bloodline

The structure became not an edifice, but an operating system.

Why Lawyers and Bankers Resist the Living Model

One obstacle to the Living Document Approach is institutional culture. Law firms are incentivised to produce final documents. Banks prefer clarity and compliance. The administrative friction of updating structures is seen as risk, not responsiveness. As a result, clients are often discouraged—subtly or explicitly—from making changes unless crisis forces them.

But from a design standpoint, this inertia is indefensible. Imagine an aircraft designed without ongoing performance checks, or a tech company that never updates its codebase. Wealth, particularly across jurisdictions, requires the same operational discipline. *The idea that legal documents "age well" is one of the great fictions of the asset protection industry.*

The Problem of Inherited Blindness

Many structures are passed down without review. Heirs assume that what protected their parents will protect them. But generational changes introduce entirely new vectors of risk. A child who becomes a public figure or political donor may invite visibility that invalidates the opacity of an earlier structure. A marriage, business failure, or relocation may invalidate the assumptions baked into old governance logic.

This is not paranoia. It's design logic. A document is only as good as its correspondence to current reality. *When assumptions outlive their authors, the structure becomes a liability.*

Living Doesn't Mean Chaotic

Critics of dynamic structuring sometimes fear that frequent changes will undermine predictability or asset clarity. But the Living Document Approach doesn't advocate for impulsivity. It advocates for *intentional review protocols*—scheduled, disciplined assessments of alignment between structure and reality.

This could mean:

Annual "philosophical audits" of whether current frameworks reflect evolving priorities

Strategic offsites with fiduciaries, key advisers, and next-generation stewards

Scenario modelling: "If the founder died tomorrow, would this structure deliver its intended outcome?"

Technical reviews of control mechanisms: "Are control roles still legally and reputationally safe?"

Living doesn't mean chaotic. It means *conscious.*

When Static Becomes Dangerous

A static structure doesn't simply fail to protect. It can actively amplify exposure. Courts often look for indicators of genuine governance. If a trust hasn't been updated in a decade, has never executed a protector action, or uses boilerplate distributions, it invites scrutiny. It implies simulation—something built to *appear* protective, but not to *function* strategically.

Similarly, tax authorities can question the economic substance of entities that never update directorships, contracts, or jurisdictional logic. Regulatory pressure is shifting from "is this legal" to "does this make sense." *If your structure no longer makes sense, it will eventually be dismantled—first reputationally, then legally.*

A Structure Is Not a Philosophy

Perhaps the most dangerous assumption in wealth planning is that once a structure exists, philosophy is no longer required. But a structure is merely a container. It reflects the thinking of its moment. If your philosophy evolves—and it should—then your structure must evolve with it. Otherwise, it becomes a shrine to an outdated risk profile.

The Living Document Approach ensures that your wealth system remains alive not just legally, but intellectually. It evolves because *you do.*

Final Insight Without Finality

Treat your documents as if they matter—not because they're perfect, but because they must keep *becoming* right. Wealth structuring is not the art of prediction. It is the discipline of responsiveness. The most resilient families, funds, and individuals are not the ones with the most expensive legal teams. *They are the ones who keep thinking.*

Chapter 8
Wealth and Identity – Who Are You Without Your Assets?

There are few questions more quietly unsettling—and yet more essential—for those entrusted with significant wealth than this: Who would you be if no one knew you had money? It's not a riddle. It's a reckoning. In the private wealth domain, identity is frequently woven so tightly with ownership, exposure, and control that to separate the self from the structure feels not only difficult, but disorienting. The net worth figure—ostensibly just a number—gradually morphs into a mirror. Not simply reflecting financial strength, but echoing assumptions about competence, status, and even worthiness. Titles stack. Shells multiply. But the individual—the human being at the centre—often fades behind the scaffolding erected to project or preserve them.

This chapter ventures into a seldom-discussed dimension of private capital: the interior life of the wealthy. Specifically, the often-ambiguous relationship between capital and selfhood. It is a terrain where strategic intent frequently collides with psychological inheritance. What may begin as a practical effort to secure privacy, manage exposure, or safeguard family wealth can slowly mutate into something more existential: a longing for affirmation, a hunger for legacy, or a need—quiet or glaring—to be seen. Strip back the layers on many of the most perplexing financial choices—ill-timed disclosures, risky investments, or legal missteps—and what often emerges isn't miscalculation. It's identity confusion.

Here's the hard truth: money can shield you from the world. But it does little to shield you from your own compulsions.

In the pages that follow, we will navigate three core themes: the unresolved emotional histories that quietly drive financial overexposure; the practice of privacy, not merely as a legal tactic but as a form of internal discipline; and finally, the strange, liberating potential of radical anonymity.

The Haunting of Unmet Narratives

It's easy to imagine that high-risk financial behaviour stems from flawed models, bad advice, or market turbulence. But in reality, much of it originates in story—early, emotional, often unexamined. Childhood deprivation. A parent's silent disapproval. The social sting of being perceived as "less than." These experiences, left unprocessed, don't simply fade. They calcify into behavioural patterns—manifesting not in the therapist's chair, but in the boardroom or the brokerage account.

The impulse to be seen, validated, or admired can disguise itself as strategy. For some, the moment they acquire real wealth becomes the beginning of a performative cycle. Assets aren't merely preserved—they are displayed. A trust becomes not just a shield, but a stage. Privacy feels suffocating. The wealth must *show up* somewhere—if not in lifestyle, then in influence, public recognition, or aesthetic excess.

These are not eccentricities. They are governance vulnerabilities.

Consider the entrepreneur who, despite holding assets through a carefully layered structure, cannot resist stepping into the public arena—podcasts, interviews, award circuits—inviting attention that contradicts every protective mechanism designed around him. Or the inheritor who "accidentally" drops numbers into a press conversation under the guise of authenticity. Or the founder who insists on micromanaging investment strategy despite lacking fluency in the subject—because to delegate feels like diminishing the self.

These are not random choices. They're efforts—often unconscious—to overwrite shame, insignificance, or early invisibility with adult agency and command. And while psychologically understandable, they are structurally dangerous.

Visibility invites inquiry. Inquiry erodes opacity. And in the world of sophisticated asset protection, opacity is not deception—it is defence.

Privacy as Discipline, Not Disguise

There is a common misconception, particularly outside private wealth circles, that privacy is simply the absence of noise. As though silence is its default state. But real privacy—the kind that preserves legacy, limits liability, and protects dignity—is work. It requires not only legal finesse and structural alignment, but emotional discipline.

Because the truth is this: until you can be comfortable not being seen, no structure can truly hold.

That is not a technical statement. It's a personal one. You may have the most elegantly drafted trust, the most obscure custodial layers, the most watertight cross-jurisdictional plan. But if your identity is still yoked to visibility—if the desire to be known, admired, or envied continues to dictate behaviour—then every structure you build becomes a fragile facade. It only takes one moment of self-revelation, one unguarded boast, one misstep in judgement, to unwind years of planning.

Privacy, then, is not a tactic. It's a temperament.

Radical Anonymity: A Thought Experiment

What if your name disappeared from every ledger? What if no transaction bore your fingerprint, no asset reflected your style, no holding could be traced back to your ambition? Would the self beneath still feel intact?

This is not an invitation to erase oneself—but to examine the degree to which visibility has become your measure of existence. In a world increasingly obsessed with being known, liked, validated, and visible, anonymity can feel like erasure. But it can also be relief. A return to something quieter, less performative. Perhaps even more free.

The most structurally resilient strategies—those that endure litigation, regime change, and generational transition—are almost always built by individuals who are comfortable with one thing: not being seen. Not hiding, but no longer needing to appear.

Because here's what rarely gets said in wealth circles: if the structures you design are stronger than the self you bring to them, the collapse will come not from outside, but within.

And so, the question is not whether you should protect your assets.

It is whether you are willing to protect your identity from being overrun by them.

Privacy as a Spiritual Discipline

In the context of wealth, discretion is often misunderstood as fear—paranoia in the face of regulation, litigation, or seizure. But for those who truly master the art of financial invisibility, privacy is not cowardice. It is discipline. It is *restraint in a culture of performance.*

We do not talk often enough about discretion as a kind of character. It requires the maturity to resist proving, the clarity to prioritise, and the strength to relinquish applause. In spiritual traditions—especially those with monastic or contemplative roots—withdrawal from visibility is seen not as evasion, but as cultivation. The less noise one creates, the more control one develops over attention, intention, and will.

Wealth has always been a loud force in society. But the wise practitioner of quiet banking and silent structuring is not simply avoiding headlines. They are cultivating a posture—one that acknowledges that identity does not need to be broadcast to be real. *Privacy, when embraced as discipline, transforms wealth from spectacle into sovereignty.*

To adopt this posture means resisting the gravitational pull of performative affluence. It means declining media invitations, turning down unnecessary board seats, anonymising charitable giving. Not as acts of withdrawal, but as acts of power. *Discretion becomes a strategy of long-term freedom—not just legally, but psychologically.*

Your Invisible Self

The most radical form of asset protection begins with the simplest of internal exercises: *Who would you be if no one could see your wealth?* If your accounts were invisible. If your properties bore no name. If your lifestyle gave away nothing. If applause ceased. Who remains?

This is not an exercise in asceticism. It is a practical test of strategic clarity. When wealth is used to construct identity, decision-making becomes distorted. Risk tolerances shift. Governance becomes personal. Oversight is resented. Control is hoarded. But when wealth is de-personalised—when it is decoupled from the ego—it becomes easier to design resilient systems, delegate power, and survive transitions.

To explore this more deeply, this chapter introduces tools and frameworks designed to help readers construct what we call their *invisible self.* These include:

Narrative reflection: tracing your financial origin story and locating emotional triggers

Exposure mapping: identifying where wealth is visible and why

Self-separation exercises: distinguishing identity from ownership, lifestyle from worth

Visibility audits: understanding what your structure *signals* to others—and whether that serves you

For many, these will be uncomfortable exercises. They will challenge habits of identity reinforcement that have been rationalised as strategic necessity. But beneath that discomfort lies clarity. And beneath that clarity lies power—the kind that doesn't depend on assets to be recognised.

The Identity Risk in Asset Structuring

It is no accident that the most complex structures often serve the most fragile identities. What begins as good-faith planning becomes an overengineered attempt to *stay visible while pretending to be invisible.* The family office that employs twenty people to monitor five is often managing insecurity, not capital. The patriarch who cannot cede trustee authority isn't managing risk—he's preserving a persona.

This is not a moral critique. It is a design vulnerability. Structures must eventually function independent of personality, charisma, or central authority. If your system cannot survive your absence, it is not an asset structure—it is an ego structure.

The most durable asset protections are rooted not just in law or finance, but in *emotional maturity*. The ability to release visibility, to separate self from spectacle, and to design from a place of psychological distance—these are the true competencies of a strategic wealth holder.

This Chapter's Promise

You've learned how to structure trusts. You've examined banking jurisdictions, layered nominees, and designed privacy-forward frameworks. But until now, much of the work has been external. This chapter turns inward. It is not asking for vulnerability in public. It is asking for clarity in private.

You will understand the hidden emotional motives that shape risk exposure

You will learn to see privacy not as a shield, but as a stance

You will discover frameworks to decouple identity from visibility, and design accordingly

What you do with this clarity is your choice. But know this: *the person who can disappear without loss of self is the person who is hardest to defeat—by courts, markets, or time.*

That is the real value of privacy. Not protection from the world, but sovereignty within it.

The Emotional Geography of Wealth

There is a paradox at the heart of private wealth: the more assets one accumulates, the more vulnerable one becomes—not to theft or taxation, but to identity distortion. While wealth may begin as a strategic pursuit, over time it begins to contour the self. People don't just own things. *Things begin to own them.*

The emotional geography of wealth is not plotted on spreadsheets or estate plans. It is charted through attachment, ego, fear, memory, and desire. Every asset has a story; every structure has a shadow. And until these unseen attachments are understood, even the most sophisticated asset protection strategies will carry invisible liabilities—anchored not in law, but in psychology.

True control begins where identification ends. This subchapter explores how our identities become entangled with what we own, why that is both dangerous and deeply human, and how strategic detachment creates a more resilient form of ownership—legally, emotionally, and philosophically.

The Illusion of Possession

Modern wealth management is structurally obsessed with control—control over tax exposure, regulatory risk, asset custody, information flow. But few speak candidly about the internal craving that underwrites these efforts: *the illusion of permanence.*

To possess is to believe that what is around us is *of* us. But control is never absolute. Even the most watertight trust can be pierced by legal innovation. Even the most anonymous entity can become exposed through data convergence or social error. And yet, many people cling to their structures as if they were unassailable, not because they believe it legally, but because they need to believe it emotionally.

This is not strategic. It is mythological. *The moment ownership becomes identity, rational governance erodes.* Individuals overcustomise legal vehicles not to serve the asset, but to mirror the self. Companies become proxies for personality. Foundations evolve into memorials. Homes become castles of ego. At scale, this leads to dangerous fragility: one reputational breach or asset loss can feel like a personal collapse.

It is only through structured detachment—deliberate psychological and operational distance from the things we manage—that true resilience becomes possible.

How Attachment Compromises Governance

Private clients often ask how to "bulletproof" their structures. What they rarely ask is whether their own identity is the biggest security flaw. An emotionally entangled principal will often reject advice that undermines their self-image, even if that advice is technically correct.

Consider a patriarch who insists on being settlor, protector, and investment committee chair for a family trust—despite international relocation plans and growing intergenerational complexity. The consolidation of roles is not about efficiency. It is about *relevance.* Letting go of control would feel like letting go of self. But a court will see that consolidation not as strength, but as vulnerability. A hostile party will not hesitate to argue de facto ownership through retained influence.

The same emotional logic explains why many founders resist asset fragmentation, even when fragmentation would reduce visibility and litigation risk. Identity seeks coherence, not obscurity. And yet, in the world of privacy and protection, *strategic incoherence*—through distance, layering, delegation—is often what shields wealth from collapse.

You cannot delegate identity. But you must delegate control. And to do that well, you must first let go of your need to be seen in ownership.

The Geography of Meaning

Assets are never just financial. They are charged with meaning. The estate inherited from a parent. The shares in a company you built. The vintage watch from the year you made your first million. The offshore trust you designed after your first lawsuit. These aren't just entries on a ledger. They are repositories of memory, emotion, and narrative.

And while such meaning can be beautiful, it also creates rigidity. We become reluctant to restructure what has become symbolic. We delay reallocation because to do so would feel like disowning the past. Wealth becomes topographical: filled with sacred zones, emotional landmarks, and forbidden terrain. But this internal map is often invisible to the lawyers and advisers asked to protect it.

The work, then, is twofold. First: *to map the meaning attached to our holdings*. Second: *to determine which meanings are strategic, and which are sentimental.* Only then can we edit the terrain with clarity.

Control as a Psychological Defence

Control is often mistaken for strategy. But for many, it is a coping mechanism. The fear of irrelevance, betrayal, or mortality is redirected into ever-more elaborate systems of ownership. We don't just manage assets—we *fortify ourselves against loss*. But no structure can fix what the psyche has not resolved.

Philosophers from the Stoics to the Buddhists have warned against the perils of attachment, not because it is immoral, but because it is fragile. *Whatever is owned out of fear will eventually become a source of fear.* The more one clings, the more one is exposed.

The most secure individuals in private finance are not those who control the most entities, but those who need to control the least. Not because they are passive, but because they are clear: about what they own, why they own it, and whether their self-worth would change if they didn't.

Strategic Detachment and the Future of Asset Design

Detachment is not abdication. It is *designing ownership without ego*. A well-structured estate plan, for example, should function without the founder's personality. An offshore structure should withstand shifts in reputation. A holding company should operate in silence—not because it hides wrongdoing, but because it is irrelevant to the personal brand of its beneficiary.

Strategic detachment requires different questions:

What would this look like if no one knew I owned it?

If I could never talk about this asset, would I still want it?

If someone else controlled it but I benefited quietly, would I still feel powerful?

These are not philosophical indulgences. They are design heuristics. Because if you cannot answer yes to those questions, then your structure is not resilient—it is performative.

Visibility is not a sign of wealth. It is often a symptom of insecurity.

The Emotional Cost of Complexity

Not all entanglement is visible. Complexity itself can become a mirror for unresolved identity. Family offices that expand into sprawling, opaque entities often do so to justify a sense of internal importance. But complexity creates its own burdens: cognitive load, legal exposure, bureaucratic drag. And if it exists to serve ego rather than strategy, it will eventually collapse under its own weight.

Clarity is not just a legal ideal. It is an emotional one. Simpler structures—if psychologically tolerable—are often stronger. But simplification requires confidence. The confidence to need less, to be seen less, to operate without recognition.

What appears strong on paper often reflects fear. What appears quiet in public often reflects power.

Exercises in Self-Separation

This article closes with a set of reflections that can serve as design filters—not only for structuring decisions but for the emotional posture behind them.

Identify which assets feel most like extensions of your identity. Ask yourself why.

Write a paragraph imagining life with no visible ownership. What would feel missing? What would feel lighter?

Audit the governance of your key holdings. Where is your name, voice, or influence concentrated? What would happen if it disappeared?

Explore whether your wealth structures reflect legacy or self-preservation. Are you building for others, or for applause?

These are not theoretical questions. They are foundational. Because the durability of a structure depends not only on legal architecture but on the psychology of the person who built it.

Final Thought

The emotional geography of wealth is invisible on a balance sheet, but deeply felt in behaviour, decision-making, and resilience. Until we understand how our identities cling to ownership, we cannot claim to be truly protected. The only real security is this: *to design as if your selfhood is already intact, regardless of what the world sees—or doesn't.*

Money Trauma and the Need to Be Seen

Wealth is not neutral. It is emotional memory made material. Every financial decision—especially those made at scale—is a psychological statement, not merely a strategic one. Behind high-risk investments, unnecessary public visibility, and compulsive acquisition, there is often not greed or ambition, but *unresolved pain.* Money trauma, though seldom acknowledged in elite circles, is a defining undercurrent in wealth behaviour. And when left unexplored, it distorts judgment, invites exposure, and sabotages even the most sophisticated financial structures.

To manage wealth effectively, one must understand the silent contracts made with the past—contracts drafted not in law, but in emotion.

This article explores how early emotional experiences with money shape adult behaviour around wealth—particularly the compulsion to be seen. It draws on psychological research, clinical observations, and real-world cases to map how trauma manifests in financial risk-taking, asset visibility, and ego-based structuring. It argues for deeper financial introspection as a pillar of intelligent privacy strategy.

Visibility as a Compensation Mechanism

The public performance of wealth—the curated lifestyle, the newsworthy donation, the headline acquisition—is often misread as confidence. In reality, *it is frequently a form of compensation.* For many, the need to be seen is not about power; it is about *proof*—proof that one has escaped scarcity, transcended a past, or earned a place in rooms that once felt unreachable.

This pattern is particularly prevalent among first-generation wealth creators. The climb is often steep, the sacrifices immense, and the internalised doubts numerous. When wealth finally arrives, it is not merely capital—it is validation. And with validation comes performance: high visibility becomes a way to say, "I exist. I matter. I overcame."

But this hunger for recognition is dangerous. It invites scrutiny, legal vulnerability, and structural fragility. And worse—it places one's internal peace at the mercy of external attention. *The louder the signal, the more fragile the signaler.*

Trauma Is Not Always Tragedy

The word "trauma" often evokes extreme scenarios—abuse, war, catastrophe. But money trauma is more insidious. It is *emotional patterning* around safety, worth, and identity, rooted in formative experiences. A parent who hoarded money and used it to control. A family that never had enough. A household where financial success was equated with love. Or shame. Or survival.

Such memories are rarely processed consciously. They become encoded as financial instincts: don't trust banks, always own property, never rely on others, keep everything in your name, prove your value constantly. These rules feel rational. They are not. They are responses to fear—shaped by history, maintained by ego, and enforced by subconscious loyalty to the past.

The tragedy is not the trauma itself. It is the fact that no one in private banking is trained to recognise it. Structures are designed around what clients say they want—not around *why* they want it. That omission is not harmless. It is a liability.

The Architecture of Overexposure

In practice, unexamined money trauma often manifests in structurally visible choices. The billionaire who insists on personal branding through company shares, despite the tax and security risks. The entrepreneur who cannot let go of founder control, making succession impossible. The family office that expands into a media-facing legacy project, purely to rival a peer. These are not strategic errors. They are *psychological projections*—acted out through legal forms.

Consider the compulsive buyer of luxury assets—supercars, watches, penthouses. These are not investments. They are mirrors. And when the individual lacks self-understanding, the mirrors become addictive. But each mirror introduces visibility. And visibility invites interest. And interest begets inquiry. Suddenly, a private individual is subject to headlines, litigation, or government scrutiny—not because of wealth itself, but because of *how* it was signalled.

Privacy cannot exist where performance is required. Until the need to be seen is interrogated, the desire for discretion will remain performative.

Emotional Self-Sabotage in Structuring

Trauma also shapes resistance to best-practice structures. Clients may *say* they want protection, but sabotage implementation:

Refusing to use nominee directors due to control anxiety

Insisting on account signatory status for emotional security

Rejecting anonymous jurisdictions due to perceived loss of visibility

Keeping assets in their own name to "feel close" to them

These are not logical decisions. They are fear-based ones. And advisers, trained in technical reasoning, often lack the language or permission to confront the emotional basis of such choices. But ignoring it is costly. It results in fragile, legally exposed, psychologically brittle systems that fail at the exact moment they are needed most.

To protect a client's assets, one must also protect them from their unresolved selves.

The Psychology of Recklessness

Some money trauma doesn't produce overexposure. It produces self-destruction. Risk-taking becomes compulsive. The client enters ventures that make no sense. Bets aggressively. Ignores counsel. Pushes boundaries until something breaks. And when it does, there is often quiet relief—because collapse confirms a deeply held internal narrative: *I don't deserve this.* Or: *it never lasts.*

This is not mere impulsivity. It is *identity congruence.* Individuals unconsciously recreate the emotional state that shaped them. If instability was normal, stability will feel wrong. If loss was formative, loss will be chased.

The irony is that wealth managers often interpret this behaviour as "appetite for risk." But it is not appetite. It is addiction—to volatility, to drama, to the emotional spike of crisis. And like all addictions, it escalates until the system breaks.

Reputation as Emotional Proxy

The need to be seen isn't always about money. It is often about *worth.* And in today's world, worth is measured in visibility—followers, features, recognition. Clients with unresolved money trauma often pursue reputation as a form of repair. But reputation is a dangerous currency. It fluctuates. It distorts. And it invites attack.

When reputation becomes the proxy for healing, structures become tools of theatre. Wealth is wielded not to secure freedom, but to reinforce identity. And the more reinforced the identity, the more fragile it becomes. The public self must be constantly curated. The private self is ignored. And the result is a hyper-visible, deeply insecure, legally exposed individual—surrounded by advisers who manage structures, but not the self who drives them.

A Strategic Case for Emotional Introspection

None of this is theory. It is governance. The most resilient wealth strategies are built not just on legal soundness, but *emotional coherence.* A client who knows their triggers, patterns, and insecurities will build better. They will accept distance. Delegate roles. Trust process. Decline exposure. Say no to applause.

Strategic introspection is not therapy. It is structural foresight. It anticipates behaviour, preempts sabotage, and aligns governance with maturity. Some family offices now employ behavioural wealth specialists to audit not just risk exposure, but *emotional exposure.* That trend will grow. Because the next frontier in wealth protection is not law. It is *identity design.*

Pathways to Emotional Neutrality

What does emotionally neutral structuring look like? It begins with truth:

What am I trying to prove through this structure?

Who am I trying to impress by owning this publicly?

If no one could see this, would I still want it?

What am I afraid will happen if I let go of control?

What unresolved memory am I protecting against?

These questions are not ancillary. They are central. Because until they are answered, every structure built will carry *emotional metadata*—data that adversaries, courts, or crises can exploit.

Final Insight

Money trauma is not an affliction to be pitied. It is a psychological residue—understandable, inevitable, and universal. But if left unacknowledged, it becomes a structural liability. The need to be seen, when unconsciously driven, is the most dangerous force in private wealth. Because it builds from within what adversaries couldn't break from without.

Only when the self no longer needs to be validated through assets can the assets themselves be truly protected.

Privacy as a Spiritual Discipline

To most, privacy is a strategy. To the wise, it is a *practice*. It is not merely a defensive measure against surveillance or asset tracing; it is a conscious philosophy—one that shapes identity, behaviour, and the very architecture of wealth. True privacy is not born from paranoia. It is born from restraint. And restraint, in a world that rewards performance, is not weakness. It is *strength of the highest order.*

Privacy, at its most refined, is not about concealment. It is about refusal—refusal to participate in the cultural assumption that worth must be validated by visibility. It is the quiet conviction that what is most valuable does not need to be seen to be secure, and what is most secure must often never be seen at all.

This article frames discretion not as legal tactics or risk management, but as a *discipline of being*—a spiritual approach to ownership, reputation, and personal identity. It draws from philosophy, behavioural science, and elite wealth practices to argue that privacy, properly understood, is not about hiding. It is about mastering one's signal in a world saturated with noise.

The Marketplace of Ego

Modern finance has become entangled with modern identity. Platforms that once connected people now function as status hierarchies. The self has become a brand; every action a broadcast. Wealth, in this context, is not used solely for security or independence—it is used for validation. Homes are chosen for how they photograph. Portfolios are curated for public narrative. Contributions are made for plaque recognition, not private impact.

This is not a by-product of modern culture. It *is* the culture. And it incentivises a fundamentally unstable posture: to equate presence with power, exposure with credibility, and access with control. It creates a psychological dependence on external signals—and in doing so, it erodes discretion at its core.

Those who choose privacy in such an environment are not withdrawing out of fear. They are *opting out of the ego economy*—a system that conflates visibility with value and performance with proof.

The Ascetic Logic of Strategic Silence

In spiritual traditions across time, withdrawal has been revered—not as escapism, but as refinement. Monastic silence, desert solitude, and the veil of anonymity were not signs of retreat. They were tools of purification. They allowed the self to re-centre away from audience, applause, and acclaim.

In high-level wealth structuring, the same principle holds. The most resilient configurations are those that require the least external validation. Entities are silent. Beneficiaries are protected. Structures are layered. Decisions are de-personalised. This isn't just for legal insulation. It's for *ego insulation.* The less one's identity is fused to their financial footprint, the harder it is to manipulate, provoke, or extract.

Privacy here functions not as secrecy, but as sovereignty.

The Detachment Principle

Philosopher Epictetus once observed that we suffer not from events, but from our attachments to them. The same holds in private wealth. Clients who are emotionally attached to control, recognition, or ownership titles are far more vulnerable than those who are not. A name on a document may offer pride, but it also creates liability. A face on a foundation may inspire prestige, but it also invites scrutiny.

True detachment is not apathy. It is intentional distance. It is the conscious decoupling of identity from assets, of public image from private control, of social signalling from internal worth. Those who practise this consistently exhibit three traits:

1. *They are calm in crisis*, because they do not derive security from external positioning.

2. *They are structurally protected*, because their planning reflects psychological maturity.

3. *They are hard to provoke*, because their sense of self is not tied to perception.

Privacy, in this context, is not concealment. It is *clarity*.

Case Study: The Silent Architect

Consider the example of a high-net-worth client whose wealth was built through software infrastructure. Despite a nine-figure valuation, he refused media coverage, declined all panel appearances, and used nominee directors across every jurisdiction. His legal presence was practically non-existent, but his influence was absolute.

When asked why he operated this way, he replied, "Visibility is vulnerability. I didn't build wealth to be seen. I built it to be free." His strategy was not born from fear of litigation. It was rooted in *self-awareness*. He knew his instincts. He knew his temptations. And he structured his world to protect him from both.

This is privacy as discipline: not reactive, but proactive. Not about avoiding threats, but about *avoiding self-sabotage*.

Discretion in Practice: A Philosophy of Restraint

Spiritual disciplines have always relied on limits to create strength—fasting, silence, seclusion. These are not acts of deprivation. They are acts of focus. They remove distraction so one can attend to what matters most. Privacy, applied correctly, performs the same function. It limits noise. It reduces exposure. It protects what is sacred by making it *unavailable to public consumption.*

This has structural consequences:

A discreet trust is stronger than a well-branded family office.

A private donation yields more control than a headline gift.

A silent partnership preserves more power than a visible stake.

Each decision to *not* signal is a form of capital protection—not just of money, but of meaning.

The Fragility of the Public Self

The opposite of privacy is not publicity. It is dependency. Dependency on reputation. On affirmation. On narrative control. Once wealth becomes an identity performance, the self becomes fragmented. You are no longer protecting what you own. You are protecting how you appear to own it. Every comment, article, or rumour becomes a threat—not to your assets, but to your *image of yourself.*

In this way, overexposure is not just a risk vector. It is a soul cost. It detaches people from themselves. And when that happens, wealth becomes hollow—protected legally but vulnerable existentially.

This is why privacy must be taught as a discipline, not a tactic. It must be cultivated—not imposed. It requires internal clarity, not just external secrecy.

Ethical Dimensions of Discretion

To practise privacy is to acknowledge ethical responsibility. Discretion is not deception. It is stewardship. It is the refusal to pollute a shared world with unnecessary signals, data, and provocations. It is the quiet confidence that not everything valuable must be visible. And not everything visible is valuable.

In an age where surveillance is ambient and oversharing is default, choosing silence is a radical act. It is, in a very real sense, *ethical rebellion*—a resistance to commodification of the self.

Exercises in Privacy as Practice

To internalise this philosophy, consider reflective prompts:

If no one knew what I owned, what would I still value?

What part of me needs others to know I'm successful?

What am I proving when I display my assets?

What would strategic invisibility feel like—relieving or frightening?

If my reputation vanished, would my identity remain intact?

These are not abstract questions. They are the foundations of mature wealth management. Because a system is only as strong as the psychology behind it. And if that psychology is dependent on being seen, no amount of structuring will provide true protection.

Final Insight

Privacy is not retreat. It is revelation. It reveals who you are when you no longer need to signal. It clarifies what matters when you are no longer performing. And in that clarity, real control emerges—not over markets or courts, but over the self.

In this light, discretion is not weakness. It is willpower. It is the discipline to say no to applause, attention, and external proof. It is the cultivation of quiet mastery in a world that demands constant display.

True privacy is not hidden. It is centred.

Your Invisible Self

What remains of you when all the external indicators of success are stripped away? No titles, no balance sheets, no curated lifestyle. Not even a last name that opens doors. Just you—unseen, unmeasured, and unrecognised. If that premise feels uncomfortable, even vaguely threatening, you are not alone. In today's economic culture, wealth is more than what we possess—it is often mistaken for *who we are.* And this confusion, while socially reinforced, is strategically dangerous. Especially for those serious about long-term asset protection.

This subchapter offers more than philosophical musing. It is an operational exploration into the idea that *emotional clarity is a financial tool.* It guides readers through a radical, structured reflection: to examine their identity apart from visibility, and in doing so, cultivate the mental resilience needed for genuinely private wealth. Because until we know who we are without our net worth, we risk building structures that protect assets, but leave the self exposed.

The Fallacy of External Identity

Wealth, particularly when self-made, has a magnetic pull on the ego. It reinforces stories of superiority, endurance, uniqueness. But these narratives—though occasionally accurate—are not neutral. They tend to conflate visibility with validation. The home isn't just shelter; it's a message. The car is no longer transport; it's proof. The social circle is not simply shared interest; it becomes a mirror of status.

Yet structures based on external identity are brittle. The more a person's sense of self relies on being *seen* as successful, the more predictable and vulnerable they become—to lawsuits, to manipulation, to public pressure. Privacy, when practiced deeply, is not just a matter of legal engineering. It's an act of *personal disentanglement* from that entire dependency.

Why This Matters Strategically

In practical terms, clients who are unable to emotionally separate their identity from their wealth consistently undermine their own protection frameworks. They insist on control clauses that signal ownership. They overexpose assets for affirmation. They resist blind trusts because anonymity feels like erasure.

But when privacy becomes *psychologically intolerable*, legal structures can't hold. They get pierced—not by courts, but by behaviour. The strategic lesson here is simple: *Emotional clarity precedes structural integrity.* A well-built trust is only as strong as the trustee's discipline. A layered asset structure is only as invisible as the client's ego allows.

Case Study: The Name on the Door

A former tech executive, worth several hundred million, had a foundation named after him. Every donation came with press. Every event bore his initials. When faced with potential litigation, his counsel advised converting the foundation into a donor-advised fund under a private entity. "But then how will people know it's me?" he asked.

That one sentence revealed the real liability—not the legal entity, but the psychological need to *be recognised.* Until that was addressed, no asset structure would fully protect him. And indeed, a year later, his high-profile philanthropy became the very breadcrumb that exposed a deeper ownership trail in court discovery.

Exercises in Strategic Disengagement

The following reflective prompts are not soft psychology. They are tools for stress-testing your privacy philosophy. They expose how much of your planning is driven by clarity—and how much by a need to *be seen.*

1. **If your name vanished from every structure, would your sense of control feel threatened?**

2. **If no one ever knew what you gave, would you still give the same amount?**

3. **If you could operate in total anonymity, what would you stop doing—and why were you doing it in the first place?**

4. **What part of you needs your wealth to be known? What, exactly, does that need protect?**

5. **If a stranger misjudged your net worth, would you feel indifference—or irritation? Why?**

These questions are designed to puncture the narrative of identity-as-balance-sheet. And the discomfort they provoke is *exactly* the signal that further exploration is warranted.

Reputation is Not Resilience

In wealth circles, much emphasis is placed on legacy, brand, and reputation. But reputation, by definition, exists only in the minds of others. It is both volatile and external. The person who builds for reputation builds on sand. A single crisis, a tabloid article, or a public betrayal can undo decades of narrative management.

The invisible self, by contrast, is resilient. Because it does not require proof. It is not subject to performance. It is not invested in audience. This detachment does not mean apathy. It means clarity. The invisible self acts *from purpose*, not performance. It knows that privacy is not absence—it is control over presence.

The Architecture of Ego-Proof Planning

True discretion does not just depend on offshore jurisdictions or nominee directors. It depends on a mindset that *does not crave exposure.* The more psychologically detached you are from performance-based identity, the more robust your structure can be. Why? Because:

You'll be willing to surrender directorship for distance.

You'll tolerate beneficial ambiguity for protective effect.

You'll prioritise functional control over formal ownership.

This requires a shift: from ego-based structuring to *integrity-based design*. It means building systems that reflect who you are privately, not who you want to appear to be publicly.

Psychology, Philosophy, and the Stoic Parallel

Marcus Aurelius, emperor and philosopher, wrote, *"Just that you do the right thing. The rest doesn't matter."* He was not poor. But he was invisible by practice. He understood that the self is most powerful when it is least entangled in appearance.

Modern privacy strategists would do well to study such models. Because the Stoics didn't hide from the world. They simply refused to let the world define them. They cultivated internal sovereignty—and that is precisely what today's privacy planning demands.

The Quiet Power of Not Needing to Be Known

The most secure individuals—financially, emotionally, existentially—do not fear invisibility. They welcome it. They are not motivated by proving anything to anyone. Their confidence is internal. Their structures are quiet. Their decisions are unprovoked.

This is not passivity. It is *power.* It is the ability to walk away from attention, because attention no longer determines value. It is the freedom to say no to showmanship, and yes to design that prioritises security over display.

The more you can tolerate being unseen, the more protection you can build.

Design Implications for Real-World Structuring

Clients with clarity on their invisible self make sharper decisions. They:

Choose fiduciaries for skill, not flattery.

Accept long-term lockups to reduce temptation.

Rely on entities that do not reflect personal branding.

Embrace generational structures that minimise personal naming.

This kind of planning cannot be reverse-engineered from spreadsheets. It must be born of philosophy. That's what this subchapter offers: not just insights, but *a method*—a way to explore selfhood as part of your privacy architecture.

Closing Reflection

The invisible self is not lesser. It is *liberated.* It is the part of you that exists whether markets crash, articles surface, or opinions change. It is stable because it is silent. Powerful because it is detached. And resilient because it is real.

Designing from this posture is not just advisable. It is essential. Because no matter how elegant your structures, they are only as strong as the mind that governs them. Build wealth from the visible self, and your empire rests on reputation. Build it from the invisible self, and it rests on clarity.

And clarity, unlike applause, does not fade.

Chapter 9
Global Arbitrage – Playing the Game Without Being Played

In a world increasingly shaped by seamless connectivity and borderless flows of information, the notion of wealth tied to a single country feels increasingly anachronistic. What's taking shape before our eyes is a quieter revolution—the emergence of stateless wealth. This is no mere technical shift in how capital is parked or moved; it's a reconfiguration of identity, of how individuals relate to the idea of place, allegiance, and control. The new stewards of wealth—global entrepreneurs, digital nomads, borderless investors—are rewriting the script. For them, geography is fluid, residency is optional, and wealth moves not with loyalty, but with logic.

This chapter ventures into that evolving landscape, one where money is no longer neatly nested under the banners of fixed nation-states but flows across jurisdictions, adapting to incentives, laws, and emerging fault lines in the global order. It is a terrain governed by a subtler kind of map—one that rewards strategic fluidity over patriotic fixity, and foresight over sentiment. What we're witnessing is the rise of global arbitrage—not merely as a tactic, but as a worldview.

To truly grasp what's unfolding, we must begin with a deeper tension that has always lurked within international finance: the friction between economic loyalty and financial self-determination. On one side stands the inherited ideal of national allegiance—the idea that where you are born, or where you hold citizenship, defines your financial obligations and moral commitments. On the other side is a newer, sharper imperative: the need to design your financial life with resilience in mind, diversifying risk across systems rather than concentrating it within any one.

This isn't some abstract ethical conundrum. It's a practical dilemma faced daily by those whose assets are substantial enough to attract scrutiny, yet mobile enough to require protection. The binary of "loyalist versus opportunist" breaks down quickly here. Real life exists in shades. A tech founder might hold citizenship in one country, domicile in another, run operations in a third, and bank in a fourth—not to game the system, but to survive and thrive within it.

One conceptual tool in this space, now in need of reinvention, is flag theory. Originally devised as a method for the wealthy to plant strategic "flags" across different jurisdictions—citizenship here, business incorporation there, banking elsewhere—it sought to distribute one's life across the global stage, optimising for privacy, protection, and profitability. But the world has changed. Regulatory regimes have tightened. Economic nationalism is resurgent. Privacy, once assumed, now demands constant defence. The old flag theory feels brittle—effective in form, but out of step in spirit.

Enter a more refined lens: flag integrity. This isn't about scattering assets to the winds or hopping borders to chase loopholes. Rather, it's about anchoring your financial and legal alignments to jurisdictions that reflect your principles and strategic vision. Jurisdictions with coherent legal systems, respect for privacy, and a stable regulatory climate. It's a framework that doesn't reject the nation-state—but also doesn't pretend allegiance should be unconditional.

This shift, from extraction to engagement, is what sets the new global arbitrage apart. It is not a game of hide-and-seek. It is a deliberate strategy to mitigate risk, preserve autonomy, and align structure with substance.

Within this chapter, readers will be invited not just to observe this evolution—but to enter it. We will examine how stateless wealth is practically structured: from the selection of jurisdictions to the nuances of multi-country compliance; from the design of legal entities that serve longevity to the calibration of visibility and control. But alongside these technical elements runs a more philosophical current. What does it mean to belong anywhere—and nowhere? How do you reconcile personal sovereignty with collective responsibility?

This isn't just about where your money sleeps. It's about where you *stand*—legally, ethically, and strategically.

Case studies and lived examples will accompany the text—not to dazzle, but to ground the reader in realities that stretch from the familiar to the unconventional. A crypto entrepreneur navigating three tax regimes. A retired executive shifting domicile for family continuity. An activist philanthropist seeking jurisdictions that honour both privacy and purpose. Through their stories, the abstract becomes tactile. The map gains texture.

By the chapter's close, the reader will see global arbitrage not as a privilege afforded only to the ultra-wealthy or the globe-trotting elite, but as a framework increasingly relevant to anyone with assets to protect and foresight to act. This isn't about fleeing responsibility. It's about recalibrating it. In a world where political flux and economic pressure erode traditional guarantees, to diversify one's jurisdictional footprint is no longer opportunism—it is prudence.

And that prudence requires not just technical fluency, but ethical depth. Flag integrity offers a compass. It suggests that one can navigate with sophistication and still hold fast to a sense of responsibility—to family, to principle, to the communities we quietly shape through the deployment of our capital.

In the end, the chapter is not merely a map. It is a mindset. It urges readers to stop thinking of themselves as passengers in a national system, and to begin acting as architects of their own financial sovereignty. The nation-state isn't going away. But nor is it the only axis around which modern wealth revolves. For those prepared to engage with nuance, think globally, and design with care, the tools are here—and the game has already begun.

"Beyond Borders: The Mobility Advantage":

There was a time when citizenship was destiny. A passport dictated not only one's national allegiance but the boundaries of their financial future, movement, and personal freedom. Today, that paradigm is dissolving. We are entering a sovereign shift—quiet but profound—in which the legal ties that bind a person to a single jurisdiction are no longer unbreakable, nor necessarily desirable. The rise of second residencies, alternative citizenships, and mobile asset structures reflects not a fringe strategy, but a systematic rethinking of what it means to be financially and geopolitically free. *The ability to move—personally, legally, and economically—is no longer a privilege of the ultra-wealthy; it is an emerging baseline for intelligent, forward-thinking asset design.*

At its core, mobility is not about escapism. It is about resilience. The individual who can pivot jurisdictions has more than optionality; they possess *leverage*. When one's wealth, legal presence, and operational base are all anchored to a single regime—whether stable or not—they are vulnerable to its whims. But when thoughtfully distributed, across jurisdictions with diverse legal traditions, economic cycles, and geopolitical climates, a portfolio becomes *sovereign*. It becomes harder to freeze, less visible, more adaptable—and ultimately more secure.

Consider the sudden collapse of banking infrastructure in Cyprus in 2013. Seemingly overnight, depositor accounts exceeding €100,000 were forcibly "bailed-in," as governments raided private capital to stabilise national finances. This event wasn't confined to a fringe economy; it was a Eurozone country under the regulatory umbrella of Brussels. Thousands of individuals—especially those with EU-only exposure—discovered that what felt like permanence was, in fact, brittle. *Mobility would not have prevented the crisis. But it would have transformed how much of one's capital was exposed to it.*

Second residencies offer a practical entry point into this world of defensive mobility. Whether through economic residency programmes in Portugal, Panama, or Malta, or via more robust pathways such as Singapore's Global Investor Programme, the aim is not merely a change of scenery. It is the layering of jurisdictional options—healthcare access, taxation flexibility, banking infrastructure, and diplomatic stability—into one's strategic design. A second residency grants more than a right to live elsewhere; it provides an exit option from instability, a soft shield against political volatility, and a future base for children or assets.

Yet the real force multiplier comes in the form of *citizenship diversification*. Citizenship-by-investment (CBI) programmes, though controversial in some circles, are among the most powerful legal arbitrage tools available. A second passport from a Caribbean nation like St Kitts and Nevis, or a European state like Austria (granted under rare discretionary pathways), is not merely a travel document—it is a legal reset. It allows the bearer to decouple personal identity from a single sovereign claim. It introduces the capacity to renounce, relocate, or redesign a life without triggering existential loss.

This is particularly critical when considering the extraterritorial reach of some tax regimes. The United States, for example, asserts global taxation rights over its citizens regardless of where they live or earn. Contrast this with nations like the UAE, Monaco, or even Switzerland under certain residency arrangements, which operate under territorial or flat tax regimes. A second citizenship may open the door to restructuring residency and domicile in a manner that aligns not only with privacy but with long-term tax planning. *But none of this is ethically tenable unless it is done lawfully, transparently, and with an understanding of responsibility—not simply opportunity.*

To operate effectively beyond borders also means mastering *geo-political asset mobility*. This refers to the design of asset holdings—bank accounts, trusts, corporations, physical property, intellectual property—in jurisdictions whose legal, political, and infrastructural characteristics differ and therefore diversify risk. The goal is not complexity for its own sake but *asymmetry*: ensuring that a single lawsuit, regulatory change, or asset freeze in one country does not cascade across the entire financial landscape of the individual or family. For instance, intellectual property registered in Singapore, held by a BVI corporation, generating royalties banked in Liechtenstein, and distributed through a New Zealand trust, is not easily dismantled by a single nation's claim.

This is not a call for concealment. It is a call for structural sophistication. Governments are increasingly collaborating to identify tax evasion, money laundering, and financial crime. Initiatives like the OECD's Common Reporting Standard (CRS) and FATCA in the US have drastically reduced the space for shadowy operations. *But lawful arbitrage—using what the law allows to design antifragile wealth structures—is not unethical. It is prudent.* It is what corporations have done for decades; it is what thoughtful individuals are now beginning to replicate with equal deliberation.

Still, the mobility advantage must be approached with philosophical clarity. What does it mean to be untethered? Does it dilute civic responsibility? Is it a rejection of nationalism or an evolution of it? These questions matter. Because with every flag planted, passport obtained, or bank account opened abroad, a deeper question arises: *who are you when no single nation defines your legal or financial identity?* The answer need not be nihilistic or purely transactional. In fact, the most powerful mobility frameworks arise when personal values, not opportunistic avoidance, shape jurisdictional choices. One might choose Estonia for its digital governance, Uruguay for its democratic resilience, or New Zealand for its rule of law. *The strategic use of borders becomes a mirror of one's worldview.*

There is, too, a psychological recalibration required. Many professionals still anchor their sense of safety to domestic regulations and institutions. To them, mobility feels risky—exotic, even suspect. But the inverse is increasingly true. *Risk now resides in immobility.* To assume that any one country will preserve its financial freedoms, tax codes, or political orientation for the next thirty years is to ignore history. Argentina has defaulted nine times. Venezuela once had the highest GDP per capita in Latin America. Even the United Kingdom has undergone dramatic financial and political upheavals in recent decades. Anchoring long-term strategy to any single jurisdiction—regardless of how familiar—invites concentration risk of the highest order.

Ultimately, *the mobility advantage is not about becoming a global ghost.* It is about becoming structurally fluid, intellectually agile, and legally resilient. It is about recognising that in a world of interconnected risks—cyber threats, political extremism, regulatory overreach—geographic diversification is not a luxury, but a strategic necessity. For the thoughtful reader, second residencies and multiple citizenships are not badges of elitism but instruments of responsible design. They are tools to ensure continuity, choice, and protection—not only for wealth but for wellbeing, legacy, and peace of mind.

The challenge is not technical—it is philosophical. Are you prepared to think like a sovereign individual, not just a domestic taxpayer? Can you embrace the discomfort of complexity for the sake of greater control? If so, then mobility is no longer a backup plan. It is your *strategic default.* Not because you are fleeing, but because you are choosing—not one system over another, but *your system, your design, your sovereignty—beyond borders.*

"The Rise of Stateless Wealth":

The most powerful assets today are not owned, they are configured. They are not buried in vaults or tied to land, but encrypted, tokenised, fractionalised, and dispersed across networks that no single government can fully regulate. *Wealth has become partially decoupled from geography—and entirely detached from borders.* It is no longer confined by the constraints of a single jurisdiction. This is not theoretical. It is observable, measurable, and expanding. The rise of stateless wealth is not a glitch in the system; it is the system evolving in plain sight.

To understand this transformation, we must recognise the convergence of three forces: digitisation, decentralisation, and mobility. These are not transient trends. They are structural shifts with legal, economic, and psychological implications. In combination, they allow wealth to exist outside traditional definitions of domicile, nationality, and regulatory perimeter. It does not mean lawlessness; it means *jurisdictional optionality.* And for a growing class of professionals, entrepreneurs, and investors—especially digital nomads—this is not only practical, but philosophical.

Start with the digital asset layer. Cryptocurrencies are often dismissed as speculative or volatile, but this ignores their deeper function: *they are borderless stores of value.* A private key does not care whether you are in Lagos, Lisbon, or Lima. Bitcoin cannot be frozen by a single authority. Ethereum-based smart contracts execute without regard for local courts. These are not theoretical advantages. They are actively used in countries where capital controls, inflation, or asset seizure are real threats—not hypothetical risks. When a Venezuelan business owner migrates with nothing but a hardware wallet, or a Ukrainian developer escapes invasion with their net worth in stablecoins, we are witnessing wealth that travels without friction, without detection, and without intermediaries.

Yet it is not only digital currency that enables stateless wealth. It is also how legal and technical infrastructure has evolved. A startup founded by a Brazilian, incorporated in Delaware, funded by

Singaporean investors, storing its codebase in decentralised repositories and billing in USDC—this is not exotic. It is increasingly normal. The company's value is not "located" anywhere in the classical sense. Its code, capital, and contracts are all cloud-native. In practical terms, it exists everywhere and nowhere. *To seize it, you must first find it. And by design, it evades centralised visibility.*

This doesn't mean these structures are beyond the reach of law. On the contrary, they require even greater legal literacy. The tax obligations of an Estonian e-resident earning crypto in Thailand while banking through a Lithuanian fintech are complex, and must be navigated responsibly. Stateless wealth, when done poorly, risks opacity, confusion, and exposure. But when executed with precision, it is a way to *redistribute risk*, not evade responsibility. It allows assets to exist in a diversified legal ecology—one where no single actor holds the keys to one's financial fate.

At the human level, this shift is personified by the digital nomad. Often caricatured as lifestyle migrants, they are increasingly becoming decentralised financial agents. These are individuals who work, invest, and move across jurisdictions with strategic intent. They may live in Mexico, file taxes in Portugal, bank in Switzerland, and store assets on-chain. Their lives are designed to avoid economic monoculture. Not through secrecy, but through *sovereignty*. They are crafting systems where control is retained by the individual—not defaulted to the state.

But this evolution raises uncomfortable questions. Where does responsibility begin and end? Should stateless wealth be viewed as an escape from civic duty or a rebuke of unjust governance? If capital has escaped the nation-state, what of citizenship? What of shared obligation? These are not merely legal questions; they are moral ones. Because the moment wealth can transcend borders, it can also detach from the consequences of place. *It can uplift or abandon. It can insulate or invest. The power cuts both ways.*

There is also the growing tension between regulatory harmonisation and technological resistance. Initiatives like the OECD's Common Reporting Standard (CRS) and the Financial Action Task Force (FATF) are explicit attempts to map and monitor cross-border wealth. But these efforts are playing catch-up against decentralised finance (DeFi), zero-knowledge proofs, privacy-preserving tokens, and encrypted peer-to-peer exchanges. The tools of enforcement are centralised. The tools of wealth are not. This is not an arms race—it is a *paradigm mismatch.*

Some governments, aware of this shift, are adapting rather than resisting. Portugal, until recently, did not tax crypto gains. El Salvador made Bitcoin legal tender. Dubai created specific zones for virtual asset regulation. Singapore formalised digital asset exchanges under the Payment Services Act. These are not ideological moves—they are competitive ones. *Jurisdictions now compete for mobile capital not just with tax rates, but with regulatory clarity.* The rise of stateless wealth is also the rise of the regulatory entrepreneur: a government that builds legal frameworks to attract decentralised wealth without undermining national security.

Yet for all its advantages, stateless wealth introduces a new challenge for individuals: *the erosion of the safety illusion.* For centuries, wealth was stored in banks, real estate, or gold. Its location gave comfort. It was visible, tangible, insurable. Today, the most sophisticated portfolios are diversified across jurisdictions, asset classes, legal wrappers, and digital architectures. This is safer in many ways—but it demands more from the owner. One must be legally literate, technologically fluent, and psychologically comfortable with abstraction. *To own stateless wealth is to accept complexity in exchange for control.*

So where is this all headed? The likely trajectory is not full escape from regulation, but *a rebalancing of power between capital and jurisdiction.* Governments will continue to attempt oversight, but those jurisdictions that offer low-friction, high-transparency, crypto-compatible frameworks will attract the lion's share of mobile capital. Individuals who embrace this complexity—and design accordingly—will gain not only resilience but leverage. Those who ignore it may find their assets overexposed, their strategies outdated, and their freedom constrained by legacy assumptions.

Stateless wealth is not a slogan. It is a structural evolution. It means assets that move without permission. Contracts that execute without borders. Value that stores without vaults. It redefines what it means to *own*, to *earn*, to *protect*. But most of all, it redefines what it means to *trust*. Because in this new architecture of capital, trust is no longer outsourced to the state. It is embedded in code, distributed across networks, and ultimately anchored in personal responsibility.

For the thoughtful reader, the imperative is clear. *Don't wait for consensus to validate this trend. Design for it now.* Think legally, act digitally, diversify structurally. And remember: wealth is no longer where it is stored, but how it is configured. Statelessness is not an escape. It is a strategy. And when done with clarity, ethics, and foresight, it is not just a financial upgrade—it is a philosophical one.

"Economic Patriotism vs. Financial Sovereignty":

Patriotism has long been an anchor of identity. People pledge allegiance, pay taxes, vote, serve, and in return expect protection, infrastructure, and a sense of belonging. But as capital globalises and jurisdictions compete, *a subtle tension has begun to surface in the minds of globally mobile wealth holders*: the tension between national loyalty and financial autonomy. This isn't merely an economic calculation—it is an identity crisis.

At the heart of this conflict is the question: *What do we owe the state once our assets, income, and even our lives become mobile?* The traditional narrative holds that citizens contribute to the nation-state because they benefit from its services. But this social contract becomes strained when an individual's wealth is earned abroad, taxed in multiple countries, held across jurisdictions, and exposed to global volatility. In such conditions, loyalty can begin to feel like liability.

This is where the concept of *economic patriotism* comes into focus. Economic patriotism refers to the belief that individuals and corporations should prioritise the economic welfare of their home nation, even when it comes at a cost to their own efficiency or optimisation. It's the philosophy that celebrates bringing capital "back home", hiring domestically, paying local taxes without legal minimisation strategies, and avoiding offshore havens. It is often used rhetorically in politics, especially during economic downturns, where offshore planning is framed as abandonment or betrayal.

But here lies the conceptual fracture: *What if the rules of the game penalise loyalty?* What if a nation-state becomes unstable, corrupt, punitive, or misaligned with your values? What if the financial system of your country becomes a source of systemic risk rather than stability? In these scenarios, the rational actor must ask whether uncritical economic loyalty is wise—or naive.

This is where *financial sovereignty* enters as a counterpoint. Financial sovereignty is not about evasion or secrecy. It is about *agency*. It is the right and capacity to design your financial architecture in a way that is resilient, adaptive, and decentralised. It means being able to choose your jurisdictions, structure your assets, plan your taxes legally, and insulate your future from the whims of any single government. In many ways, it is the economic extension of the freedom of thought and movement.

The internal conflict arises when these two values—patriotism and sovereignty—are both deeply held. You may want to contribute meaningfully to the nation that raised you, while also protecting your assets from bad legislation, inflation, or political instability. The tension is not always financial. It is *emotional.* It is the discomfort of feeling like a defector when in fact you are simply diversifying. It is the anxiety of seeming disloyal, when your strategy is driven by prudence, not greed.

Consider the example of entrepreneurs in high-tax jurisdictions. A founder in France or California may build a company from scratch, hire locally, pay employment taxes, and contribute to GDP—yet face a marginal tax rate that discourages reinvestment and growth. When this founder explores relocating to Portugal or Estonia for a more balanced tax regime, the backlash is not technical—it is moral. The implication is that she is abandoning her duty. But is it abandonment if the system penalises productivity? *Or is it a rational response to distorted incentives?*

This debate is not confined to individuals. Corporations, too, are under scrutiny. When Apple holds its cash reserves in Ireland or Starbucks structures through the Netherlands, critics call it profit shifting. But defenders argue these moves are not just legal—they are required by fiduciary duty. Who, then, defines what is patriotic? And what happens when laws lag behind innovation?

What we are confronting is the need for a more mature framework—*a vision of responsible globalism*. This does not mean a libertarian fantasy of no oversight, nor a statist insistence on total capital control. It means acknowledging that loyalty and strategy can coexist—but only if both are redefined.

Responsible globalism begins with transparency. Financial sovereignty should not depend on obfuscation. You can structure your assets legally across borders, declare your income, and remain fully compliant—*while still refusing to be economically captive to a single system.* The key is design, not escape.

It also means *contribution by choice, not coercion.* When individuals feel respected and understood by their governments—when taxation is fair, services are delivered efficiently, and legal systems are predictable—they are far more likely to contribute voluntarily.

Economic loyalty is a function of trust, not guilt. Nations that foster environments of mutual respect and competitive policy will attract and retain the most productive citizens, even when they have options elsewhere.

There's a historical dimension here, too. The modern state was built on assumptions of immobility: that people would live, earn, spend, and retire in the same country. Today's reality is different. A British investor may hold real estate in Dubai, equities in the US, crypto in cold storage, and spend winters in Thailand. To treat this person as a "taxpayer" in the 19th-century sense is intellectually dishonest. Their economic life spans time zones, legal systems, and asset classes. Their obligations should reflect that complexity—*without moral panic.*

This doesn't mean every form of capital flight is ethical. Moving assets to escape legitimate debts, dodge civic responsibility, or undermine shared institutions is not sovereignty—it's selfishness. But the opposite extreme is also dangerous: guilt-driven financial martyrdom in systems that offer diminishing returns. Somewhere between these poles lies a pragmatic ideal: design a resilient, transparent global structure, pay fairly where value is created, and *refuse to be manipulated by outdated moral narratives.*

One must also confront the psychological undertow. Many successful individuals report that the greatest challenge in pursuing financial sovereignty is not technical—it is *emotional permission.* The sense that "good people don't do this." That real patriots don't optimise. But these are residues of outdated systems. Today, responsible actors must unlearn the false dichotomy between ethics and strategy. It is entirely possible to be *loyal by principle, but sovereign by design.*

The coming decade will test this balance. As geopolitical instability rises, as tax regimes harden, and as wealth becomes more portable, the divide between economic nationalism and global resilience will widen. Those who cling to blind loyalty may find themselves vulnerable. Those who chase aggressive avoidance may find themselves isolated. The thoughtful middle path—the one defined by transparency, ethics, and strategic design—will be harder, but far more durable.

In the end, the question is not whether you "believe" in your country. It is whether your country believes in *your ability to act intelligently on its own terms*. Economic patriotism is admirable when it is reciprocated. But it becomes coercive when it is used to trap. Financial sovereignty, at its best, is not a rejection of community—it is a demand for *earned allegiance*.

Design wisely. Contribute fairly. But never apologise for protecting yourself intelligently. This is not betrayal. It is the future.

"From Flag Theory to Flag Integrity":

The original premise of flag theory was simple, almost seductive: plant different aspects of your life in different jurisdictions, and you'll achieve freedom, safety, and tax efficiency. Originating in the mid-20th century and popularised by perpetual travellers and privacy seekers, the "five flag" model proposed separating citizenship, legal residence, asset domicile, business base, and lifestyle hub across multiple countries. It was designed as an escape hatch—an elegant strategy for personal sovereignty at a time when governments were tightening their fiscal grip.

But what began as a framework for strategic freedom has, in some cases, devolved into a checklist for arbitrage without accountability. The original ideals—sovereignty, decentralisation, risk dispersion—remain valuable. Yet the modern landscape demands more than modular mobility. It calls for *integrity*.

Flag integrity is the evolution of flag theory. It is not a rejection of jurisdictional diversification, but a refinement of its purpose. Where traditional flag theory asked, "Where can I go to minimise exposure?" flag integrity asks, "How can I design a global structure that reflects both my strategic interests and ethical values?" It moves beyond the mechanical scattering of legal affiliations and into a deliberate, principle-aligned architecture of life and capital.

This shift is not cosmetic—it is structural. Consider the difference between building a tax structure purely to reduce your liability, versus building one that is *also aligned with your identity, transparent to stakeholders, and resilient under scrutiny*. Flag integrity doesn't view compliance as a nuisance to be navigated; it treats it as a design challenge to be mastered. It does not treat sovereignty as escape, but as stewardship.

The need for this evolved lens has grown more urgent as jurisdictions evolve in real time. Nations are no longer passive backdrops. They are active participants—tightening anti-avoidance laws, enforcing information exchange treaties, and developing ever more sophisticated compliance technologies. The global tax and regulatory ecosystem is converging. The margins for irresponsible arbitrage are shrinking. What remains is a new space—*a space for intelligent, transparent, value-consistent structure.*

Flag integrity begins with rethinking the assumptions baked into the original model:

1. Citizenship is not just a passport; it is a relationship. The traditional flag theory often treated citizenship as a liability—a tax anchor to be neutralised through second passports or expatriation. While this is still a legitimate strategic move in certain high-burden jurisdictions, flag integrity compels us to go deeper. If you are abandoning your birth nation's citizenship, what values are you gaining—or losing? Is your new passport just a transactional hedge, or is it tied to a nation where you would actually participate, contribute, and be protected?

2. Residency is not a loophole; it's a contract. A common tactic among digital nomads is to "reside nowhere," seeking perpetual motion as a shield against tax residency rules. But in reality, most tax regimes operate on substance over form. If you spend enough time in one place, establish routine ties, or even run a business remotely, your floating lifestyle may not protect you. A better model is to *select jurisdictions where your presence, taxes, and expectations are in harmony*—not where the rules are simply lax or poorly enforced.

3. Asset location matters as much for ethics as for efficiency. Where your money lives signals what you believe about governance, risk, and security. Placing assets in unstable or opaque jurisdictions might offer short-term privacy but expose you to long-term instability or seizure. Flag integrity means selecting jurisdictions with rule of law, reciprocal treaty frameworks, and tested financial institutions. Not just because it's safe—but because it's right. Capital placed in dark corners corrodes trust and legitimacy.

4. Business base is not just operational—it's reputational. The legal entity from which you invoice clients or hold intellectual property is a public statement. A BVI shell may offer low taxes, but it also invites scrutiny. A regulated company in Singapore, the UK, or Switzerland might cost more—but it sends a message of seriousness, continuity, and accountability. When your business is embedded in a sound legal framework, your credibility increases. Your access to banking, capital, and partners improves.

5. Lifestyle base is not just comfort—it's alignment. The original fifth flag was about choosing a pleasant place to live—preferably with low taxes and high quality of life. But today, the question is sharper: does your chosen lifestyle jurisdiction reflect your personal values, your family's needs, and your risk tolerance? Does it offer safety, education, mobility, and access to healthcare? Are you merely consuming sunshine, or integrating meaningfully into the local community? Flag integrity includes *moral coherence*—not just strategic optimisation.

Importantly, flag integrity is not moral puritanism. It does not require sacrificing efficiency or opportunity. Rather, it insists that these be pursued in a way that can withstand challenge. That you can look at your own structure and say: *this was designed intentionally, not opportunistically. This is resilient, legal, and true to who I am.*

There's also a psychological dividend. Traditional flag theory often carries the weight of constant vigilance—wondering whether your setup will survive the next treaty, regulation, or whistle-blower. Flag integrity offers relief. When you build structures that are rooted in both law and logic, you can operate confidently. You stop hiding. You start leading.

We've already seen glimpses of this evolution in practice. Consider the rise of "values-aligned" banking—offshore institutions that comply with Common Reporting Standards (CRS) but also uphold privacy, customer service, and robust cybersecurity. Or the growth of multi-national family offices that coordinate assets across borders while prioritising philanthropy, sustainability, and next-generation education. These are not flag theorists in the old sense—they are practitioners of *integrity-based global design.*

Critically, this approach is not only for billionaires. Even mid-level entrepreneurs and professionals can apply flag integrity by asking sharper questions when setting up their companies, selecting their banks, or choosing a residence programme. *Is this just the cheapest? Or is it the most coherent for my long-term goals and values?*

There is also a geopolitical context to this shift. As nationalism rises in some regions and surveillance capitalism expands in others, the individual is caught between state overreach and market extraction.

Flag integrity is one way to reclaim *individual sovereignty without abandoning civic responsibility*. It offers a blueprint for ethical mobility, not just tactical evasion.

From a legal standpoint, flag integrity also hedges against regulatory fatigue. Governments are not blind to the abuses of old-school flag theory. Whether through Base Erosion and Profit Shifting (BEPS), beneficial ownership registries, or blacklists, the tide is turning. Compliance is no longer optional. Integrity, therefore, is no longer luxury—it is necessity.

But the most compelling case for flag integrity may be *philosophical.* In a world increasingly defined by polarisation, opacity, and distrust, those who structure with clarity and principle will stand apart. Not as targets, but as examples. Not as manipulators, but as *designers of thoughtful, coherent lives.*

Flag theory got us moving. Flag integrity keeps us grounded. It is how you build not just protection, but credibility. Not just mobility, but meaning.

In a world of shifting borders and surveillance regimes, *the only true sovereignty is that which you can explain, defend, and sleep soundly within.* That is the future of global structuring. Not flags for the sake of flags—but flags that represent something more enduring: alignment, coherence, and trust.

Chapter 10
Legal Doesn't Mean Obvious – The Art of Subtle Compliance

There is a quiet, almost architectural elegance in understanding the law well enough to work within its margins—not to evade, not to subvert, but to inhabit its contours with precision and depth. In a world increasingly ruled by algorithms, institutional vigilance, and regulatory reflexes, the distinction between merely being legal and being intelligently compliant has never mattered more—and never been so subtle. This chapter explores that boundary, not as a technicality, but as a deliberate craft.

We are conditioned to equate legality with tidiness—as though what's compliant must, by default, look standard, transparent, and easy to explain. But such assumptions ignore a deeper truth: the law is not a closed equation. It is a language, filled with nuance, contextual silence, and interpretive drift. Those who operate at the higher levels of international finance, asset protection, or transnational structuring do not rely on the obvious. Their tools are nuance, foresight, and structural patience. Their aim is not to manipulate, but to outlast.

There exists a pervasive suspicion—often unspoken—that complexity is somehow unclean. That the more layers one adds to a financial or legal structure, the more likely it is to be evasive or unethical. And yet, paradoxically, some of the most transparent, lawful, and ethically grounded frameworks are the ones that appear, at first glance, overly elaborate. Complexity, when done well, is not concealment. It is defence. A structure with depth, like a building designed for siege, can frustrate superficial probes but still withstand forensic scrutiny. There's strength in that—though not everyone recognises it.

Take, for instance, asset protection trusts in jurisdictions like the Cook Islands or Nevis. To the untrained observer, their layered

composition—settlor powers, discretionary trustees, protector clauses—may seem needlessly dense. But to a seasoned legal strategist, each moving part carries distinct function: isolating control, defining liability, resisting court challenges. Their complexity isn't arbitrary. It is what allows them to remain upright in a regulatory storm. That's not deception. That's design.

The first mental shift this chapter demands is to separate legality from optics. The law doesn't reward simplicity; it rewards coherence. The question is not "does this structure look neat?" but "will it stand, under pressure, with integrity and within the letter of the law?" When done right, compliant complexity builds so intelligently that it never needs to hide.

The second—and arguably more important—shift is away from the adversarial mindset. Far too often, individuals with newly acquired wealth, or entrepreneurs navigating expansion, treat regulation as something to be outmanoeuvred. They brace against the tax code, flinch at compliance, and view oversight as the enemy. It's an outdated posture, and more than that, it's strategically unsound. The savviest operators today don't resist the system. They learn its rhythms and move with them.

Consider how real estate investors in the United States use depreciation allowances not to cheat the system, but to participate in it with precision. Or how high-net-worth families in civil law countries use insurance wrappers not to obscure, but to align their planning with frameworks that privilege policyholder rights over asset exposure. These aren't loopholes. They're harmonies—designs that honour the spirit and the letter of the law simultaneously.

This is what we call subtle compliance: not hiding behind forms, but understanding form as function. To do it well, one needs counsel who don't merely recite statutes, but read patterns—who grasp how law behaves across systems, how precedent speaks, and how regulatory moods shift. Sadly, many advisors don't operate this way. Their instinct is self-defence. "No" is safer than "let's think it through." So you end up with conservative recommendations—not because they're wise, but because they're easy to justify in hindsight.

Which leads to an overlooked form of leverage: the calibre of your team. As we move through this chapter, we'll explore how to identify legal counsel who aren't just competent, but compositional thinkers. They aren't always the ones with the glossiest offices or most LinkedIn endorsements. Often, they're the former regulators who now structure quietly. The lawyers who ask the right questions, who draft with restraint, and who view discretion as foundational rather than ornamental. These are people who build as though privacy were a structural load—not an afterthought.

And it's not only the global elite who benefit from such thinking. Even purely domestic structures—small family trusts, holding companies, profit-sharing agreements—can reflect this ethos. Take the irrevocable trust with a retained power of appointment. On the surface, it seems contradictory. But properly constructed, it offers flexibility without sacrificing protection. Or consider intellectual property revenue flows structured through controlled entities with third-party pricing methodologies. Complex? Absolutely. But also clear, lawful, and, if challenged, defensible.

Every intelligent structure must answer three questions: Is it legally sound? Can it adapt? And is it ethically durable? These filters matter not just because they protect, but because they predict. A structure that cannot evolve, or that cannot be defended with moral clarity, is a structure waiting to fail. The point of subtle compliance is to avoid that failure before it materialises—not by reacting faster, but by designing better.

This is not a manual of tricks. It's a philosophy. And once adopted, it changes how you approach everything: your advisors, your jurisdictions, your timing, your exposure. You begin to view compliance not as a box-tick, but as a form of architecture—measured, elegant, and anticipatory.

To build this way is to make peace with complexity. Not noise, not gimmickry, but depth that reads as grace under pressure. The kind of structure that can be placed before a judge, regulator, or sceptic and still stand—precisely because it doesn't rely on hiding. It relies on having thought it through.

In an era where simplicity is often equated with virtue—and where visibility is both exploited and misunderstood—there is a certain power in building quietly. In layering not to confuse, but to clarify. In choosing structures that don't seek applause, but endure.

This is subtle compliance. And if done well, it becomes not just a legal advantage, but a strategic signature.

Transparency vs. Exposure

Teaches the nuanced line between disclosure and damage—how to be visible to regulators but invisible to threats.

There is a profound difference between being transparent and being exposed. One is a deliberate act of clarity—calibrated, compliant, and controlled. The other is a vulnerability—accidental, unprotected, and often irreversible. For anyone engaged in wealth structuring, especially across jurisdictions or regulatory regimes, this difference is not just semantic. It's strategic. And misjudging it can mean the collapse of everything you've built.

We live in an age where disclosure is no longer optional. From automatic exchange agreements like the Common Reporting Standard (CRS), to Know Your Customer (KYC) and Anti-Money Laundering (AML) obligations, the architecture of global finance is increasingly tilted toward visibility. *But visibility to regulators is not the same as visibility to adversaries.* The problem is not that governments know where your assets are. The problem is when litigators, extortionists, or commercial competitors do.

Many asset protection strategies fail not because they're illegal or non-compliant, but because they confuse formality with foresight. They assume that ticking regulatory boxes guarantees safety. It doesn't. *True safety lies in controlling the vector of exposure—not eliminating it, but directing it intentionally.* This means designing structures that satisfy disclosure laws without broadcasting strategic information to those who might misuse it.

To understand the stakes, consider this: a wealthy individual complies with CRS by disclosing an offshore trust to their home country's tax authority. That act is not, in itself, dangerous. But if the same individual uses their personal name on public land registries, appears as the director of a holding company, or is publicly associated with luxury assets, they've created a data constellation. One that can be pieced together by anyone with basic digital tools. Journalists. Civil litigants. Hackers. Divorce attorneys. *Exposure is not about what you declare—it's about what others can infer.*

The philosophical underpinning of this discussion is simple: *you can be fully legal and fully vulnerable at the same time.* This dissonance is poorly understood by both advisors and clients. The financial system rewards disclosure in one dimension—vertical clarity toward regulators. But the threats clients face often operate horizontally: leaks, social engineering, reputational attacks, commercial espionage. You must design for both.

This is where many default compliance strategies fall short. They're written to satisfy institutional checklists, not to defend against asymmetric threats. For example, it's perfectly legal to list a beneficial owner on a trust register. But if that register is leaked (as happened with the Panama Papers), the implications can be reputationally catastrophic, even if nothing illegal occurred. *Transparency does not mean publicity. And compliance does not mean immunity.*

The art, then, is to engineer visibility without vulnerability. This begins with a crucial mindset shift: *compliance is not the ceiling—it's the floor.* A properly structured entity, trust, or financial relationship must pass through three lenses simultaneously:

1. **Legal Legibility** – Does it comply with current laws, reporting frameworks, and treaty obligations?

2. **Operational Opacity** – Does it minimise unnecessary attribution, ownership trail clarity, or symbolic visibility?

3. **Strategic Ambiguity** – Does it introduce interpretive distance between control and title, ownership and benefit?

Let's take a practical example. Suppose you hold a valuable intellectual property portfolio. You could register it under your name, house it within a domestic company, and license it directly to your operating entity. That would be tax-compliant, visible, and straightforward—and disastrously exposed. A better design would house the IP within a purpose-built offshore company, owned by a trust, administered by a licensed fiduciary, with layered licensing agreements back to the commercial operations. Every element would be declared to tax authorities where required. But to the outside world, the owner of record, the controlling mind, and the economic beneficiary would be separate. *That's the difference between transparent and targeted.*

It's critical to understand that overexposure often stems not from legal failure, but from *psychological overconfidence.* Many successful individuals believe that compliance buys them reputational protection. It doesn't. The public doesn't distinguish between legal complexity and evasion. A trust that appears in a data leak—regardless of its legality—is often interpreted as sinister. The court of public opinion is rarely calibrated to nuance.

This is why discretion must be an explicit design goal—not an accidental outcome. Anonymity is increasingly difficult to achieve in a digitised compliance environment. But *controlled discretion* is still very much possible. This includes:

Separating legal ownership from beneficial use

Limiting name-based associations with registrable assets

Using nominee structures with audit-proof documentation

Ensuring data minimisation in legal disclosures

There is a delicate balance here, and it's not binary. You don't need to disappear. You need to *be seen strategically*. Being too visible makes you a target. Being completely opaque invites suspicion. The optimal point is *legible to regulators, irrelevant to attackers*.

Critically, this balancing act is not static. Laws evolve. Treaties expand. Databases get hacked. Political climates shift. A structure that is private today may be exposed tomorrow under new regulatory rules or investigative journalism. This is why privacy, like compliance, must be a process—not an event. Regular reviews, jurisdictional diversification, and real-time threat modelling are essential to staying ahead of both regulation and retaliation.

And yet, even this level of sophistication is often undone by human error. It only takes one casual interview, one social media post, or one indiscreet advisor to unravel years of carefully designed privacy architecture. Therefore, the human element—training, mindset, discipline—matters as much as legal structure. If your lifestyle is loud, no structure will silence the exposure. *The most robust design is defeated if the client behaves like an open-source database.*

From a legal philosophy perspective, this raises an important ethical tension: how much privacy is defensible in a transparent world? The answer depends on intent. If privacy is engineered to conceal wrongdoing, it's indefensible. If privacy is built to preserve dignity, security, or strategic sovereignty, it is not only legitimate—it is essential. *There is a moral difference between hiding and protecting.* One seeks to deceive. The other seeks to endure.

In the chapters that follow, we will explore how to construct structures that satisfy this higher threshold—structures that are audit-proof, legally clean, and psychologically grounded. You will see how legal design, behavioural restraint, and strategic signalling can combine into something far more powerful than secrecy: *resilience.*

Visibility is no longer optional. But exposure is. The difference lies in your design. Choose wisely.

Compliant Complexity

Explores how legal complexity can be a form of protective architecture, not confusion.

Complexity in wealth structuring is often maligned. To the casual observer, intricate trusts, layered holding companies, cross-border asset vehicles, and jurisdictional hybrids can appear convoluted, opaque, even suspicious. Yet to the seasoned practitioner—and the strategically aware client—*legal complexity is not evidence of obfuscation, but of design.* It is a conscious architecture, constructed not to confuse, but to defend. The distinction is subtle but critical.

Too often, simplicity is romanticised in legal affairs as if elegance and minimalism are virtues unto themselves. In many domains, they are. In asset protection, they are frequently liabilities. *The real world does not reward simplicity—it rewards resilience.* And resilience, in law, is engineered through depth, redundancy, and optionality. These require structure. They require complexity. Most importantly, they require compliance—*not in spite of the structure's intricacy, but because of it.*

Let us begin with a clear premise: a complex structure that is fully compliant with all relevant laws is not only defensible—it is often unassailable. Complexity, when aligned with regulation, introduces both strategic ambiguity and jurisdictional insulation. The result is not chaos but coherence, distributed across multiple legal frameworks, none of which individually controls the whole. This is the principle of *modular opacity*: no single court, authority, or claimant can dismantle the system without intersecting other legal regimes that operate on different logic, rules, or timelines.

To illustrate, imagine a scenario where a high-net-worth individual holds a portfolio of real estate, intellectual property, private equity, and cash equivalents across four continents. A simplistic strategy would be to consolidate assets under a single holding company, ideally located in a low-tax jurisdiction. This might offer ease of management, but it also creates a single point of failure. A legal attack, seizure order, or political shift in that jurisdiction could threaten the entirety of the estate. *Simplicity, in this case, is not elegance—it is exposure.*

Contrast this with a legally compliant multi-layer structure: real estate held through local entities in each jurisdiction, owned by regional subsidiaries, which are in turn owned by an offshore trust. Intellectual property sits in a dedicated IP-holding company in a treaty-friendly jurisdiction, licensed through arm's-length agreements. Cash reserves are distributed across multiple custodial banks, tied to different entities. The structure appears complex, but it is transparent to regulators and tax authorities. Each component has a rational legal, operational, and commercial purpose. And critically, the architecture ensures that no single attack vector compromises the entire estate.

This is not about hiding—it's about *engineering lawful distance between control and exposure.*

Historically, legal complexity has served the same role as physical fortification did in ancient societies. Walls, gates, moats, and layers of security were not designed to confuse invaders; they were built to slow them down, tire them out, and force them to fight on multiple fronts. The legal analogue is the multi-jurisdictional, cross-functional structure that requires claimants to navigate divergent legal systems, languages, evidentiary burdens, and procedural thresholds. *Every layer is lawful. Every layer is documented. Every layer buys time, space, and negotiation leverage.*

Yet even in today's sophisticated circles, this perspective meets resistance. Some advisors insist that "keeping it simple" is the best policy—citing auditability, cost efficiency, or reputational optics. There is some merit to these concerns. Over-complexity can become a risk if it is not managed properly. Structures must be intelligible to those who administer them, and must avoid artificiality, sham arrangements, or the appearance of bad faith. The line is not between complexity and simplicity. The line is between *functional complexity and performative complexity*. One strengthens the structure; the other invites scrutiny.

Compliant complexity is not the same as evasion. In fact, it is the opposite. It embraces regulation fully—and uses the logic of each jurisdiction to produce a legally sound result. The laws of one country may prioritise beneficial ownership disclosures; another may privilege fiduciary control; a third may favour settlor intention. A well-designed structure maps these differences into a unified defensive grid. *What looks complex to an outsider is, to the insider, a rational distribution of legal attributes.*

This approach also allows for what might be termed *regulatory asymmetry*: the ability to fulfil all local disclosure and tax obligations while minimising practical visibility across the public domain. A trust may be fully disclosed to a tax authority, while remaining invisible in asset registries. A company may comply with filing requirements while its shareholders remain protected by nominee services. This is not secrecy. It is selective visibility—*engineered disclosure calibrated to the role and risk of each actor.*

The psychological barrier for many is accepting that legal opacity is not moral opacity. There is a deep cultural bias, particularly in common law societies, that complexity implies wrongdoing. This is a relic of narratives that equate simplicity with virtue. In reality, some of the most ethical, compliant, and professionally managed structures in the world—those serving philanthropic families, cross-border entrepreneurs, or politically exposed persons—are legally complex by necessity. *When your operating environment spans multiple jurisdictions, complexity is not indulgence. It is a tool of stewardship.*

There is also a technical reason why compliant complexity must be embraced: legal arbitrage. Different jurisdictions offer different protections—not just tax rates, but rules around asset protection, bankruptcy, data privacy, trust interpretation, and regulatory enforcement. No single jurisdiction offers everything. Designing a structure that draws selectively from multiple regimes—*without triggering conflict-of-law vulnerabilities*—requires intellectual rigor and architectural fluency. The end product is not confusion. It is coherence through multilateral calibration.

Critically, this type of complexity does not absolve the client of responsibility. It demands more from them: higher levels of documentation, more sophisticated counsel, and a proactive approach to governance. Structures must be maintained, not merely created. Minutes must be kept. Trustees must be briefed. Compliance reports must be submitted. Advisors must be synchronised. The reward for this effort is not just resilience, but legitimacy. *A well-maintained complex structure is both audit-proof and strategically valuable.*

There is, however, a cautionary edge to this philosophy. *Complexity without clarity is just noise.* Many structures collapse not because they were illegal, but because they were mismanaged. Trustees who don't understand their role. Clients who commingle personal and trust assets. Companies that fail substance requirements. These are not failures of structure—they are failures of execution. Complexity is only powerful when it is matched by *comprehension and care.*

To ensure this, professionals should approach structuring with a mindset closer to systems design than legal drafting. Every layer must serve a function. Every role must be clearly delineated. Every disclosure must be accounted for. Just as engineers build redundancies into critical infrastructure, advisors must build jurisdictional and operational redundancies into legal frameworks. Not to obscure, but to endure.

Ultimately, *compliant complexity is not a loophole—it is a language.* A language spoken by those who understand that the real world is volatile, that single points of failure are unacceptable, and that law—when used intentionally—can be as much a shield as a sword. For those serious about wealth preservation, security, and transgenerational continuity, simplicity is not an ideal. It is a vulnerability. The future belongs to those who can navigate—and master—the art of lawful complexity.

Working With (Not Against) the System

Shows how to ethically use the law's own blind spots and defaults to your benefit

The greatest legal advantages are often not invented—they are discovered. In the world of private wealth, those who succeed most durably are rarely the ones who attempt to outwit the system through evasion or secrecy. Rather, they are the ones who understand the system deeply enough to *cooperate with its internal logic while sidestepping its unintended punishments.* To work with the system is not a concession.

It is a strategy of *asymmetric mastery*—leveraging the law's own architecture to design invisibility, insulation, and lawful advantage.

The core principle is this: *the law is a construct of generalisations*. Statutes, codes, treaties, and regulatory regimes are designed to govern the average case. They are built to be enforceable, not perfect. As a result, legal systems everywhere possess *blind spots, defaults, and discretionary thresholds*—not by negligence, but by necessity. These imperfections are not inherently sinister. They are opportunities for interpretation. And interpretation, handled ethically, becomes a tool for strategic design.

Take, for example, the principle of tax residency. Across the globe, most countries apply residency-based taxation, citizenship-based taxation, or territorial taxation. Each of these systems, however internally consistent, contains built-in assumptions about individual behaviour, location, and reporting. A person who lives in multiple jurisdictions, spends fewer than 183 days in any of them, and earns foreign-source income through structures domiciled elsewhere, may—entirely legally—fall outside of the taxable reach of any one country. That is not avoidance. That is *structural participation* in the rules as they were written. The law cannot demand from a person what it has not anticipated.

This is not a technical loophole—it is a constitutional feature. Courts in common law and civil law jurisdictions alike have ruled, repeatedly, that tax minimisation achieved within the boundaries of the law is not criminal intent. Indeed, the most authoritative legal maxim in this area comes from Lord Tomlin in the 1936 UK case *IRC v Duke of Westminster*: *"Every man is entitled if he can to order his affairs so that the tax attaching under the appropriate Acts is less than it otherwise would be."* What has changed since then is not the principle, but the sophistication required to apply it.

To work with the system, then, is first to *understand what the system cannot do.* It cannot legislate for every anomaly. It cannot foresee all future behaviours. It cannot force individuals to act contrary to their self-interest, provided those actions remain lawful. The system is therefore filled with defaults—rules that only activate if you fail to provide an alternative. Probate is one such example: if you do not establish a trust, the law provides an intestacy framework. If you do not appoint guardianship for your children, the court will decide. If you do not declare your domicile, the system will presume one. *Silence becomes the state's proxy for consent.* But if you articulate your own structures—again, lawfully—you are no longer bound by the system's assumptions. You have overridden the defaults.

That is not resistance. That is participation on superior terms.

There is also an ethical dimension to this philosophy that is routinely overlooked. Too often, public discourse conflates structural design with subversion. This is an error born of moral superficiality. To comply with the law is not merely a minimum threshold—it is a civic posture. But compliance is not passivity. True compliance means understanding the law well enough to align with it on your own terms. Consider the difference between a passive taxpayer who simply remits what their accountant tells them, and a strategic wealth holder who *proactively arranges their affairs to honour the letter of the law while optimising their position within it.* The latter is not more aggressive; they are more *engaged.* It is precisely this level of intentionality that the system, ironically, rewards.

Take international asset protection trusts as an illustration. Jurisdictions such as the Cook Islands, Nevis, and Belize offer trust statutes with unusually strong asset protection features. These laws were not crafted in secrecy; they are published, debated, and internationally recognised. They include specific timeframes for creditor challenges, burden of proof provisions, and conflict-of-law clauses. A person who uses such a trust is not "hiding assets". They are *exercising a legal right to forum selection*—a right embedded in international private law. No legal system can claim to be neutral while denying its subjects the right to choose better protections elsewhere.

Similarly, controlled foreign corporation (CFC) rules, reporting thresholds, and beneficial ownership registries all rely on defined criteria. They do not demand omniscience. They demand *precision.* A structure that stays beneath disclosure thresholds—not by deceit, but by design—is not non-compliant. It is simply *non-triggering.* That is the difference between evasion and discipline. The former conceals. The latter constructs.

Yet to execute this strategy responsibly requires more than technical knowledge. It requires *philosophical clarity.* The question is not merely what the law allows, but how your use of it shapes the world. If wealth holders consistently weaponise complexity only for concealment, they erode the legitimacy of lawful structuring itself. Conversely, if they use these tools to protect their families, their intellectual property, or their philanthropic legacies from capricious regimes or frivolous litigation, then they are enacting *protective pluralism*—an ethos that values self-determination within lawful parameters.

This is where the concept of *regulatory aikido* becomes instructive. Aikido, the Japanese martial art, is based not on resistance but redirection—using the opponent's energy to your advantage. In legal terms, this means *using the inertia and scope of the law itself as a protective force.* For instance, if a foreign jurisdiction offers stronger protections for digital assets, placing an NFT or smart contract-based protocol under that jurisdiction's governance is not about avoidance. It is about aligning with the legal framework that best fits the asset's nature. The result is structural harmony—each asset governed by the law most coherent with its purpose.

Blind spots and defaults also appear in areas as banal as reporting requirements. FATCA, CRS, DAC6—all of these are designed to enhance transparency. But they are also inherently *rule-bound.* They apply based on definable relationships—residency, control, beneficial interest. When you design a structure that separates legal ownership from beneficial enjoyment in accordance with trust law, you are not evading disclosure—you are *structuring around it in full view.* The tax authority sees what you have disclosed. What it cannot see is what was never within its jurisdiction to begin with.

This approach demands a high level of intentionality in professional relationships. Working with the system means choosing advisors who understand this interpretive logic. A lawyer who drafts documents to meet statutory minimums is not the same as one who designs frameworks for multi-jurisdictional durability. An accountant who files returns is not the same as one who maps the tax implications of various domiciles across generational timeframes. A compliance officer who reacts is not the same as one who pre-engineers transparency windows to anticipate regulatory changes. The difference is not academic—it is existential.

The quiet power in this approach is that it *de-escalates conflict.* When your affairs are structured to pre-empt the most common vectors of legal threat—litigation, tax reassessment, expropriation, reputational attack—you are no longer operating from a position of fear. You are operating from foresight. And foresight is what turns the legal system from an adversary into an instrument.

Ultimately, the goal is not to disappear from the system. It is to *design your interaction with it so carefully that your position becomes unassailable.* You are not invisible—you are frictionless. To most observers, you seem to be everywhere and nowhere: present where required, protected where it matters, exposed only where advantageous.

This is not magic. It is mastery. It is what happens when law ceases to be a threat, and becomes a medium.

And to those who say this is too complex, too strategic, or too elite, the answer is simple: the system is already complex. The only choice is whether you drift through it on default settings—or take control of your own operating framework.

Working with the system means playing the long game—*ethically, intelligently, and with eyes wide open.* The future belongs not to those who fight the law, but to those who understand how to *align with its hidden geometry.*

Your Personal Counsel Strategy

Offers a framework for choosing lawyers, advisors, and teams that understand this philosophy of quiet power

The highest form of legal strategy is not found in courtroom theatrics or grand declarations—it is embedded, preemptive, and silent. Wealth, especially when it is mobile, diversified, and designed for generational endurance, demands a very particular kind of counsel. Not just competent legal technicians, but *architects of discretion.* Not simply advisors who know what is allowed, but professionals who understand *why* certain permissions should be exercised *and when they should remain dormant.* In a world where visibility invites risk and sophistication can invite scrutiny, the composition of one's legal and advisory circle becomes a form of self-protection—if not self-definition.

Most wealthy individuals acquire advisors reactively: a lawyer for a property transaction, an accountant for filing taxes, a banker for asset custody. But these roles are transactional by default, not strategic by design. To operate with quiet power—to align one's structure with lawful invisibility and regulatory foresight—requires *an entirely different premise for how counsel is selected and deployed.* You are not buying legal services. You are curating an ecosystem of interpretive intelligence.

The first principle of such a strategy is to reject linear thinking. Wealth today exists across multiple vectors: digital assets, multinational businesses, cross-border residences, philanthropic initiatives, and increasingly, reputational and privacy considerations. Each of these vectors operates under its own legal regime, tax implication, compliance burden, and geopolitical exposure. There is no single advisor who can—or should—manage all these threads. What is needed instead is a *multi-disciplinary structure* where each actor understands their functional depth *and the strategic meta-logic* guiding the entire design.

Choosing personal counsel, then, is less about *what* a lawyer knows and more about *how* they think. Are they structurally literate across jurisdictions, or merely fluent within one? Do they see the law as a sequence of static rules, or as a dynamic environment of incentives and defaults? Do they instinctively seek control through complexity, or clarity through intentional design? These are not soft questions. They are *qualitative proxies* for how your advisor will respond when the landscape changes—when regulation tightens, when litigation arises, or when your wealth structure must flex in response to personal or political shocks.

Consider the difference between two lawyers: one who drafts a standard discretionary trust because "that's what everyone does," and another who designs a hybrid trust with integrated offshore governance, variable protector powers, and succession protocols tied to real-time residency status. Both may technically meet your needs—but only the latter anticipates *what the law doesn't say* and *how it might shift.* That difference is not about cost. It is about *philosophical alignment.*

Quiet power—the core ethic of this book—is built not on secrets but on strategic silence. Your counsel must be selected accordingly. The best advisors are not those who promise total secrecy, but those who understand the nuances of *selective disclosure*, *defensive transparency*, and *jurisdictional separation*. They will not only protect your privacy; they will teach you *why certain forms of visibility are structurally necessary*—for regulatory compliance, legitimacy, or insulation from reputational harm. They know that visibility to regulators is not the same as exposure to threats. They help you remain *auditable to the system, but invisible to predators*.

This requires counsel who are not only legally sharp but emotionally intelligent. Especially in family governance, estate planning, or philanthropic design, decisions are rarely driven by logic alone. They are shaped by fear, ambition, memory, loyalty. Advisors who can read those dynamics—who know when to slow down a structure to accommodate relational pacing, or accelerate it in anticipation of external events—are worth far more than transactional speed. *Emotional fluency is a risk-management skill.*

Equally critical is your advisor's relationship to ambiguity. Any counsel who insists on certainty in cross-border affairs is either inexperienced or disingenuous. The legal landscape is evolving: tax treaties are being renegotiated, beneficial ownership registries are expanding, and financial institutions are increasingly functioning as soft regulators. The question is not whether your structure will ever be questioned—it's whether it was *built to withstand questions before they arise*. Advisors who only see problems once a letter arrives from a tax authority are not strategists; they are liabilities. You want people who *pre-empt stress tests*, who simulate scrutiny before it happens, who understand *which parts of your structure should be defensible by logic, which by law, and which by jurisdictional boundary*.

Another often ignored yet essential criterion is *ego*. Many highly credentialed advisors are deeply uncomfortable operating in service of structures they did not invent. This is dangerous. The counsel you retain must be philosophically aligned with the role of *serving a larger strategy*, not centring their own legal authorship. If your offshore lawyer cannot coordinate comfortably with your tax advisor, or your compliance consultant undermines your estate planner out of professional insecurity, then your risk profile increases *regardless of the technical soundness of each component.* Quiet power depends on harmony across domains.

That harmony is built through *deliberate team design.* High-net-worth families often benefit from establishing an internal general counsel or trusted strategic lead—someone who understands the entire structure and can coordinate external specialists as needed. This person acts as a conductor, ensuring that advice is not only legally accurate but *contextually integrated.* It prevents fragmentation and guards against jurisdictional myopia. Without this role, even the best advisors can end up solving problems in isolation while exposing the client to unintended consequences elsewhere.

A well-formed advisory strategy also requires *jurisdictional diversity.* It is unwise to anchor all legal thinking within one country—even if that country is your current residence or citizenship. Lawyers trained in the UK or United States, for example, often carry assumptions about control, fiduciary duty, or tax planning that do not translate cleanly across borders. Including counsel from civil law jurisdictions, trust jurisdictions, and non-Western financial centres provides a more complete risk lens. It also forces your structure to be legible from multiple legal angles—a critical advantage in an age of regulatory convergence.

Finally, the question of trust. This is not about blind loyalty or personal rapport. It is about structural trust: *can this advisor function with your interests in mind even when doing so complicates their own role?* Will they flag a conflict they are not legally required to disclose? Will they recommend a simpler solution that earns them less billable time?

Will they step back when another expert's domain is more relevant? These are behavioural markers of long-term alignment. Advisors who pass this test are not employees. They are *custodians of strategy*.

And strategy, here, means more than wealth preservation. It means reputation management. Succession integrity. Jurisdictional neutrality. Philosophical coherence. You are not merely asking for tax savings or legal protections. You are building a structure that should reflect your values, safeguard your legacy, and remain adaptive across decades. The people you involve must be selected as if you were choosing *the future guardians of your decisions*—because in many ways, you are.

Quiet power begins with internal clarity. But it is sustained by external discernment. The law will always contain noise—overlapping jurisdictions, shifting rules, competing claims. Your counsel must bring signal. Choose them accordingly. Not for their title. Not for their firm. But for their *ability to make complexity protective, silence strategic, and legality sovereign.*

Chapter 11
In Case of Emergency – Resilience Tactics for Wealth Survival

The illusion of permanence may well be the most costly delusion in the entire scaffolding of private wealth. Structures—legal, financial, reputational—are too often erected as if tomorrow will unfold more or less like today, give or take a headline or two. But the foundation of resilience lies in a refusal to mythologise stability. Wealth doesn't hover, untethered, in some sterile vacuum. It is enmeshed in political systems, legal regimes, infrastructural realities, shifting cultural sentiments, and brittle technologies—any of which can unravel with little notice. The most intelligent wealth strategies don't depend on continuity. They are engineered for rupture.

That is, in essence, the terrain we explore here: how to think structurally when things don't just veer off course, but come undone entirely. Not the garden-variety tremors—market downturns, regulatory tweaks, the odd audit—but the tectonic kind. What happens if your assets are frozen without warning? If your main jurisdiction destabilises overnight? If a reputational crisis strips you of access to capital, however temporarily? Such scenarios might sound theatrical to the unseasoned, but for those stewarding serious, mobile capital, they're less about panic and more about prudence.

Resilience, in this domain, has nothing to do with blind optimism or institutional trust. It is instead defined by layered optionality: the systematic embedding of redundancies, exits, and counterweights into the very DNA of your architecture. Not because failure is inevitable—but because you refuse to be at its mercy when it arrives.

We begin with what may be one of the most quietly potent strategies available today: Second-Layer Contingencies. These are the shadow structures—legally distinct, pre-positioned, and intentionally dormant. They might include reserve banking arrangements in politically neutral territories, alternative trusteeships already in motion, or shelf companies with no current operational purpose, yet fully compliant and ready to activate. Their elegance lies in their silence. Like a fire door in a quiet hallway, their value is not in constant use, but in reliable presence. When crisis strikes, they turn existential risk into a solvable logistics problem.

And then there's something more radical: the Exile Protocol. It's not metaphor. It's a stress test. The prompt is blunt: if you had 72 hours to leave your country—no forewarning, no favours—could your financial life come with you? Would your structures function without you at the helm? Are your cryptographic keys decentralised, your digital residency pathways unlocked, your governance frameworks unbound by your geography? The Exile Protocol isn't dystopian theatre. It's a tool of sober design. It separates those who merely own assets from those who understand sovereignty.

Let's be clear: this is not an argument for fear-based strategy. It is a case for first-principles thinking. Which brings us to something more philosophical—The Moral of Redundancy. In mainstream finance, redundancy is often equated with waste. Two accounts where one might do. Parallel systems that seem to slow things down. But in complex systems—ecological, electrical, or financial—redundancy is precisely what makes survival possible. It's the humility to admit that no matter how brilliant your assumptions, the world is still more unpredictable than your models. And that's a moral insight as much as a technical one.

From here, the implications become pragmatic. How to build bank relationships across multiple jurisdictions that are insulated against capital controls. How to fragment control rights and beneficial ownership to mitigate direct seizure. How to design trustee relationships and nominee appointments that don't trip automatic disclosures under pressure. How to install off-grid access mechanisms—dead man switches, decentralised signatories—that allow movement of key assets when you're not available to do it yourself. These aren't for the conspiratorially minded. They are sober, practical measures for anyone paying attention to the merging trajectories of transparency mandates, political risk, and reputation-driven vulnerabilities.

The underlying thesis, though largely unspoken, is this: resilience isn't a product. It's a cultivated mindset. Too often, emergency planning is delegated to others—insurance providers, wealth advisors, compliance departments. But true strategic autonomy begins when you yourself understand how your structures behave under strain. When you're not just briefed on what's legal today, but when you have a map of how legality itself might shift tomorrow. Because the future rarely changes the facts—it changes the meanings.

You must prepare not only for risk, but for redefinition. For the moment when lawful becomes suspect. When the private becomes reportable. When the protected becomes politically expendable. The lesson is not merely to be compliant, but to be adaptive—to have built in such a way that you can reposition without rupture.

Legal form, in isolation, will no longer suffice. What matters is how intelligently your wealth moves, how discreetly your structures respond, how robustly your identity—your family, your freedom, your intentions—can function beyond any single bank, nation, or advisory firm.

This chapter is not about contingency plans in the narrow sense. It's about a philosophical stance. A commitment to structural realism. A willingness to imagine interruption not as exception but as inevitability. It's about building systems of capital that anticipate friction, rather than collapsing at its arrival. That understand the paradox: the most powerful safeguards are often invisible, and the smartest structures are the ones no one notices—until they're needed.

And most of all, it's about responsibility. For the design of your own survivability. For not outsourcing your sovereignty to institutions whose incentives don't always align with your own. This is not alarmism. It's architectural maturity. A shift from passive security to active structural intelligence.

Stress-Test Your Empire

Most people believe their wealth strategy is strong because it hasn't been tested. That illusion—of strength mistaken for durability—is perhaps the most dangerous form of complacency in capital preservation. Structures that perform well under normal market conditions or tax audits may quietly disintegrate under actual stress: litigation, sanctions, political seizure, or catastrophic financial downturns. To operate in today's environment without a formalised, adversarial rehearsal of your systems is not just negligent—it is *arrogant.* The real question is not "how well is your empire performing?" but rather *"how well would it survive a multi-vector assault?"*

Stress-testing your wealth structure is not paranoia—it is discipline. And more than that, it is strategy. Military war games, pressure testing in engineering, and scenario planning in aviation all share a singular logic: *resilience cannot be assumed; it must be demonstrated under force.* For wealth, that force may arrive as a lawsuit, a reputational attack, a banking freeze, or a shift in political tides. The aim of stress-testing is to rehearse those shocks on paper—before they happen in reality.

To do this well, one must abandon the comfort of assumptions and adopt the mindset of a hostile interrogator. What would an adversarial regulator see if they scrutinised your asset flow? Could a court claim you were the beneficial owner of an entity you thought was safely distanced? If your most trusted jurisdiction imposed sudden capital controls, what liquidity would remain accessible? And perhaps most importantly, how quickly—*and legally*—could you regain control in a crisis?

This chapter introduces a framework that moves beyond the theoretical. It is a working checklist—not one filled with banalities or generalised 'tips', but a series of conceptual load-bearing questions designed to identify real structural vulnerabilities. These are not questions about wealth accumulation. They are about *wealth survivability*.

We begin with the foundational principle: *jurisdictional spread is not diversification unless it is asymmetric*. Many high-net-worth individuals believe they have international diversification because they hold assets in multiple countries. But if all those countries are allied through shared intelligence networks (such as the OECD's Common Reporting Standard), legal reciprocity, or political sympathies, then geographic spread does *not* equal protection. Effective jurisdictional strategy demands *contradiction*. If one node is under attack, another must remain legally uncooperative—not due to criminal intent, but to maintain lawful insulation.

The second axis is *control redundancy*. In engineering, redundancy means the duplication of critical components to maintain function under failure. In wealth architecture, it means retaining operational access to accounts, trustees, signatories, and key documents across different pathways. If your entire empire is reliant on a single custodian bank or cloud-based vault, you are not sovereign—you are merely unchallenged. True control requires contingency: multiple access routes, non-correlated gatekeepers, and pre-scripted emergency triggers that shift authority if a party becomes unavailable, compromised, or hostile.

Next comes the *liquidity stress*. Can you access 30% of your net liquidity within 48 hours without triggering tax events, reporting thresholds, or reputational alerts? Many structures look clean on paper but are fatally illiquid. Real estate portfolios in politically unstable zones, equity in opaque private trusts, or complex offshore holding companies with frozen banking infrastructure can all function well—until they don't. What you need is not just capital, but *usable capital under duress*. That is a very different filter.

Now consider *legal survivability*. If your name becomes publicly associated with scandal—whether justified or malicious—how many of your structures are legally insulated from reputational risk? This is not simply a matter of hiding ownership, which is both unethical and legally dangerous. It is about designing structures where *beneficial ownership is distinct from visible control.* Through the careful use of nominees, directed trusts, or fiduciary segregation, one can ensure that even under reputational attack, the assets themselves remain untouched—because their legal logic has been architected for separation, not concealment.

Let us now interrogate the *human dimension.* Who are the people who hold keys to your system? Do they understand your values, your tolerances, and your philosophy of discretion? Stress-testing your empire also means stress-testing *your advisors.* If your trust lawyer panics under media scrutiny, if your banker has no framework for operating under political seizure, if your accountant defers entirely to compliance checklists without understanding your structural intent—you are not protected, you are exposed through delegation. *Quiet power requires counsel who can perform under pressure.*

One critical layer is psychological: *your own response under pressure.* Have you rehearsed this? Do you have decision protocols, contingency checklists, offshore communication networks, or encrypted storage systems that you can access in exile? If you had to leave your country tomorrow, could you reconstruct your empire from a laptop and a satellite phone? This isn't fantasy; it is operational clarity. And the act of stress-testing must include *you*, the principal—not just the paper.

Now, let us examine specific adversarial scenarios and the structural responses they demand:

Civil Litigation: If sued, can your wealth structure demonstrate clear arm's length separation between you and your assets? Is there plausible fiduciary distance? Are trustees independently located and documented as acting without your direct control?

Tax Authority Audit: If audited, can your asset flows withstand a forensic review? Are there ambiguous transactions, intra-family transfers, or routing decisions that would appear suspicious without clear legal narrative and supporting documentation?

Bank Freeze or Seizure: If one of your major accounts were frozen, how long before operational liquidity is restored elsewhere? Are your banking relationships diversified across jurisdictions with differing regulatory postures? Do you maintain active banking credentials in neutral states?

Political Sanctions or Exile: If politically targeted, are your residencies and citizenships activated and in good standing? Are your key documents replicated across legal vaults or diplomatic storage? Are there dead man triggers or power-of-attorney structures that activate in your absence?

Each of these questions is more than academic. They are *diagnostic.* And while most readers may never face all of them, *those who prepare for them hold a quiet strategic advantage over those who do not.*

The final insight is perhaps the most difficult: stress-testing cannot be fully outsourced. While you will rightly rely on expert advisors to guide you, the integrity of your empire depends on *your understanding of its logic.* You must know the why behind the structure—not just the names of the entities, but the philosophy behind their arrangement. Only then can you test that logic under pressure. Only then can you adapt when the terrain shifts.

This is not about fearing collapse. It is about refusing to be caught off-guard by it. Stress-testing your empire is not a luxury. It is a fiduciary responsibility—*to your future self, your heirs, and your mission.* Done well, it is not merely protective. It is *clarifying.* It reveals weaknesses, strengthens governance, and forces a level of operational honesty that many families of wealth have never been forced to confront—until it is too late.

And so the question remains: not "is your structure compliant?", but *"is it survivable?"* That is the standard. That is the test. And that is where true wealth protection begins.

Second-Layer Contingencies

Resilience is not redundancy—it is the intelligent layering of function. In the architecture of enduring wealth, nothing should hinge on a single point of failure. The more sophisticated a system becomes, the more vulnerable it is to the silent failure of one overlooked cog: a signatory lost, an account frozen, a jurisdiction compromised, a fiduciary who turns rogue or incapacitated. True sovereignty demands a second layer—not a clone of the first, but an alternate logic of continuity. *Second-layer contingencies are not optional upgrades. They are foundational to any strategy that aspires to be robust under real-world pressure.*

To design second-layer contingencies well is to admit an uncomfortable truth: *no structure is as secure as it appears in peacetime.* A primary account with excellent reporting, strong legal wrappers, and the right jurisdiction may still be locked for review if a single transaction is flagged. A well-crafted trust may become an entanglement if the trustee is compromised, unresponsive, or under pressure from local regulators. Nesting structures, in this context, is not about obscurity—it is about *operational agility.* When your first layer is disrupted, does the second layer activate quietly and legally, or are you left exposed, with your tools frozen mid-crisis?

The central idea of second-layer design is not about hiding wealth. It's about ensuring *access and function under duress.* Think like an engineer: planes don't carry extra engines because they expect them to fail, but because the cost of not having one if failure occurs is existential. Wealth structures should be built with the same logic—where secondary systems are dormant, autonomous, and *ready*.

Take secondary accounts, for instance. A common mistake is duplicating banking relationships across the same institution or within the same jurisdiction. This is not contingency; it's correlation. A regulatory freeze, court order, or compliance audit can cascade through these accounts in a matter of hours. A second-layer banking relationship must be *jurisdictionally, institutionally, and operationally distinct*. If your primary accounts are in Switzerland, your contingency accounts might be in Singapore—structured through a separate holding entity, with independent signatories and access mechanisms.

More advanced families implement *cascading liquidity thresholds*. For example, if primary liquidity is inaccessible for more than 72 hours, predefined protocols activate to release funds from a secondary vehicle. These vehicles are not backups in name only—they are deliberately funded, legally ringfenced, and kept lean enough to respond without triggering visibility or bureaucratic friction. This is where backup trusts come in.

A backup trust is not simply a clone of the main family trust. It is a *differentiated risk profile with an autonomous trustee relationship*. Ideally, it exists under a different trust law regime, one that is strategically dissonant with the jurisdiction of the primary trust. If your first trust is in the Channel Islands, the second-layer trust might be under Cook Islands law or a U.S. domestic asset protection trust—chosen for distinct legal characteristics, not brand familiarity.

This distinction becomes critical in litigation scenarios. Suppose your primary trust becomes entangled in a lawsuit through claims of constructive control or fraudulent conveyance. A backup trust—properly designed and funded well in advance—can remain untouchable, provided it operates under a clear, independent mandate with credible fiduciary distance. *That is not loophole design. That is legal foresight.*

Nested entities further strengthen second-layer strategies. A nested structure is not about complexity for its own sake. It is about creating internal compartments that isolate specific assets or functions. Think of it like a submarine: if one chamber floods, others remain sealed. In practice, this might mean separating intellectual property holdings, operating companies, and investment portfolios into distinct legal wrappers—each with its own governance, reporting, and jurisdictional logic.

These compartments also allow for tailored responses. If one sector of your wealth is attacked—say, a business facing a class action lawsuit—it does not automatically jeopardise real estate assets or passive investment income. This isn't just legal safety. It is *psychological clarity* under crisis. Nested structures reduce panic by containing damage.

A critical feature of second-layer design is *trigger logic*. Many structures exist on paper but fail in execution because no one knows when or how to activate them. A second-layer plan should include pre-agreed conditions for activation, protocols for communication, and designated individuals (or entities) with the authority to act. These should be reviewed, rehearsed, and legally documented. Crisis is not the time to read instructions for the first time.

There is also a *human layer* to consider. Many wealth structures rely too heavily on a few key individuals—lawyers, trustees, CFOs, or patriarchs/matriarchs—whose unavailability can paralyse operations. A well-constructed second layer anticipates this. It incorporates successor signatories, backup trustees, alternative legal counsel, and even *disaster-tested digital access infrastructure*. Your wealth's continuity should not depend on the health, goodwill, or availability of any one person.

Modern second-layer strategies are increasingly integrating *technological redundancy*. Digital vaults (such as decentralised encrypted storage), cold wallets, and time-locked smart contracts allow for asset access and transfer outside traditional banking systems. These tools are not for speculation—they are for *resilience*. For example, a cold wallet containing stablecoins or tokenised sovereign bonds, stored offline but activated through a smart contract in the event of a bank failure, can serve as a tactical liquidity tool during blackouts.

Yet none of this matters without clarity of *ownership logic*. Who truly controls what? Who is the legal signatory, the beneficial owner, the operational controller? Structures often fall apart because they are misunderstood—not by outsiders, but by the family itself. A second-layer plan should be accompanied by plain-language documentation: a private "continuity brief" explaining what exists, how it works, who holds the keys, and when to use them. Confidential, yes—but accessible to those who need it, when they need it.

Critics argue that such layering is unnecessary for the average high-net-worth individual. But *average* is the wrong metric. Risk is not distributed evenly—it is asymmetric, situational, and reputational. If you operate in multiple jurisdictions, hold politically sensitive assets, or have a complex family structure, your exposure is not theoretical. It is *probable*, given a long enough timeline. Second-layer contingencies are not for the paranoid. They are for the *prepared*.

This preparedness has a moral component. Second-layer contingencies are not designed to evade accountability or responsibility. They are designed to uphold *stewardship*. When you are responsible for significant capital, whether personal or generational, your duty is not just to grow it—it is to *protect it through foresight*. Contingency is not about pessimism. It is about *designing for the unexpected without sacrificing ethics, legality, or integrity*.

Ultimately, second-layer contingencies represent a quiet kind of power—not loud, not public, but deeply strategic. They allow you to respond with precision instead of panic. They reduce fragility without resorting to opacity. And most importantly, they honour the truth that *wealth is not secure simply because it is large, but because it is wisely architected.*

Ask yourself: if your primary systems failed tomorrow—by force, fraud, politics, or simple error—what remains operational? Who has access? What remains protected? What continues? If the answers are unclear, you don't need more complexity. You need *contingency*.

The Exile Protocol

If you had 72 hours to leave your country—what would break, and what would function?

It's not a rhetorical question. It's a forensic diagnostic tool designed to measure *systemic fragility* across your wealth, citizenship, communication, and physical security infrastructure. The Exile Protocol is not about paranoia or prepping for Armageddon. It is about clear-sighted scenario planning for plausible future disruptions—geopolitical, legal, or reputational—that could force a sudden dislocation from the nation-state you rely on today.

We live in a world where mobility is both increasingly accessible and perilously constrained. Passports, banking access, personal safety, asset protection, legal representation—all are jurisdictionally bound. You can have impeccable structures in place and still be immobilised when those structures rely on the cooperation of a single government, a local notary, or a frozen digital identity.

The Exile Protocol poses a deceptively simple challenge: *Could you function—legally, financially, operationally—if you were forced to evacuate with little more than what fits in a backpack and what you remember in your head?*

This is not fantasy. History is thick with examples: from Jewish families fleeing Nazi Germany to Hong Kong dissidents transferring digital assets via encrypted seed phrases; from Chilean executives during the Pinochet coup to Russian entrepreneurs facing international sanctions. In every instance, *the ability to move was inseparable from the ability to act. Those who planned survived not because they had more, but because their systems were mobile.*

So, what does it mean to *plan for exile*—and more importantly, how do you do it without turning your life into a bunker?

The Exile Protocol begins with a core insight: *Jurisdictional concentration is vulnerability.* The moment your identity, wealth, access, and operations are all tethered to one legal system, one language, or one cultural assumption, you are exposed. You may be compliant today, even admired, but law is not fixed—neither is power. Reputational winds shift. Political climates harden. Compliance regimes expand their reach, often retroactively.

To be clear: this is not a call for escape, nor a strategy for criminal evasion. It is an exercise in *responsible detachment*: designing sovereignty *within* the law so that you are not wholly at the mercy of any one nation's political, financial, or ideological upheaval.

At its most practical level, The Exile Protocol begins by stress-testing four foundational domains:

1. Identity Mobility

Do you hold more than one citizenship? If not, could you acquire a second within 12 months through legal investment, ancestry, or extraordinary talent channels? Citizenship-by-investment programmes are often viewed solely as status symbols—but they are strategic infrastructure. A second passport is not just a travel document; it is *a legal identity contingency*. It can mean the difference between having a legal right to enter a country or being stateless in an airport lounge.

Equally important are permanent residencies with path-to-citizenship timelines. Portugal's Golden Visa, Uruguay's residency-for-presence model, or Thailand's Elite Visa offer vastly different geographies, tax environments, and geopolitical alignments. A strong protocol balances at least two jurisdictions: one for safety, one for optionality.

2. Asset Accessibility

Imagine needing to access liquidity from abroad while under investigation, blocked from using your domestic banking infrastructure. Could you do it—without triggering visibility that exposes your entire portfolio?

Assets must not just be safe; they must be *liquidatable without signalling*. This requires secondary accounts, legal wrappers in jurisdictions that respect privacy while maintaining OECD-aligned compliance, and digital wallets with multi-signature redundancy. Your wealth's portability is its *true resilience*. A private trust in Guernsey with an overseas trustee may technically exist, but if the trustee refuses to act under pressure—or worse, complies with an overly broad freezing order—your sovereignty evaporates.

Designing for exile means ensuring there are *functioning pathways to funds* that don't rely on a phone call to the wrong government, the goodwill of a single custodian, or visibility in a country where your status has just turned volatile.

3. Communications Autonomy

Too often overlooked is the reality that *data is a jurisdictional asset*. Your phone, your email, your cloud storage—are all tethered to infrastructure controlled by nation-states. In a forced-exit scenario, your ability to communicate privately, without surveillance or disruption, becomes existential.

The Exile Protocol demands encrypted, jurisdiction-agnostic systems: secure messaging apps like Signal or Threema, password vaults stored via decentralised networks, and digital identity tokens that can be authenticated independently of a compromised device or SIM card.

Even more, your communication infrastructure must be *redundantly accessible*: ideally through memorised seed phrases, biometric-recovery mechanisms, and pre-shared contingency plans with trusted individuals. Think like an intelligence operative, not because you're hiding, but because *you're designing for durability in degraded conditions*.

4. Legal Readiness

If you needed to prove ownership, instruct counsel, or authorise the movement of assets while in exile, could you? Who knows where the documents are? Who understands the system well enough to execute it without calling you every five minutes?

The Exile Protocol requires a *continuity dossier*: a private, legally robust instruction set distributed across secure channels. This includes notarised powers of attorney, digital signatures that remain valid in alternate jurisdictions, and pre-retained legal advisors across at least two legal ecosystems. Your legal authority must not depend on your physical presence.

And then there is the *human capital layer*: your family, your team, your advisors. Who stays? Who travels? Who knows how to lead in your absence? Exile is not just an individual test. It is a system-wide simulation. And in many cases, the weakest link is not infrastructure—but untrained human response.

Some may argue this is all too extreme, that planning for exile suggests a life of anxiety and mistrust. But that is a misunderstanding of what this protocol offers. The purpose is not fear—it is *clarity*. Just as military units train for worst-case scenarios to perform better under normal conditions, scenario planning sharpens *every other part* of your system. It clarifies what is essential. It exposes latent fragilities. And it provides *the confidence to act decisively* should crisis erupt.

Crucially, the Exile Protocol is also a values filter. When everything is stripped down—your location, your language, your leverage—what remains? What are you committed to protect? What are you willing to rebuild? The 72-hour window forces existential questions: What matters most, and what was only performance?

Throughout history, those who survive exile don't just adapt. They often emerge more focused, more integrated, more deliberate in how they design their next move. Think of Victor Hugo in Guernsey, Nabokov in America, or the wave of Hong Kong entrepreneurs now reshaping Singapore's financial ecosystem. *Exile, properly understood, is not disappearance—it is recalibration.*

For the modern sovereign individual, The Exile Protocol is not about hiding. It's about *designing life so that it can continue—with integrity, legality, and agency—regardless of what regime controls the airspace*. If your structures can pass the 72-hour test, they're likely to function in any other scenario too. If they can't, the question isn't if you'll face risk—but when.

You don't need to live in fear to prepare. You need to build as if *sovereignty is something you steward, not something you assume*. Because one day—quietly, suddenly, or predictably—you may have to walk away from your country. And when that day comes, everything you've built must either come with you or be left behind.

Choose now. Design wisely.

The Moral of Redundancy

Redundancy is not inefficiency. It is civilisation's insurance policy—an architecture of margin, optionality, and foresight, designed not for paranoia but for permanence.

In wealth strategy, the idea of doing something "twice" often evokes discomfort. We've been trained—by efficiency-maximising economics, minimalist design, and lean startup philosophy—to equate duplication with waste. Yet this thinking, while elegant in theory, collapses under volatility. When systems fail, it is rarely for lack of optimisation. They fail for lack of resilience.

At the elite level of wealth planning, redundancy is not a flaw—it is *a design ethic.* It signals seriousness about permanence, about stewardship, about responsibility not just to self, but to lineage, to partners, to the complexity of the modern world. Redundancy is the quiet architecture of sovereign families, decentralised organisations, and multi-jurisdictional investors who understand that *single points of failure are the enemy of sovereignty.*

This subchapter does not advocate duplicating everything blindly. Instead, it argues that layered safety—redundant accounts, redundant identities, redundant infrastructure—is not only practical, but *moral.* Not because we fear collapse, but because we respect the unpredictable terrain through which capital, law, and politics now move.

From Aviation to Asset Protection: Why Redundancy Matters

Every commercial aircraft carries at least three independent flight control systems, two navigation radios, and multiple hydraulic backups. Not because airlines are inefficient, but because they are serious about *not crashing.* Aviation treats redundancy as sacred. Not one pilot has ever complained about having a second altimeter when the first goes dark.

Apply the same principle to wealth. If your family office operates from a single legal jurisdiction, if your personal liquidity relies on one bank, if your offshore trust hinges on a single point of contact—you are flying blind in bad weather with one dial. That may be fine in calm conditions, but *resilience is not tested in calm conditions.*

The question is not whether your structures are efficient on paper. The question is whether they survive stress—regulatory change, reputational attack, custodial freeze, or political instability. And the answer, in nearly every case, comes down to *redundancy*.

Redundancy as a Form of Respect

At its core, the philosophy of redundancy is about respect—for the complexity of reality, for the fallibility of systems, and for the stakes of getting it wrong. To build redundancy is to acknowledge that even the best structures—legal, financial, or technological—are susceptible to disruption, misinterpretation, or failure.

It is no accident that the most enduring institutions—central banks, military intelligence agencies, diplomatic corps—are redundancy-obsessed. They rotate personnel, replicate secure comms, maintain shadow copies, and simulate failure modes regularly. Not because they expect to fail, but because *they cannot afford not to survive.*

For the serious wealth holder, this is not paranoia. It is *governance maturity*.

Case Study: The Dual Trustee Framework

Consider a high-net-worth individual who establishes a private trust in Jersey with discretionary powers held by a single offshore trustee. All appears robust—until the jurisdiction passes sweeping new legislation increasing disclosure requirements, and the trustee, under political pressure, halts disbursements. Access is stalled. Courts are consulted. Months pass. The structure holds—but the individual's sovereignty *does not.*

Now contrast this with a similar trust—same assets, same jurisdiction—but with a dual-trustee model: one primary, one standby, operating under a mirror deed in a separate jurisdiction, with automated trigger clauses and pre-approved legal validity. The cost difference? Marginal. The outcome? Uninterrupted continuity. *This is the moral of redundancy.*

The Psychology of Redundancy Aversion

Why, then, is redundancy so often resisted?

Partly, it's cultural. Modern professional training—from MBA curricula to engineering workflows—teaches us to optimise. Duplication is seen as lack of rigour. The ideal is sleek, consolidated, efficient.

But wealth management is not a start-up. It is not a software sprint. It is, if done properly, *intergenerational infrastructure.* And infrastructure is not optimised for elegance; it is optimised for survival. Bridges are over-engineered. Water systems are looped. Data is backed up threefold.

Redundancy is not wasteful when the thing being protected is irreplaceable.

Redundancy vs. Hoarding: A Crucial Distinction

Critically, redundancy is not hoarding. Hoarding is reactive, disorganised, and emotionally driven. It creates chaos, not resilience. Redundancy, by contrast, is *planned, deliberate, strategic.* It is a system of *fallbacks*, not a pile of extras.

A second residency is redundancy. Ten shell companies with no purpose is hoarding. A secondary access key to your crypto wallet is redundancy. Fourteen cold wallets scattered without documentation is noise. The difference lies in intentionality—and the ability of the system to *function under pressure.*

Moral Clarity Through Redundancy

The real insight here is that redundancy is not just technical—it is *moral.* Why?

Because the absence of redundancy often places others at risk. Your family. Your clients. Your philanthropic obligations. When a patriarch centralises all access, and dies suddenly with no redundancy in place, the family does not just lose control. They lose trust, cohesion, time, and sometimes decades of compounding capital.

To plan for failure is *an act of care.* It signals seriousness. It acknowledges your fallibility without diminishing your authority. It says: *I don't assume everything will go to plan. I take stewardship seriously enough to prepare for when it doesn't.*

Three Layers of Intelligent Redundancy

For those seeking to apply this principle practically, redundancy operates at three essential levels:

1. *Structural Redundancy* — Jurisdictional diversification of entities, trustees, and residencies. This includes backup legal domiciles, asset-holding companies with mirrored mandates, and secondary citizenships with path-to-engagement features.

2. *Operational Redundancy* — Duplicated access pathways for digital assets, financial authorisations, and institutional relationships. This may include secondary signatories, multi-factor authentication using multiple geographies, and legally-valid proxies held in escrow.

3. *Human Redundancy* — Trained successors, empowered lieutenants, and contingency instruction sets. Wealth is often undone not by legal design, but by *lack of capacity in people.* Redundancy must be human as much as it is legal.

Conclusion Without Calling It That

You are not redundant because you create redundancy. You are responsible.

You are not wasteful because you plan fallbacks. You are wise.

Redundancy is not fear-based. It is *reality-based.* The world is complex. Systems fail. Laws change. Relationships fracture. In that context, redundancy is the quiet language of the prepared.

In truth, there is no permanence without redundancy. What survives—what endures—is not the sleekest structure, but the one built to lose a part and still function. That is the heart of sovereign architecture. Not just having something—but *being able to keep it under stress.*

Redundancy doesn't ask: "What's the best-case scenario?" It asks: "When the worst happens, what still works?"

The answer to that is not luck. It is design. Thoughtful, layered, mature design. And that, ultimately, is not just technical strategy. *It is the ethics of responsibility in an unpredictable world.*

Chapter 12
The Quiet Billionaire Mindset – Principles for the Next Era

Wealth, in its conventional pursuit, has become misaligned with the very environment in which it now must be preserved. The tactics that once elevated prior generations—high-octane returns, conspicuous dominance, the almost theatrical declaration of success—are no longer just losing their edge. In today's climate, saturated by systemic volatility, digital hypervisibility, and a kind of cultural exhaustion, these strategies are becoming liabilities. This chapter is not a sermon on motivation or grit. It is a strategic reckoning—a pivot away from performative success and towards principled endurance; away from volume and towards nuance; from extraction to deliberate construction.

The core proposition is unflinching in its clarity: the most resilient wealth today is not the most rapid, nor the most optimised, nor even the most diversified. It is the most intentionally structured. Quietly so. Thoughtfully, even artfully, so. It is wealth that resists detection not through concealment, but through design. What's being advocated here is not a retreat from ambition, but a redirection—a move from trying to outshine to learning how to outlast.

This isn't about romanticising restraint or engaging in curated humility. The figure of the "quiet billionaire" is not some eccentric introvert cloaked in anonymity, nor a monk draped in cashmere. It is, rather, a strategic archetype. A conscious choice to forgo spectacle in favour of sovereignty. Not a withdrawal from power, but an elevation of it—channeled, precise, and anchored in integrity. This isn't asceticism. It's engineering.

It marks a deeper shift: from wealth as spectacle to wealth as substrate. Not the shining facade, but the architecture beneath a life that answers to no script but its own. The visible trappings of success—recognition, applause, social signalling—may still seduce, but they no longer insulate. And insulation, now more than ever, is the measure of maturity.

To move in this direction requires not just a new playbook, but a different question altogether: What would it mean to build capital structures not to impress, but to endure? What if the goal wasn't to be seen owning, but to remain sovereign over what matters, without having to advertise that control?

The challenge, of course, is that endurance isn't flashy. It doesn't lend itself to headlines or algorithms. It demands patience, discretion, a tolerance for being underestimated. It demands the discipline to let go of the need for narrative triumph—and instead pursue structural clarity. That kind of wealth doesn't need defending. It defends itself.

And so, the invitation here is subtle but radical: to step away from the compulsion to outperform, and instead cultivate the resilience to persist. Not through hiding, and certainly not through cynicism, but by crafting ecosystems of capital that are legally elegant, psychologically liberating, and ethically defensible. That kind of wealth does not announce itself. It simply survives—quietly, intelligently, and on its own terms.

The Fallacy of the Next Big Yield

Contemporary financial culture is addicted to immediacy. Risk models are compressed into weeks. Success is benchmarked quarterly. Tech valuations swing violently on a whisper. In this atmosphere, the person who *does nothing*—who holds, watches, refines—is seen as passive. But true wealth preservation often involves subtractive discipline: not buying, not chasing, not intervening.

Too many asset holders have internalised a false equivalence between *motion* and *mastery*. The result is portfolios riddled with fragile leverage, entities formed without sovereignty in mind, and decision-making driven by dopamine rather than design. These are not investors; they are speculators in drag.

The first provocation of this chapter is this: *What would your capital look like if you stopped chasing yield altogether?* What if the goal wasn't accumulation for its own sake, but the crafting of a coherent future ecosystem—of values, relationships, and assets—that could survive you? The answer is not an investment thesis. It is a worldview.

Quiet Growth as Strategic Advantage

There is a critical distinction between *getting rich* and *building wealth.* The former can happen overnight. The latter cannot. Wealth—real, transferable, intergenerational wealth—is an act of *slow accretion.* It involves strategic redundancy, jurisdictional diversification, embedded legal foresight, and infrastructural patience. None of this makes headlines. That's exactly why it works.

Quiet growth rejects both the spectacle of sudden gain and the austerity of permanent retreat. It is not about hiding. It is about *detaching from public metrics as the measure of value.* A well-built holding company in Liechtenstein may never trend on social media, but it will outlast the flamboyant founder whose assets are still personally held in Delaware and broadcast monthly on LinkedIn.

Examples abound. Consider the private European dynasties whose capital has moved silently through trusts, foundations, and tax-exempt vehicles for 150 years. Or the discreet Singaporean family offices that control vast infrastructure portfolios without ever appearing in rankings. These actors understand something profound: *visibility is not influence. Design is.*

The Psychological Economics of Silence

To live quietly is not to renounce ambition; it is to master the conditions under which ambition is meaningful. The quiet billionaire mindset reframes wealth not as performance, but as *infrastructure for freedom.* This infrastructure does not crave applause. It craves resilience. It is less concerned with winning and more concerned with *not losing what matters most*—time, privacy, mobility, dignity.

This philosophy also liberates one from the corrosive economics of comparison. When wealth is internalised as a public narrative—when every acquisition must be signalled, every move defended, every win amplified—then wealth becomes *a liability of the ego.* Quiet wealth, in contrast, is unburdened by audience. It is private not because it is secretive, but because it is *secure enough not to need approval.*

This approach is not theoretical. Numerous studies in behavioural economics demonstrate that financial satisfaction correlates poorly with absolute wealth and strongly with perceived autonomy and control. By engineering wealth structures that minimise reputational exposure, reduce operational dependence, and allow for dignified silence, one regains *psychological sovereignty*—an asset more scarce than yield.

Designing for Legacy, Not Reaction

The world is changing too fast to build for speed. The serious question is not, "What will return 20% next year?" but rather, *"What will still serve my descendants 60 years from now—even if no one ever hears my name?"* That question reshapes everything. It reorients planning around durability, not novelty. It rewards system design over personal flair. It prizes coherence over expansion.

This is where architecture replaces ambition. Holding structures become legally multilingual. Trustees are rotated. Multiple residencies are maintained not to escape tax but to secure mobility. Documents are drafted with succession triggers, power contingencies, and escape clauses—not because collapse is likely, but because *it is plausible.* None of this looks like success on a spreadsheet. But it is the foundation of a *sovereign life.*

Wealth, in this model, becomes less about the person and more about *the protocol.* It is sustained by rhythm, not reaction. It is informed by philosophy, not price. And its true test is not growth in a boom, but *stability under siege.*

Living with Dignity in a Loud World

We now live in an environment where self-worth is confused with visibility, where algorithmic approval substitutes for genuine accomplishment, and where to be unknown is often equated with failure. The quiet billionaire rejects this framework entirely.

To live quietly is not to vanish—it is to *redefine success as internal coherence.* It is to craft a life where wealth amplifies one's values, not one's visibility. Where freedom is experienced privately, not paraded publicly. Where legacy is embedded structurally, not scripted theatrically.

There is immense dignity in knowing you have nothing to prove. In knowing your assets are protected, your family is provided for, your advisors are aligned, and your life is your own. That dignity is not born from status. It is born from *clarity*—about what matters, what endures, and what no external applause can ever provide.

What This Chapter Offers

This final chapter is not a summary. It is a reorientation. You will not find hacks, checklists, or shortcuts here. What you will find is a distilled framework for designing wealth in a way that is architecturally sound, psychologically liberating, and morally coherent.

We will challenge the obsession with visibility and performance. We will explore the ethics of sovereignty and the aesthetics of restraint. We will outline the building blocks of quiet power—slow accretion, legal foresight, redundancy without noise—and suggest how they can be implemented practically and sustainably.

Above all, we will ask a final, provocative question: *If no one ever knew how wealthy you were, would the life you've built still make sense to you?* If the answer is yes, then you are not only sovereign. You are *free.*

Welcome to the quiet billionaire mindset. It's not a status. It's a decision. And from here, everything you build will last longer—because it was never built for applause. It was built to endure.

No Audience, No Applause

Modern wealth is not only counted in assets—it is performed. Visibility has become a proxy for value, and applause is often confused with affirmation. The algorithms reward revelation. Influence is measured in impressions. Quiet success, however potent, is overlooked if it cannot be monetised into a personal brand. In such a climate, choosing discretion over display is not just unconventional—it is psychologically radical.

This subchapter explores the deep inner strength required to operate without validation, without performance, and without the need to be seen. Not as a moral exercise, but as a strategic stance. This is not a discussion about modesty or humility. It is about *power without permission*, *impact without announcement*, and *freedom without surveillance.*

To live without applause requires a deliberate rewiring of the instincts that social architecture has rewarded for millennia. Status once conferred protection and resources in tribal societies. Today, the digital world weaponises that instinct into compulsive signalling. But a sovereign individual—particularly one managing private wealth—must develop the capacity to be invisible not just in law, but in psyche. *To act without performance is the rarest form of discipline.*

Validation as a Modern Addiction

To understand the strength of silence, one must first grasp the mechanics of attention. Neuroscience has shown that social validation triggers the brain's reward system in much the same way as addictive substances. Dopamine spikes reinforce the behaviours that earn likes, comments, applause—even when these rewards are fleeting and ultimately meaningless.

This is not confined to teenagers or influencers. High-net-worth individuals are equally susceptible. For many, the yacht is less about leisure than leverage. The art purchase is less about passion than positioning. The philanthropy becomes performance. But the moment wealth becomes performative, it is no longer private—it is hostage to the audience.

The solution is not asceticism. It is detachment. *The ability to act without needing to be seen is one of the highest forms of self-possession.* To build something exceptional, then say nothing. To move capital wisely, then disappear. To lead with clarity, then decline the podium. This is not anonymity. It is sovereignty.

Case Study: The Unbroadcast Dynasty

In the early 20th century, an American industrialist family quietly transferred their wealth into a matrix of irrevocable trusts. Over a century later, the family remains among the top 15 wealthiest in the world—without a single public figure, scandal, or televised succession drama. They do not sit on magazine covers. Their names are largely unknown outside of legal and banking circles. But they own stakes in global logistics, aerospace, and infrastructure. Their governance model is lean. Their succession planning is silent. And their strategy? *No public profile. No cultural footprint. Maximum continuity.*

Contrast this with another family of equal wealth who chose visibility—art, politics, public statements, recognisable heirs. They endured multiple lawsuits, hostile media campaigns, and fractured succession. Their influence decayed not from poor investing, but from overexposure.

This is not a call to retreat. It is a call to reframe the purpose of wealth: *not to win in public, but to persist in private.*

Strategic Invisibility vs. Passive Obscurity

It is critical to differentiate *strategic invisibility* from *passive obscurity*. The former is intentional. It is not about hiding; it is about declining irrelevant battles. It is about creating structures, identities, and systems that allow one to act without spectacle. The latter—obscurity—is often involuntary and stems from disempowerment.

Strategic invisibility is an *asset*. It allows individuals and families to move across jurisdictions, structure holdings, make acquisitions, and engage in conflict resolution without attracting unnecessary adversaries. In legal strategy, as in martial arts, *the quiet fighter always holds the advantage.*

For instance, a litigation-resistant trust structure does not rely on opacity—it relies on design. It does not scream its protections. It simply enforces them with quiet effectiveness. Similarly, multi-jurisdictional holding companies do not broadcast their footprints. They are present where necessary, silent where strategic.

In each case, the lack of visibility is not a weakness. It is a decision. *Not all victories need a headline.*

The Psychological Cost of Being Seen

There is also an immense cognitive cost to maintaining visibility. Public figures—even those in business—suffer higher rates of anxiety, hypervigilance, and burnout. The performative layer of wealth management requires energy that could otherwise be spent on innovation, legacy design, or time with family.

Living without applause is not deprivation. It is *conservation of willpower.* The more one depends on external affirmation, the more fragile one's internal compass becomes. Wealth that requires continual broadcasting is wealth that cannot tolerate solitude. That is not freedom. That is a performance contract.

The antidote is not silence for its own sake, but *selective withdrawal.* Saying less when others shout. Choosing privacy when others signal. Opting out of unneeded debates. Resisting the demand to explain every decision, every restructure, every jurisdictional move.

Consider the most effective operators across finance, diplomacy, and intelligence. Their power rests not in their visibility, but in their *opacity*. The less predictable your intentions, the more optionality you retain.

Designing a Life with No Audience

What would your lifestyle look like if you engineered it for no applause? Not just privately held assets, but *private intentions*. Not just off-market transactions, but *off-narrative living*.

The principles might include:

Homes that are comfortable but not demonstrative

Travel patterns that avoid spectacle

Social media abstention or pseudonymous presence

Legal structures that shield, not shout

Relationships based on trust, not networking

More importantly, it requires inner architecture—an identity decoupled from social metrics. This is the most difficult kind of redesign: *to measure yourself by your standards, not the market's.*

In psychological terms, this is called internal locus of control. It is the core trait of sovereign actors. They do not need to be told who they are. They already know.

Why This Matters Now

The 21st-century economy is not just fast—it is *surveilled.* Every public declaration, every transaction, every digital trace becomes data. In this environment, performative wealth is not merely foolish. It is *vulnerable.* The more visible your identity, the more predictable your decisions. The more you are known, the more you can be targeted—legally, socially, or reputationally.

Quiet wealth is not just safer. It is *harder to manipulate.*

And as regulatory landscapes become more complex, geopolitical tensions rise, and digital scrutiny intensifies, the ability to *operate without applause* may become not only strategic—but existential.

No Applause, No Regret

To end, consider this mental experiment: if every audience disappeared—if social media vanished, media mentions stopped, awards ceased to be given—*what choices would still make sense to you?* What structures would you still build? What values would you still protect?

The answer to that question is your actual strategy.

To live a life that is coherent even in silence—that is not waiting for likes, headlines, or admiration—is to live *freely.* That freedom is the truest wealth of all.

No audience. No applause. No regret. Just clarity. And power. And peace.

From Chasing Returns to Designing Futures

There is a silent crisis in modern capital: an addiction to velocity. Financial discourse is saturated with alpha-seeking, quarterly benchmarks, and short-term gains dressed up as strategic thinking. But what if wealth creation was less about movement and more about meaning? Less about return on capital and more about return on design?

This subchapter is not a treatise against growth. It is an argument for *purposeful architecture*. It challenges the dominant mindset of transactional investing and replaces it with a higher-order lens: *legacy as a design problem, not just an inheritance event*. It asks the reader to shift orientation—from optimisation to orchestration. From outperformance to endurance. From spreadsheets to structures.

The Tyranny of Yield

Yield obsession is not a modern invention, but the tools of modern finance—real-time data, algorithmic trading, social investing platforms—have intensified its grip. Today's investor is rarely thinking in 25-year horizons. Even institutions, whose portfolios ought to outlive any single CIO, are often governed by annualised metrics.

What is sacrificed in this haste is *narrative coherence*. Wealth becomes fragmented across funds, jurisdictions, advisors, and strategies. There is growth, but no story. Returns, but no rhythm. *Capital is moving, but the owner is standing still.*

The investor who chases yield without design is like an architect who adds storeys without blueprints—eventually, the structure collapses under the weight of its own improvisation.

Design Thinking for Capital

Design thinking—imported from architecture and engineering—offers a powerful reframing. Rather than ask, "What can this asset return in 12 months?" the better question is: *What role does this asset play in the future I am building?*

To design a future with capital means thinking in nested layers:

Personal Sovereignty: What structures guarantee freedom, flexibility, and privacy regardless of jurisdictional or political shifts?

Intergenerational Integrity: What values, frameworks, and assets will outlast your direct influence?

Cultural Contribution: What impact will your capital have on the communities and ideas that matter to you?

The point is not to moralise capital, but to *structure it with intention.* Capital without direction will always default to the logic of the market. And the market has no concern for legacy.

Case Study: From Trading Desk to Civic Foundation

Consider the trajectory of an equity trader who spent two decades generating outsized personal returns. By 45, he had exited with substantial liquidity, only to realise that his portfolio was optimised for a life he no longer wanted. The volatility tolerance, the geographic exposure, the risk posture—it had all been designed for someone chasing exit multiples, not stewardship.

Over the next five years, he restructured. Converted high-beta equity into private trust assets. Reinvested in regional infrastructure with 20-year timelines. Built a fund for civic entrepreneurship where returns were measured in durable local jobs, not IRR. Not philanthropy. *Design.*

The wealth did not shrink. But its rhythm changed. It began to build a future—not just finance a lifestyle.

The Failure of Succession Without Strategy

Too often, legacy is confused with inheritance. But distribution is not design. A poorly architected estate—no matter how large—invites legal chaos, moral confusion, and structural fragility.

True legacy planning involves more than family constitutions or trust instruments. It is about designing capital flows that reflect values, governance frameworks that encode clarity, and asset maps that remain resilient across decades, not just fiscal cycles.

And this requires departing from yield-maximising behaviour. The asset that compounds silently across generations may underperform your favourite venture fund for five years—but it will outperform chaos every time. *Quiet, principled growth beats noisy arbitrage.*

The Psychology of Enough

Designing futures requires not just financial acumen, but *psychological discipline.* The biggest obstacle to long-term thinking is not technical—it is emotional. Investors who chase perpetual growth often do so because they cannot define *enough.* And without enough, there is no end. Without an end, there is no design—just accumulation.

Modern capitalism conflates movement with success. But there is wisdom in stillness. It is entirely possible for a portfolio to grow and a life to feel hollow. For assets to outperform and yet fail to outlast.

The design mindset says: *decide first what you want your capital to do—then select assets accordingly.* This is inversion. And it is rare.

From Portfolio to Platform

What if you treated your capital not as a portfolio to outperform, but as a *platform to enable*?

This shifts the focus:

From asset allocation to institutional architecture

From liquidity events to legacy vehicles

From tax optimisation to jurisdictional resilience

From quarterly reviews to generational narratives

The most powerful families and funds in history did not merely seek returns. They *shaped epochs.* The Rothschilds did not just bank—they constructed networks of influence. The Medicis didn't just lend—they underwrote culture. The modern equivalents operate silently, but with the same mindset: *capital as foundation, not fuel.*

Modern Tools, Ancient Wisdom

Technology now offers tools to structure capital with precision: decentralised assets, programmable trusts, algorithmic compliance, reputation-led deal flow. But the wisdom required to use them well is ancient: patience, restraint, clarity, and commitment to something larger than self.

Designing futures requires *a different tempo.* It refuses the dopamine of quick wins. It honours risk, but within a canvas large enough to absorb losses. It respects complexity, but enforces simplicity at the core.

Why This Mindset Matters Now

We are entering an age of increasing volatility: geopolitical flux, institutional fragility, environmental instability. In this context, designing futures is not luxury—it is *a hedge against chaos.*

The investor who operates with design is not reactionary. They are not dependent on trend cycles, policy shifts, or memetic markets. Their capital is configured to bend, not break. To evolve, not pivot. To survive, even when systems around them do not.

That is the power of architecture. *Not to forecast, but to withstand.*

A Final Question

If your capital vanished tomorrow, what remains?

If the answer is "returns," then you were chasing. If the answer is "structures, people, values, and capability"—then you were designing.

To move from chasing returns to designing futures is to stop asking, "What can I earn?" and start asking, "What can I build?"

And once you answer that, you no longer need applause, headlines, or outperformance.

You have *direction.* And that is the most sovereign return of all.

Quiet Growth: A Philosophy of Accretion

In a world increasingly obsessed with speed, visibility, and instant results, the most subversive wealth strategy may be *restraint.* Not inaction. Not stagnation. But deliberate, principled, *invisible progress*—growth so structurally sound it doesn't need to advertise itself. This is the essence of accretive wealth: *quiet, layered, unshakeable.*

Quiet growth is not merely a temperament. It is a discipline. It is the difference between volatility and viability, between being rich and becoming *anti-fragile.* It is about building systems that compound—not just financially, but in strategic optionality, jurisdictional flexibility, and moral clarity. It is not driven by markets or hype, but by internal design and intentional opacity. And in a world of accelerating noise, this philosophy is more relevant than ever.

The Illusion of Speed and the Cost of Visibility

Contemporary finance rewards those who move quickly, scale visibly, and signal success before it is real. Venture capitalists chase growth at the expense of coherence. Founders raise valuations instead of revenue. Influencers masquerade as thought leaders. In this climate, growth becomes a spectacle—a marketing function rather than a structural outcome.

But *speed often conceals fragility.* Rapid expansion typically outpaces operational integrity. Public visibility invites scrutiny before you're defensible. Most critically, *growth that demands attention also invites opposition*—from competitors, from regulators, from unstable partners. Quiet growth inverts this: *it grows behind the wall, beneath the radar, and within the law.*

What Is Accretive Wealth?

To accrete is to grow by gradual addition, by accumulation without rupture. In geology, accretion is how continents form—layer by layer, without fanfare, over millennia. In private wealth, accretive growth is achieved not through sudden exits or flashy returns, but through *cumulative alignment.* That alignment occurs across five dimensions:

1. **Structural** – Are your entities and trusts designed to grow without reinvention?

2. **Jurisdictional** – Do your assets reside in environments that favour longevity, privacy, and continuity?

3. **Ethical** – Are you building in ways that can endure scrutiny, rather than evade it?

4. **Psychological** – Are your expectations calibrated to decades, not quarters?

5. **Strategic** – Is each layer of growth connected to a broader architecture?

Each of these layers compounds in the same way as capital—but with a far greater resilience multiplier. *What matters is not that you grow faster than others, but that you never need to reset.*

Case Study: The Hidden Billionaire's Architecture

Consider the story of a logistics magnate whose net worth, though exceeding a billion, never appeared in any Forbes profile or public company ledger. Over three decades, he constructed a layered architecture: land held in trusts in agrarian zones with low regulatory volatility, operating companies split across multiple jurisdictions, and liquidity mechanisms that relied on family-office-level structures rather than public markets. He refused private equity, rejected exit offers, and never raised external capital.

On paper, his profile looked modest. But his *accretion rate*—the rate at which he quietly added permanent advantages—outperformed flashier peers in every respect: taxation, litigation exposure, political risk, and generational continuity. He was not rich in narrative. He was rich in resilience. And when crises emerged—COVID, currency devaluations, tax code reforms—he did not pivot. *He remained still while others scrambled.*

The Psychology Behind Quiet Growth

This approach requires a psychological posture that runs counter to cultural norms. It requires:

Low time preference: A mindset that values the distant future more than the near-term dopamine of quick wins.

Ego containment: The willingness to succeed without credit, applause, or visible dominance.

Strategic boredom: The ability to tolerate simplicity and repeatability, resisting the urge to over-optimise or complicate.

This posture is rare. It is not taught in business schools, which teach scaling. It is not rewarded on social media, which rewards signalling. But among the most durable families, foundations, and sovereign entities, it is the norm.

Quiet growth is not an absence of ambition. It is ambition with composure.

The Power of Structural Patience

When you design for quiet growth, your strategy shifts from returns to configuration. The goal is not to win big—it is to become *undislodgeable.* This demands structural patience: the ability to build with tools that do not pay off immediately but generate *cascading advantage.*

Examples:

A trust structure that defers distribution for 15 years may seem restrictive—but it allows assets to compound with legal shielding.

A multi-jurisdictional holding company may add complexity—but it builds sovereignty against regulatory overreach.

Reinvesting into low-visibility assets (like agricultural land or long-cycle infrastructure) may seem unsexy—but they outlast hype cycles.

These are not tactical choices. They are *design philosophies.* They imply a posture toward time that prioritises *durability over display.*

Contrast: Explosive vs. Accretive Growth

Explosive growth is not inherently wrong. It creates empires. But it also attracts parasites, lawsuits, and unpredictable attention. It can be derailed by PR crises, capital calls, or executive ego.

Accretive growth, by contrast, is rarely vulnerable to a single point of failure. Its momentum is not centralised in a product, person, or market. It is diversified across time, form, and geography.

To illustrate:

Growth Type	Visibility	Volatility	Strategic	Reputation Risk	Duration

			Resilience		
Explosive	High	High	Fragile	High	Short
Accretive (Quiet)	Low	Low	Durable	Low	Long

The less visible the growth, the harder it is to attack.

Why Quiet Growth Outperforms in Crisis

The philosophy of accretion becomes most visible during downturns. When markets crash, those who rely on leverage, narratives, or public goodwill lose footing. Those who built quietly, with layered redundancies, lose little—and sometimes gain.

During the 2008 crisis, those with overexposed portfolios and public-market dependence were decimated. Those with income-generating real assets and multi-entity structures weathered the storm.

In 2020, businesses reliant on media-driven growth collapsed overnight. Meanwhile, family offices with boring portfolios—utilities, food supply chains, insurance back-ends—barely flinched.

This is not coincidence. It is *philosophy in action.*

Living Wealth, Not Just Growing It

Quiet growth is not about passive hoarding. It is about *active positioning.* The wealth is alive: self-perpetuating, self-defending, self-governing. But it does not need an audience to function. It is not tied to personality brands, cultural relevance, or institutional favour.

The ultimate test of wealth is not how fast it grows in peacetime, but how well it survives disruption. Quiet growth thrives in silence because it is *built for reality, not attention.*

A Final Insight

You are not required to announce your success to legitimise it. You are not required to prove your value to anyone outside your architecture. And you are not required to chase opportunities that cannot withstand scrutiny.

The quietest structures often become the most permanent. The slowest systems, the most trustworthy. And the wealth that grows with principle and patience—*that wealth owns the future.*

Living with Dignity in a Loud World

There is a certain dignity in choosing silence when noise is the currency of attention. In a time when algorithms reward outrage, metrics confuse visibility with value, and influence masquerades as integrity, to *not* perform for the crowd is a form of self-mastery. Dignity today is not merely a moral ideal—it is a strategic decision. It is the posture of those who understand that *freedom is inversely correlated with dependence on recognition.*

This subchapter does not concern itself with branding, optics, or winning the narrative. It concerns itself with the question: *What kind of life is worth living once the applause stops—or never arrives at all?* And more critically: *What systems, habits, and internal frameworks can preserve your autonomy in a civilisation addicted to exhibitionism?*

The Performance Trap: Wealth in the Age of Spectacle

To live with dignity requires resistance to the ambient pressure to perform. This pressure is structural, not just psychological. In the modern world, almost every domain of life has been nudged towards public consumption: meals are photographed, decisions explained, earnings flaunted, values signalled. Even privacy has been commodified—marketed as a lifestyle rather than practiced as a principle.

Within wealth culture, this has metastasised into something more toxic: *the conflation of net worth with personal worth.* Investment success is no longer enough unless it's captured in a tweet thread. Philanthropy must be accompanied by a press release. Career pivots demand a LinkedIn manifesto. This relentless broadcasting imposes an external dependency: the need to *be seen* in order to *feel real.*

But real wealth—the kind that outlasts news cycles and social feeds—does not require validation. *It simply is.* And the individuals who own and wield it effectively often do so in silence, protected by a firm grasp of what matters privately rather than publicly.

Freedom from Recognition as a Form of Power

Recognition, for all its appeal, is a form of soft captivity. The more you rely on it, the more you curate yourself for an audience rather than for truth. Living without it is not a rejection of human connection—it is a recalibration of sovereignty. It is the ability to make decisions that honour your values, your structure, your time horizon, regardless of whether they are understood or praised.

This is especially relevant in wealth governance. Quiet actors design their financial and legal structures not for accolades, but for *utility*: privacy, jurisdictional control, tax strategy, family continuity. They do not need others to know what they own. They do not need applause to feel agency. They prioritise *freedom of movement over freedom of narrative.*

Dignity, in this context, is the byproduct of operating with full alignment and *zero explanation.* It is the confidence to decline opportunities that look good but compromise structure. It is the calm rejection of vanity metrics—be they followers, speaking invitations, or glossy magazine spreads.

Case Study: The Invisible Philanthropist

One European family office, established in the early 1980s, has quietly deployed over €500 million into refugee education, water access, and regenerative agriculture. Yet the beneficiaries, the governments involved, and even many NGOs have no idea who the benefactor is. Funds move through irrevocable donor-advised trusts, multi-jurisdictional LLCs, and embedded legal intermediaries. There are no media interviews, no public credit. The family doesn't view this as secrecy. They see it as *integrity*. As one trustee told me, "Visibility is irrelevant. Impact is not."

This is dignity operationalised: when *action* becomes its own justification.

Stoicism, Status, and the Quiet Life

Philosophically, the blueprint for this mindset is not new. The Stoics, most notably Epictetus and Marcus Aurelius, warned against seeking reputation as a source of meaning. Their view was clear: status is arbitrary, opinions are fickle, and virtue—understood as disciplined internal coherence—is all that truly endures.

Modern science corroborates this. Studies in behavioural psychology suggest that those who derive self-worth from internal metrics (such as mastery, contribution, or alignment with values) experience greater psychological resilience than those who chase external metrics (likes, promotions, media attention). *Freedom from applause is not just noble. It is neurologically liberating.*

This isn't merely abstract. It has concrete implications for wealth holders and creators:

You will decline more than you accept.

You will build for permanence, not performance.

You will have fewer public allies, but deeper private leverage.

You will be misunderstood—sometimes deliberately.

And yet, from this posture emerges a different kind of power: *indifference to the performative economy.*

Designing for Dignity: Practical Considerations

Dignity is not only internal. It must be embedded in how you design your life, wealth, and time.

Time blocking for solitude, to preserve clarity amidst noise.

Legal firewalls and entity design, to prevent scrutiny from becoming intrusion.

Reputation risk controls, including pre-emptive digital hygiene and controlled disclosures.

Delegation to low-profile counsel, who share your philosophical posture of quiet competence.

These are not defensive gestures. They are deliberate acts of design, choosing *who sees what, when, and why.* They reflect the belief that *control is not about publicity; it is about sovereignty.*

The High Cost of Needing to Be Seen

There is a hidden tax on visibility. It invites litigation. It attracts regulators. It distorts incentives. Most dangerously, it skews decision-making. When you live publicly, you make choices for optics. And when you do that, you stop designing your future—you start performing a role in someone else's theatre.

Living with dignity in a loud world requires *rejecting the theatre entirely.* You step off the stage, not to retreat, but to *build without distraction.*

To parent without posting. To earn without flaunting. To give without credit. These are not limitations. They are markers of the *truest kind of wealth*: self-direction.

Silence as a Strategic Asset

In military doctrine, silence is often more valuable than noise. An operation that cannot be tracked cannot be disrupted. A leader who does not speak cannot be quoted. A plan without press is a plan without preemption.

The same applies to sovereign wealth. When no one knows what you are building, they cannot interfere. When no one knows where you reside, they cannot control. And when no one expects your next move, you retain *maximum optionality*.

Dignity is not aloofness. It is the restraint to stay still when the world demands movement. It is the confidence to *play long games without announcing your plays*. And it is the ethic of protecting what matters—not for secrecy's sake, but because *privacy is a form of reverence*.

The Final Posture

To live a life of dignity without needing to prove it is not about austerity. It is about intentionality. It is about *building impact without dependency*, *amassing leverage without spectacle*, and *living fully without exhibition*.

The quiet billionaire mindset is not limited to billionaires. It is a philosophical and strategic commitment to *be more than you appear, and to appear only as much as necessary*.

You don't need an audience to be significant. You don't need applause to be effective. You need coherence. You need leverage. And you need the courage to let your actions speak *only to those who matter*.

Conclusion
Legacy Without Spotlight

Legacy, as it's commonly conceived, is often a performance—etched in plaques, commemorated in foundation names, or enshrined in public tributes. It leans heavily on visibility. The idea, broadly accepted if rarely questioned, is that to matter in posterity, one must be seen. A name carved in stone. A biography circulated. A memory preserved in the minds of others. But this final chapter takes a sharp turn away from that well-trodden path. It proposes something less comfortable and far more enduring: that true legacy requires no spotlight. That permanence can exist without performance.

To adopt this view demands a certain bravery—the kind that lets go of applause and instead asks: What remains when the story no longer centres on you? What still functions, with quiet precision, when your name fades from memory? What mechanisms persist—not in tribute, but in utility? These are not the questions of ambition. They are the questions of builders.

Here, the thread running through this book begins to weave tightly: sovereignty over symbolism, structure over status, continuity over credit. This chapter does not attempt a conclusion in the traditional sense. Instead, it invites elevation—a move beyond the tactics of wealth management toward the philosophy of permanence.

Still, the tension remains. We are, by nature, creatures who want to be remembered. Legacy, in the conventional sense, is emotional infrastructure—it soothes the ego with the promise of continuity. But those who operate at a more structural altitude—legal architects, financial designers, institutional thinkers—understand something deeper: the more a structure depends on its creator, the more fragile it is. A robust family office doesn't unravel with the founder's passing. A trust that spans generations doesn't hinge on personality but on principle. True continuity is independent of charisma.

Which brings us to the paradox that sits at the heart of enduring influence: the most effective legacies are often anonymous by intent.

This is not an argument against recognition. It's an argument against dependence on it. The seasoned strategist, the discreet magnate, the quiet builder—these figures don't eschew visibility out of modesty, but because they understand its limitations. They know that if a structure only works in their presence, it was never truly stable to begin with. Their satisfaction is not in the monument but in the mechanics. They leave behind systems—legal, financial, institutional—that operate invisibly, quietly serving those they were designed to protect.

Take, for instance, the family that encodes philanthropic intent directly into their holding companies, binding commercial success to societal return, without fanfare. Or the global citizen who scatters jurisdictional presence across continents—not out of evasion, but as a gift of continuity to descendants who may never know their name. Or the founder who chooses not to crown their eldest child, but to appoint a council—an act of systemic confidence over sentimental hierarchy. These aren't gestures of disappearance. They are acts of permanence.

And this leads us to perhaps the most difficult part of legacy building: letting go. Letting go of the need for authorship. For attribution. For centrality. That is not resignation. That is mastery. It is a deliberate decentring of self so that the system may survive. In today's culture—obsessed with personal brands and digital memory—this seems almost radical. But it's far from new. Many of the world's most enduring institutions weren't built to glorify founders. They were built to endure. Their resilience is rooted not in personality, but in design.

This orientation requires a shift in time horizon. From immediate impact to long arc. From living beneficiaries to unseen inheritors. From headlines to governance clauses. It means crafting articles of incorporation with the same intentionality as one might write a personal memoir. That, in essence, is the distilled mindset of the quiet billionaire: to build in such a way that remembrance is optional, not essential.

And so legacy, when re-examined through this lens, becomes less about remembrance and more about resonance. Did your values survive you in the form of functional systems? Did your contracts speak louder than your accolades? Did your heirs inherit not just capital, but competence? These are the deeper metrics. This is the architecture of legacy that cannot be erased because it doesn't need to be praised.

To that end, this chapter moves beyond theory. It unpacks practical ways to embed this ethos: trust structures that obscure the founder while empowering the mission; cultural norms that prepare stewards to carry weight without craving visibility; multi-jurisdictional frameworks that dissolve dependency on any single legal system or figurehead. Even simple design prompts that ask: would this structure survive without my name?

There's power in restraint. Not just as a moral virtue, but as a strategic imperative. There's power in opting out of narrative and choosing instead to express values through mechanics. In an age where every public gesture risks commodification, anonymity isn't erasure—it's insulation.

Which is why this final chapter is not a bow or a curtain call. It's a handover. A transition from protagonist to architect. From being the focal point to becoming the scaffolding. From living your legacy to engineering its quiet endurance.

And if, in the end, what you've built continues without you—without applause, without revision, without needing to mention your name—that may be the most profound legacy of all.

One that persists not because it is remembered, but because it was built to last.

The Legacy Vault

Wealth, when stripped of its values, becomes a vessel without direction—a store of power awaiting either stewardship or entropy. This is the philosophical fault line that distinguishes mere inheritance from legacy. To transfer assets is administrative. To transfer values is architectural. And in the architecture of enduring families, foundations, and private wealth structures, *the most valuable capital is often intangible.*

The modern wealth holder operates in a paradox: they are more equipped than ever to protect financial capital, yet often ill-prepared to encode the principles that justified its creation. Trusts can secure assets. Legal wrappers can defer tax or shield exposure. But values—moral codes, personal philosophies, behavioural heuristics—cannot be locked in a safe or outsourced to fiduciaries. They must be authored, contextualised, and conveyed with clarity, or else they evaporate in a single generation. The *Legacy Vault* exists to prevent that evaporation.

This article examines the tools and methodologies through which families can pass down more than money. It explores letters of intent, ethical codicils, intergenerational mentorship frameworks, and the emergent category of wisdom trusts—constructs designed not to control heirs, but to orient them. *The objective is not to bind the future, but to inform it with intelligence from the past.*

The impulse to preserve values through generations is ancient. Roman testators attached moral expectations to bequests. Confucian dynasties encoded ancestral instruction into governance. In Jewish tradition, ethical wills (tzava'ot) have long been used to transmit not just blessings but also responsibility. What modern wealth holders now face is the need to systematise this desire using contemporary tools—without reducing wisdom to platitudes.

Begin with the **letter of intent**. Though not legally binding, it is strategically vital. A well-crafted letter of intent does not simply state "what" to do with the wealth—it articulates "why." It offers context: why assets were placed in certain trusts, why beneficiaries were selected or omitted, why specific clauses exist. It humanises the legal structure. It transforms a sterile distribution schedule into a narrated mission. When written with discipline, it becomes a psychological compass—guiding rather than dictating.

Yet a letter is not enough. In many cases, ethical **codicils**—addenda attached to wills or trusts—offer a formal mechanism to express philosophical commitments. These are not moral sermons. They are designed to clarify principles, not enforce behaviour. For example, an ethical codicil might express the testator's support for philanthropy grounded in impact rather than vanity, or warn against asset allocation strategies that prioritise speed over sustainability. Done well, these statements influence trustee discretion and interpretive fidelity without drifting into moral micromanagement.

A more ambitious development is the emergence of **wisdom trusts**. These are not separate legal entities per se, but embedded provisions within discretionary trusts that prioritise the transmission of intellectual and ethical capital. In practice, this might include:

– Curated libraries of personal letters and decision rationales
– Mandated mentorships with long-standing advisors
– Scheduled family councils to debate mission continuity
– "Living archives" of founder decision logs, explaining both successes and failures

The wisdom trust model treats insight as an asset class, one that requires stewardship and intentionality. It assumes that heirs do not need instructions—they need exposure to how and why decisions were made under uncertainty. In essence, it replicates proximity to the founder long after their death.

Importantly, these tools are not about control. They are about *coherence.* A founder who has spent decades building a multi-jurisdictional asset protection structure, selecting trustees with precise skill sets, and designing nested vehicles for flexibility should not stop short of encoding *why* those decisions were made. Without that encoding, even the most sophisticated architecture becomes hollow—a structure built with tools, but devoid of direction.

Consider the case of a Singapore-based entrepreneur who scaled an international logistics firm across emerging markets. His estate included equity in five countries, offshore accounts in Liechtenstein, and a family office split between Hong Kong and London. But his true legacy was a set of hard-won philosophies: *Never scale without redundancy. Never mistake liquidity for safety. Trust, but always cross-reference.* These principles had protected him in three financial crises and two hostile takeovers. So he embedded them into his estate documentation—not through rigid rules, but through narrative. His heirs were not left a playbook. They were left a worldview.

This approach requires psychological maturity on both ends. Founders must be willing to expose the logic—and fallibility—of their thinking. Heirs must be trained to absorb this material not as dogma, but as *design input.* It also requires humility from legal counsel and advisors, who must integrate these value-transference tools into estate design without diluting their meaning into checkbox formalities.

Wealth that is decoupled from values risks becoming corrosive. The empirical data supports this. Studies from institutions like the Williams Group suggest that *over 70% of wealth transitions fail by the second generation*, not due to tax or legal friction, but because of "a breakdown in communication and trust." This is not a problem of capital. It is a problem of continuity. And it is solvable—if the vault is not just physical, but *philosophical.*

There is also a geopolitical dimension to this. In a world where jurisdictional arbitrage is the norm and cross-border structures proliferate, values become the only universal anchor. Law varies. Tax codes shift. But an ethical instruction written clearly, with context, can influence trustee behaviour in the Cayman Islands as much as in Canada. It is, in a sense, a meta-jurisdiction: *a moral code that transcends legal boundaries.*

Nor should this be limited to the ultra-wealthy. Middle-class professionals with modest estates can also benefit from Legacy Vault principles. A father who explains to his children why he chose to fund public infrastructure rather than private charities teaches something more enduring than asset allocation. A mother who records the principles behind her investing decisions—calculated risk, informed patience, refusal to chase market noise—gives her children more than an inheritance. She gives them *orientation.*

Ultimately, the Legacy Vault is not a single document or mechanism. It is a mindset operationalised through tools. It reflects the belief that *what is preserved is not merely what is protected—but what is explained, narrated, and contextualised.* Legal robustness is not enough. Clarity of intent, continuity of philosophy, and exposure to real decision-making under pressure—these are the true safeguards of legacy.

The world does not need more instruction. It needs more coherence. Letters of intent, wisdom trusts, and ethical codicils are not substitutes for trust—they are instruments of transmission. They exist not to bind future generations, but to equip them. And in that equipping, a deeper kind of continuity becomes possible: *not of wealth alone, but of worldview.*

That is what the Legacy Vault protects. Not a fortune—but a philosophy. Not a name—but a navigational system. And not an ego—but a lineage of thought that deserves to endure, even if quietly, and even if anonymously.

About the Author

Matthias Lorenz is a European wealth strategist, legal architect, and privacy advocate who has advised families, entrepreneurs, and sovereign individuals across three continents. With a background in international law and a fascination for the psychology of wealth, Lorenz crafts strategies that prioritise control without visibility, legality without exposure, and legacy without noise. His work blends old-world discretion with modern global intelligence, offering a rare lens into the hidden architecture of private finance. He writes for those who would rather be secure than famous—and believe that real power is never loud.

www.ingramcontent.com/pod-product-compliance
Lightning Source LLC
Chambersburg PA
CBHW031338230926
51848CB00002B/289
9789371343763